IMAGES
of America

GROTON REVISITED

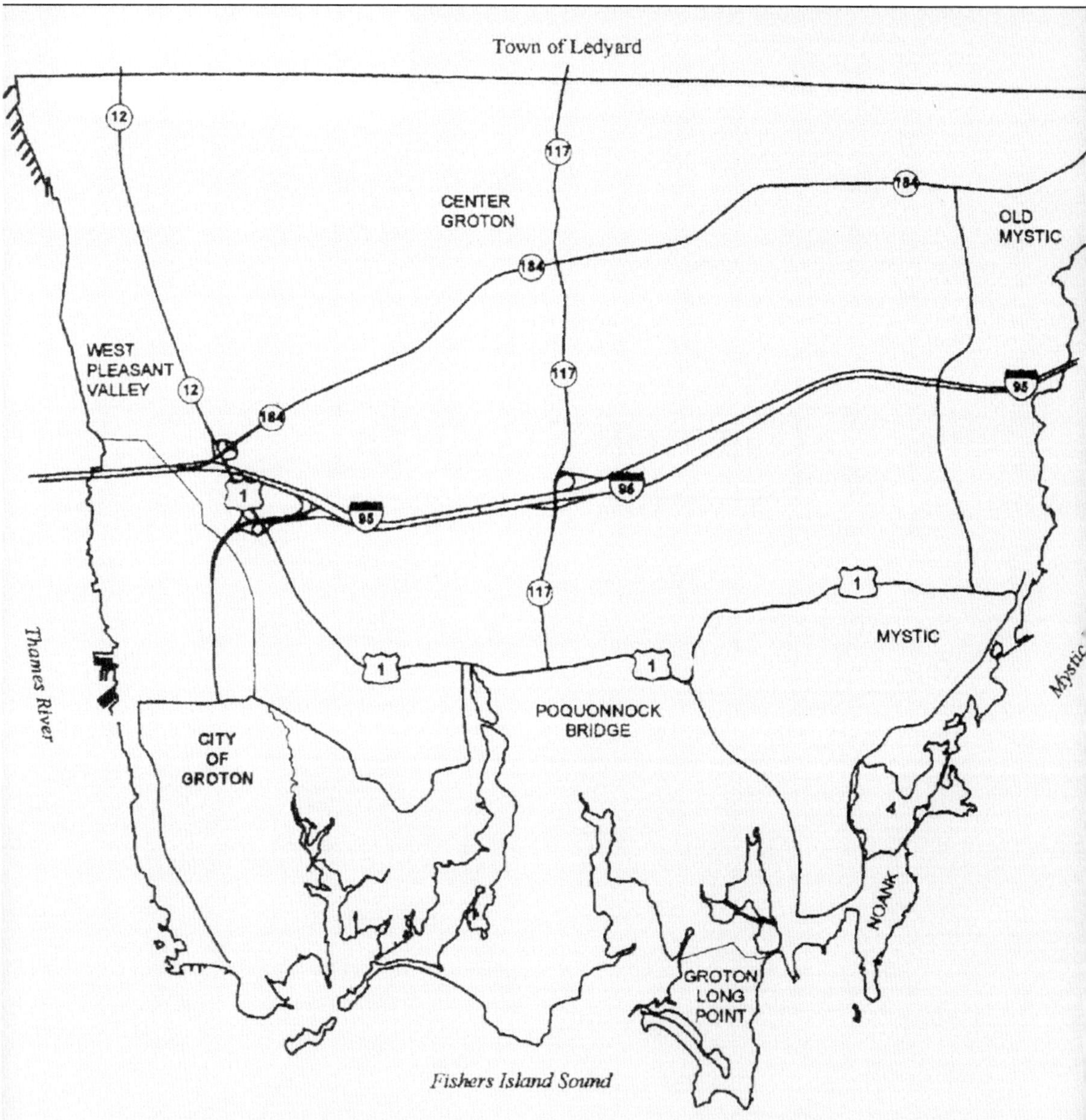

This map shows the town of Groton.

On the cover: Please see page 12. (Bob Irons.)

IMAGES
of America

GROTON REVISITED

Carol W. Kimball, James L. Streeter,
and Marilyn J. Comrie

ARCADIA
PUBLISHING

ISBN 978-0-7385-5490-7

Published by Arcadia Publishing
Charleston SC, Chicago IL, Portsmouth NH, San Francisco CA

Printed in the United States of America

Library of Congress Catalog Card Number: 2007927693

For all general information contact Arcadia Publishing at:
Telephone 843-853-2070
Fax 843-853-0044
E-mail sales@arcadiapublishing.com
For customer service and orders:
Toll-Free 1-888-313-2665

Visit us on the Internet at www.arcadiapublishing.com

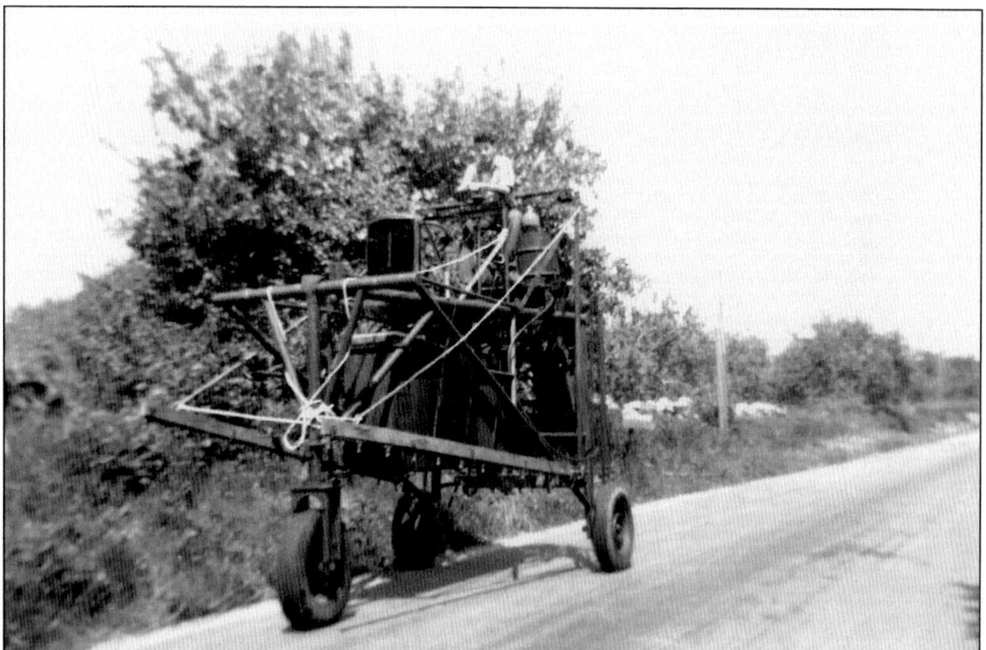

Robert Whittle works on the family's Willow Spring Farm on Noank Ledyard Road in Mystic. This Rube Goldberg–like spraying rig, a contraption that shows some real Yankee ingenuity, was engineered by the Whittles to spray their apple and peach orchards. (Whittle family.)

Contents

Acknowledgments		6
Introduction		7
1.	Shoreline Activities	9
2.	People	23
3.	School Days	39
4.	Bridges	51
5.	The 1938 Hurricane	67
6.	Villages	83
7.	Borough of Groton	95
8.	Here and There	109

Acknowledgments

The authors of this book thank the following people for contributing photographs and information: Bob Irons, the LaRoue family, Robert Bankel, Winifred Newbury, William N. Peterson, Sal Giordano, Janet Crossman, Sally Allyn Brousseau, Marty Artale, the Westerly Sun, Amby Burfoot, Bill Memorial Library, the Connecticut Department of Transportation, Mystic River Historical Society, the Fish family, the Ackley family, Jack Bucklyn, Wally Troland, the Spicer family, Mariellen French, Tom Migliaccio, the United States Navy, Al Chapman, Ed Stebbins, Avery-Copp Museum, John Scott, Groton Utilities, John Santacroce, Mike Boucher, Bill Sanford, Helen Kortesis, Betsey Allyn VanDressie, Dorothy Chrissos, Henry Haley, the Johnson family, Paul Ingle, George Edwards, Anne and Alan Bentz, Groton Ambulance Association, Grace McGrath, Dale Treadway, Ann C. Brown, Barbara Parfitt, Eleanor Byles, Groton Town Police, City of Groton, Town of Groton, Lil Hansen, Town of Groton Department of Public Works, Shennecossett Yacht Club, the Whittle family, Kay Gremley Hill, Bea Thomson, Indian and Colonial Research Center, Barbara Tarbox, Gloria Gavert, Irma Streeter, Larry Jacobsen, Harold C. Cornet, and Jonathan Lincoln.

INTRODUCTION

Groton, first and foremost, is a maritime community. From its beginnings as part of New London, to its incorporation as a town in 1705, through America's many wars, and up to the present, shipbuilding has been at the center of its commerce.

Its shipyards have turned out clipper ships that set sailing records that still stand today. It built an ironclad that aided the Union cause in the Civil War and produced America's first nuclear-powered submarine, USS *Nautilus* SSN 571, which is now permanently berthed on the Thames River in Groton at the Submarine Force Library and Museum adjacent to the naval submarine base.

In this book, Groton's maritime history will be interspersed with a look at other parts of the community. The town, for example, is bordered on two sides by rivers, the Mystic River on the east and the Thames River on the west. Over the years, many bridges have spanned the rivers.

In the early part of the 20th century, as the automobile became popular, it took long years of lobbying by local legislators, businessmen, and residents to convince the Connecticut General Assembly in Hartford that a motor vehicle bridge was needed over the Thames River that did not impede the flow of boat traffic.

Hartford's first solution was to convert the former railroad swing bridge for motor vehicles. But as motor vehicle traffic grew, as well as boat traffic with the naval submarine base now upriver, a swing bridge was impractical, causing traffic jams on both sides of the river.

For 15 years, from 1924 to 1939, southeastern Connecticut lobbied for a cantilever bridge. The state finally concurred, resulting in the original span of the Gold Star Memorial Bridge.

Groton's villages are also unique. Mystic was a thriving shipbuilding center in the 19th and early 20th centuries. Today the village, with its quaint shops and river views, is the state's number one tourist destination. Noank, at the mouth of the Mystic River, Old Mystic at the head of the river, Poquonnock Bridge with its flat landscape, and Center Groton, where the town was first established, all add a flavor to Groton's character.

The borough of Groton, now the city of Groton, has long been the economic center of the town. With Electric Boat and Pfizer, it is home to Groton's major industries. Thames Street and Groton Bank, since the town's early days, have been a thriving business community and an area of significant Colonial and Victorian architecture.

Groton also has had some interesting citizens in its 300 years. Two winners of the Boston Marathon called Groton home, as did two Medal of Honor winners from the Civil War. The woman who designed Connecticut's state flag lived on Monument Street in the shadow of Fort Griswold.

The town honored two of its significant citizens by naming schools for them. Carl C. Cutler, for whom Mystic's middle school is named, devoted much of his time to preserving 19th-century American maritime history. He was a founder of Mystic Seaport Museum, a place where the heyday of wooden shipbuilding could be honored and shared with the public. In 1941, he brought the country's last surviving wooden whaling ship, *Charles W. Morgan*, to Mystic, where it remains anchored on the Mystic River, the centerpiece of the museum.

Mary Morrisson, who fought tirelessly for women's rights and helped get the 19th Amendment passed, which gave women the right to vote, lived in Groton for 60 years. A local elementary school bears her name.

Groton's history has also included disaster. The town was badly damaged in the Great Hurricane of 1938. Connecticut's three easternmost towns, New London, Groton, and Stonington, along with Rhode Island, suffered the greatest damage from the storm because open ocean lies to their south. The rest of coastal Connecticut was protected from the storm surge by Long Island.

The 30-foot-high storm wave slammed into Groton, destroying homes and businesses, flooding downtown Mystic, eroding the shoreline, and toppling thousands of trees. It took years to recover and repair the damage.

Today Groton remains a maritime community and claims title as "the submarine capital of the world." Electric Boat continues to build submarines that allow America's nuclear navy to run silent and run deep. And upriver, many of those submarines are homeported at the naval submarine base.

Groton Revisited celebrates in photographs the people, places, and events that have made Groton a vital part of Connecticut's history and economy for more than 300 years.

One

Shoreline Activities

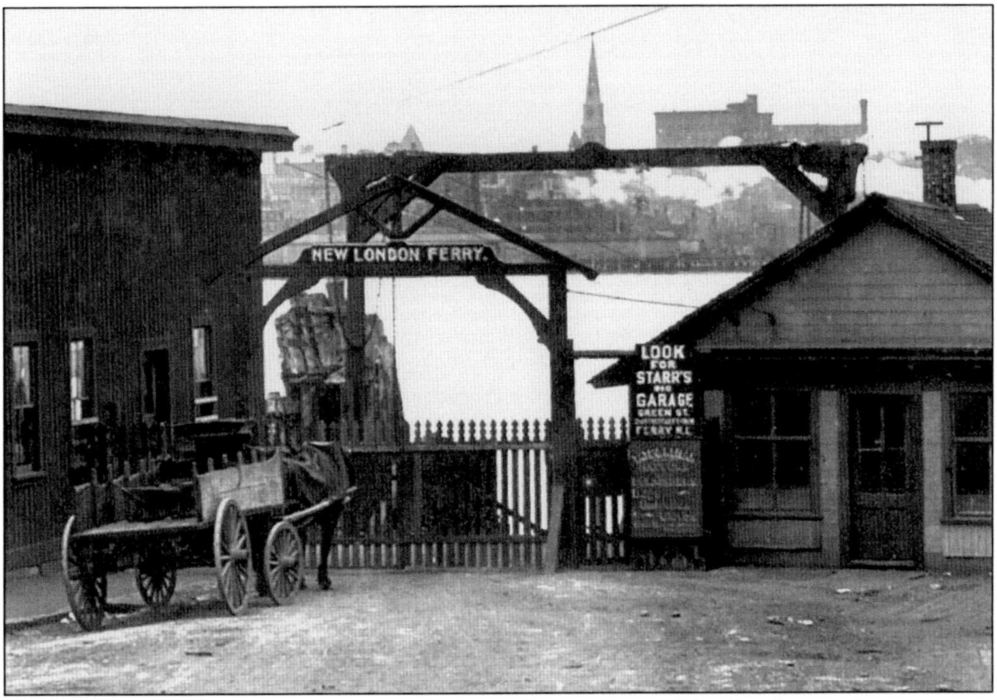

A horse and wagon wait at the ferry landing on Thames Street. The first ferry, a dugout canoe, crossed the Thames River in 1651. In 1654, Cary Latham and his family took over the ferry, which was the only way for people to cross between Groton and New London until the first highway bridge opened in 1919. Ferry service ended in 1929. (James L. Streeter.)

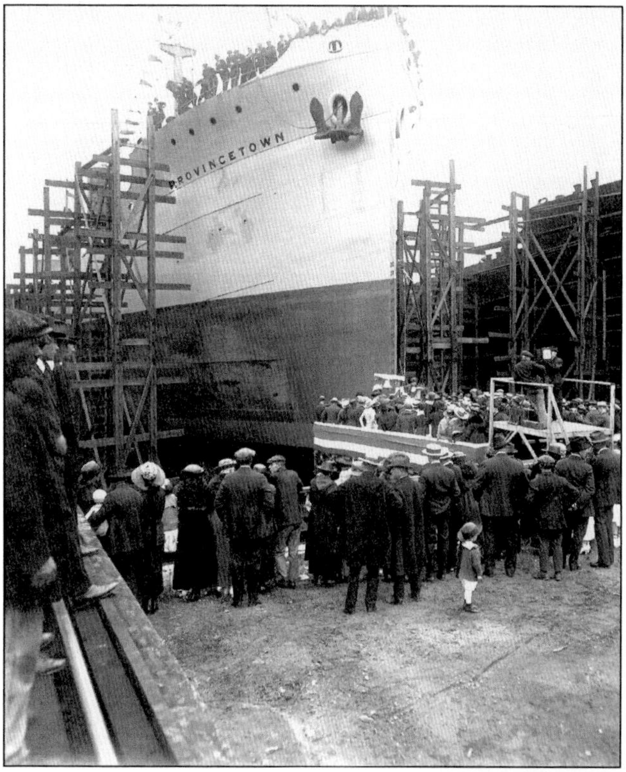

A crowd gathers at the Groton Iron Works shipyard on the Thames River for the launch of the steel freighter *Provincetown*. In November 1916, Charles W. Morse of the United States Steamship Company bought 30 acres at Eastern Point to build the freighters as transport ships for World War I. At one point, 4,500 men worked at the yard. The company failed when the bottom dropped out of the shipping market. The land later was the site of Electric Boat's Victory Yard and today is the site of Pfizer. (Carol W. Kimball.)

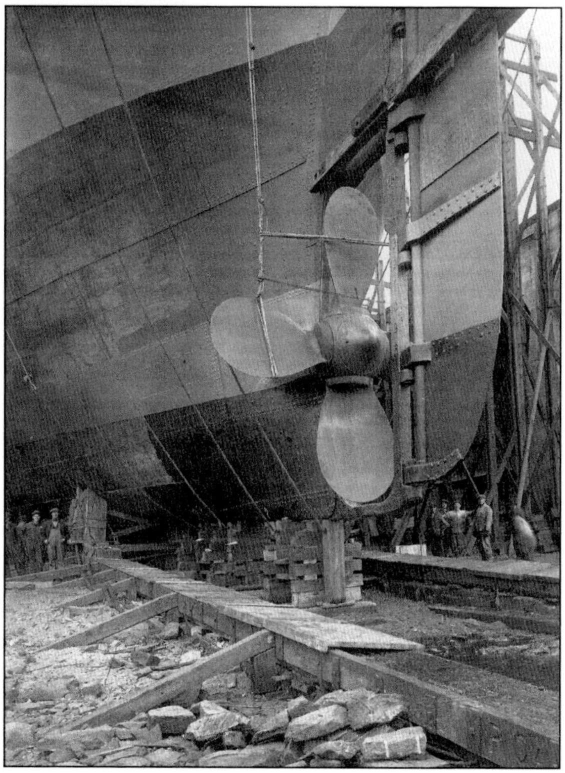

The huge steel freighters built at Groton Iron Works on the Thames River averaged 3,800 tons in displacement. The size of the ships can be imagined by noting the height of the giant propeller of the vessel pictured here, compared to the men standing alongside it. (Carol W. Kimball.)

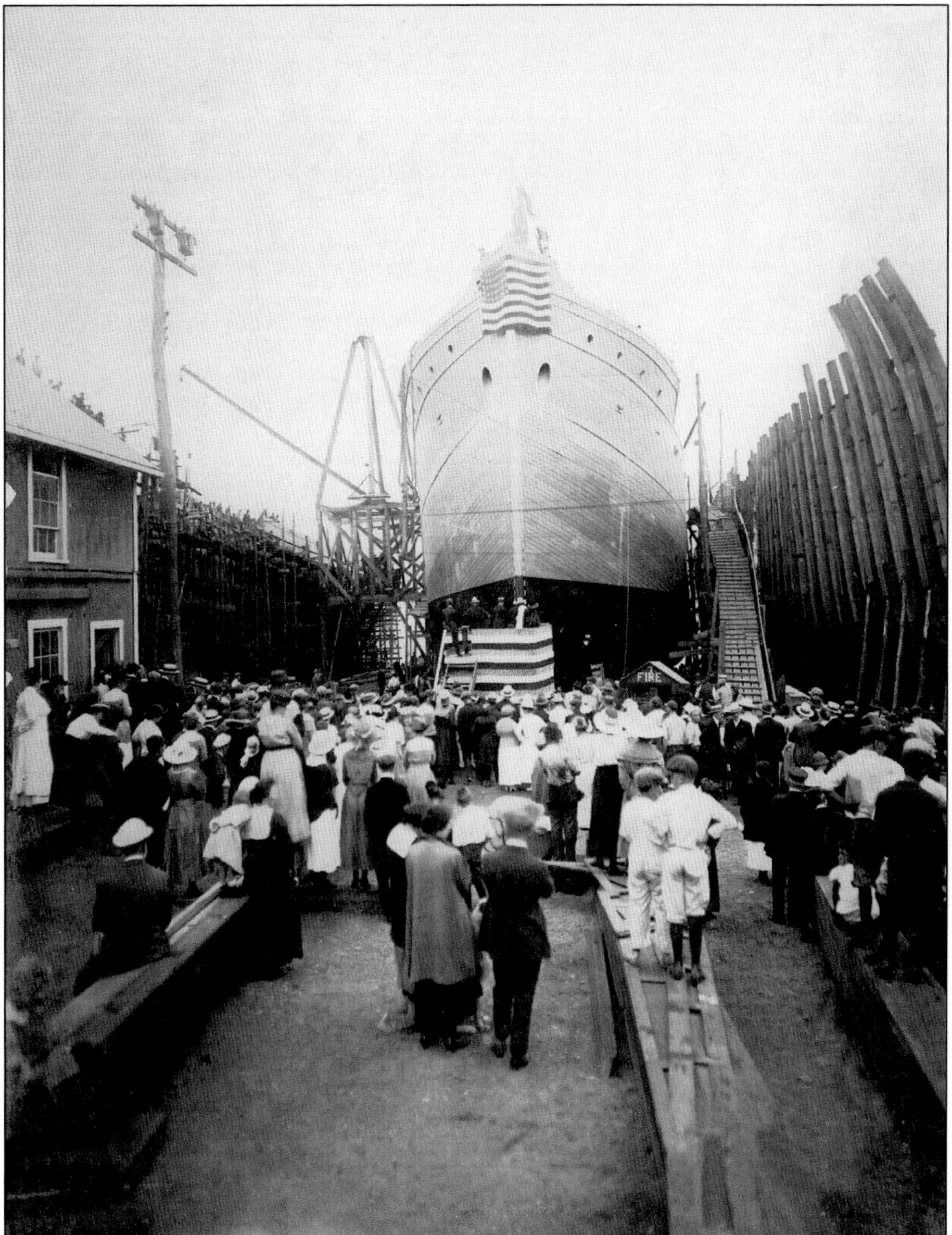

People turn out for the September 7, 1918, launching of the *Berea* at the former Palmer Shipyard in Noank, acquired by Groton Iron Works. The company had contracts to built four wooden vessels at the yard, which employed 1,500 men. Three vessels, *Berea*, *Baltso*, and *Hokah*, were built there. The yard was destroyed by fire in May 1924. (Carol W. Kimball.)

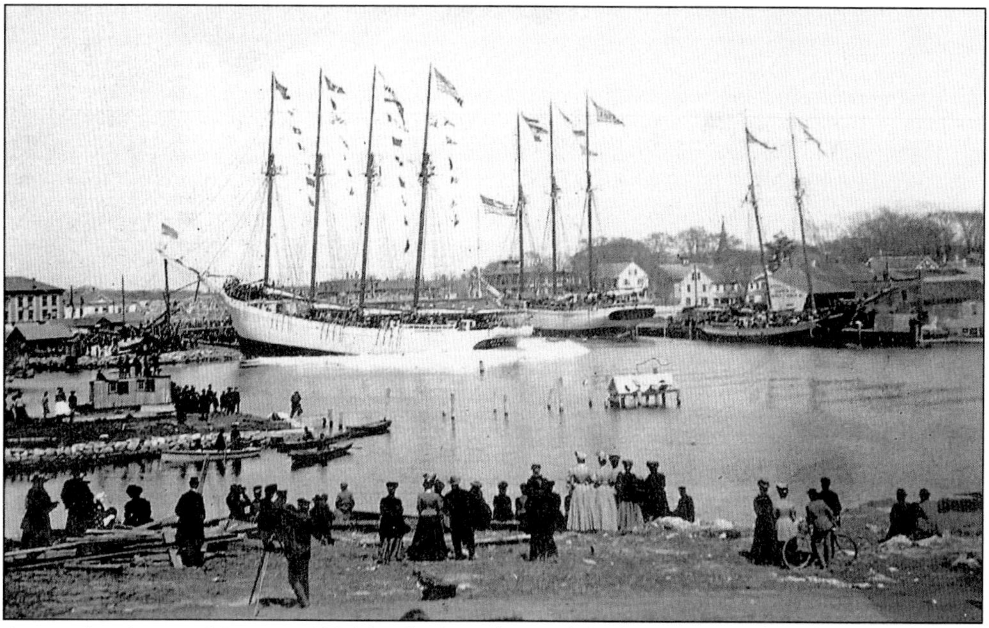

A crowd gathers in Mystic in 1906 for the launching of the four-masted schooner *Marie Gilbert*, built by the Gilbert Transportation Company of Mystic. Its shipyard was just south of the highway bridge on the Groton side of the river. The vessel represented the last gasp of the age of sail. It was short-lived. The vessel was stranded near Mayport, Florida, in 1907. (Bob Irons.)

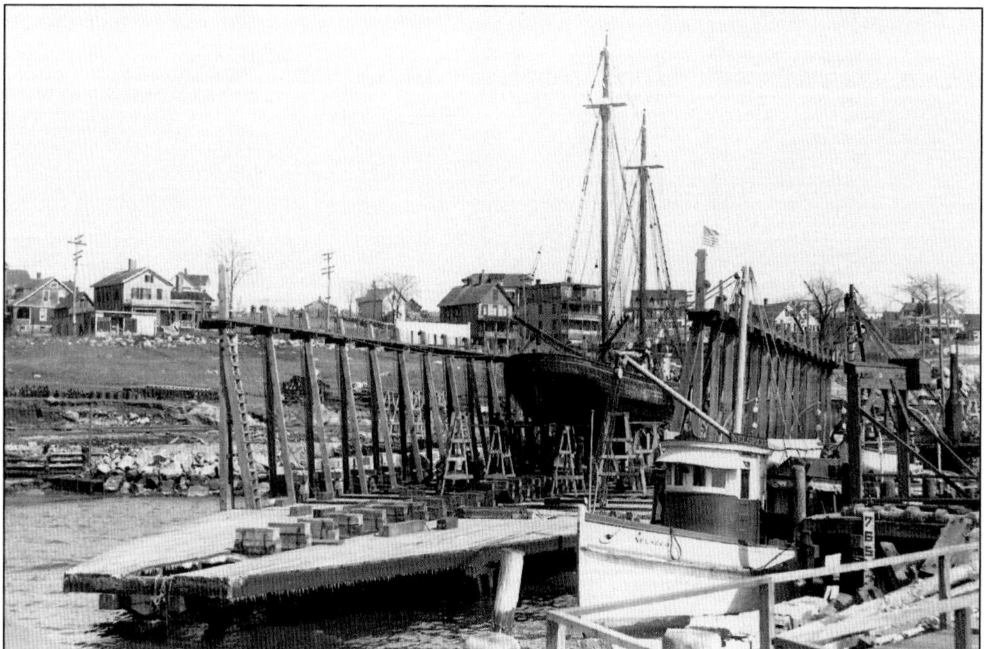

The Electric Boat Marine Railway was built in 1923 to accommodate S-class submarines after Electric Boat received a contract in 1922 to overhaul 30 of the vessels. The contract prompted Electric Boat to establish its own shipyard in Groton. The schooner on the ways in this photograph, taken about 1925, is the *Lucia*. (James L. Streeter.)

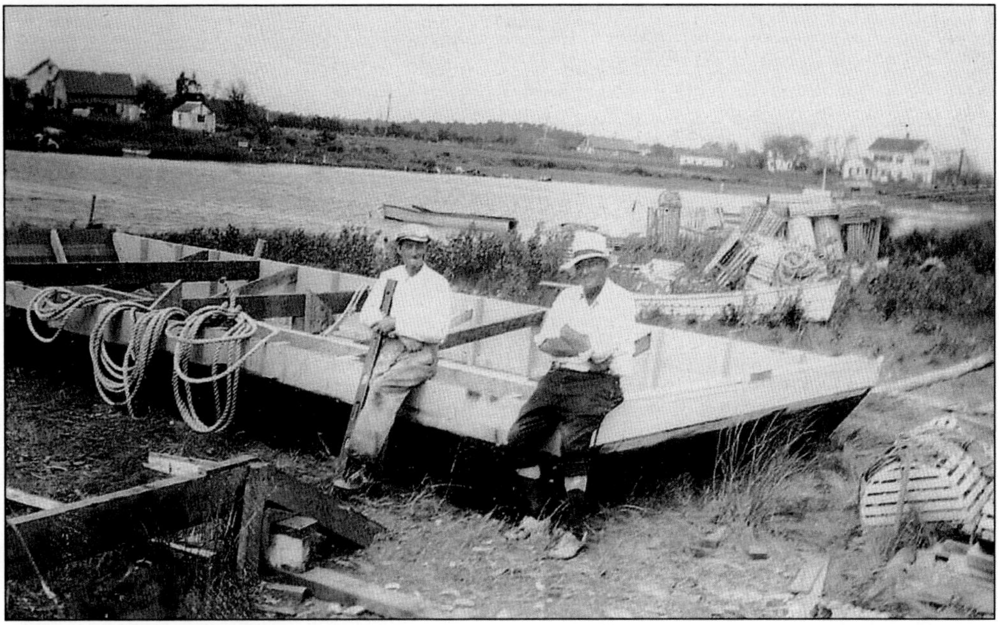

Clarence Hill and a friend sit on the foundation of a houseboat being built on the Poquonnock River in the 1930s. (Bob Irons.)

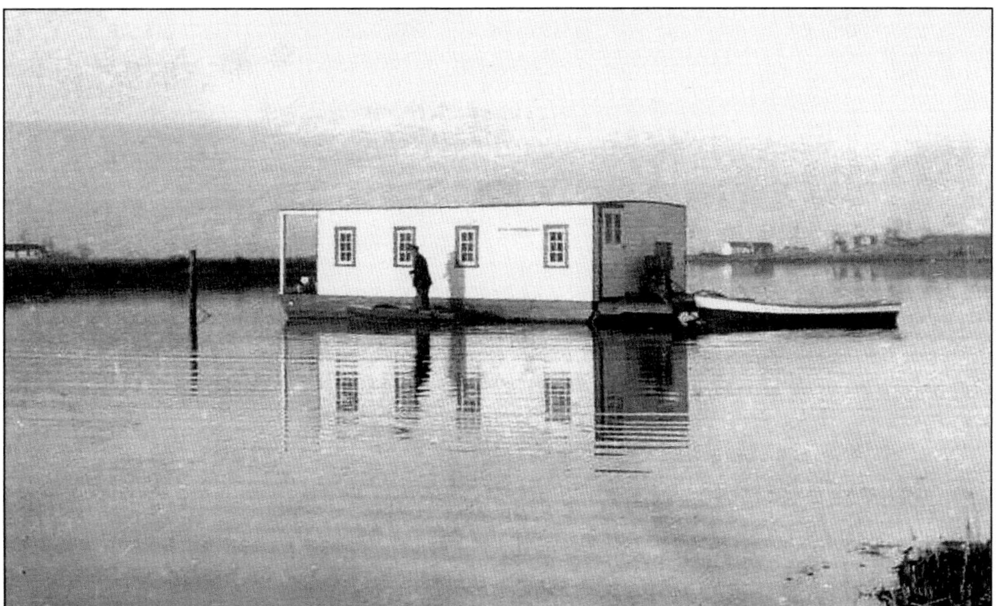

The finished houseboat, built by the men in the photograph above, floats on the Poquonnock River near Jupiter Point in this 1930s photograph. (Bob Irons.)

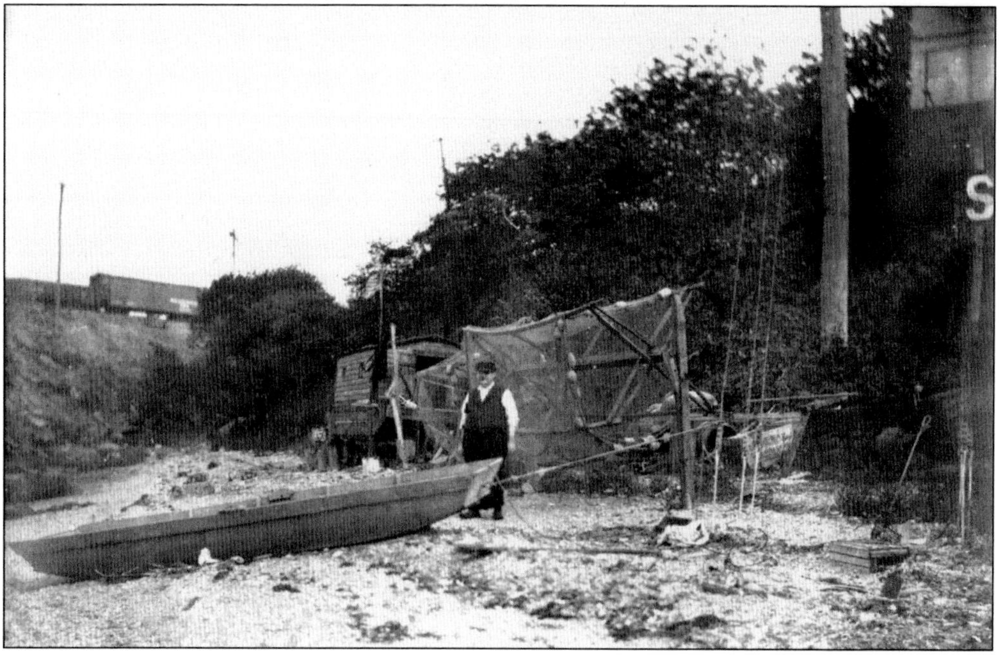

This *c.* 1905 photograph shows the Voyageurs Boatyard, which was north of the Spicer Coal Company and just south of the Thames River railroad bridge. The yard was home to the Voyageurs Canoe Club, whose participants practiced aquatic athletics on the Thames River. (James L. Streeter.)

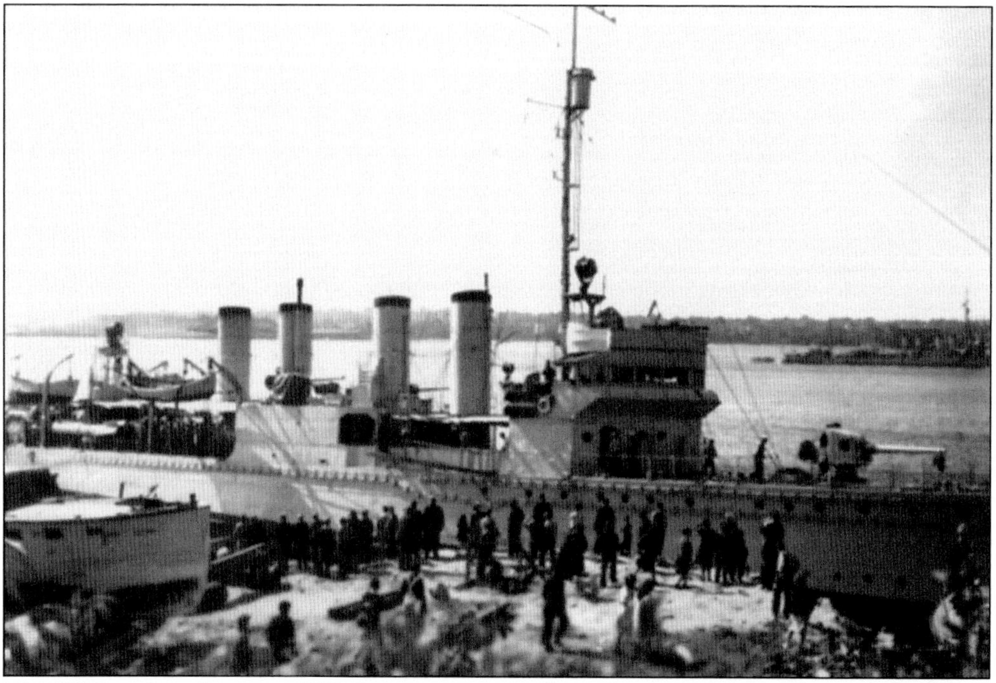

The Wickes-class destroyer USS *Roper* ran aground on the rocks of the Thames River as it accompanied Pres. Franklin D. Roosevelt to town in this pre–World War II photograph. (James L. Streeter.)

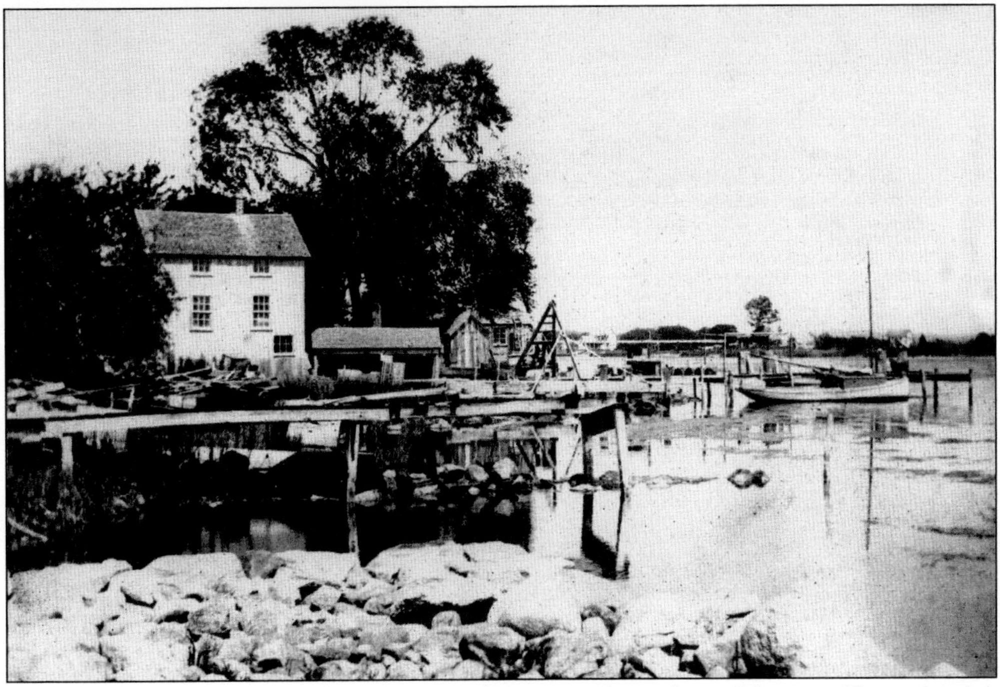

The Hill house sits at Baker's Cove. Moses Hill was an early resident of the area. (Spicer family.)

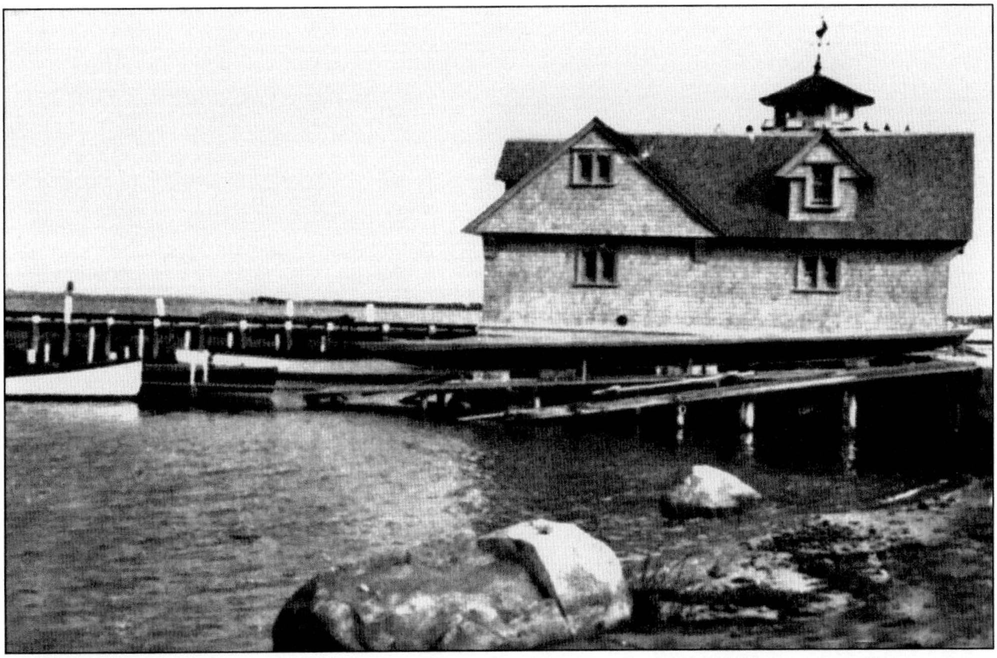

Morton F. Plant built this boathouse on Pine Island Bay in the early 1900s as part of his summer home, Branford House, at Avery Point. The long dock accommodated the family's two yachts. Today it is used by Project Oceanology, a marine science and education program used by local schoolchildren. (James L. Streeter.)

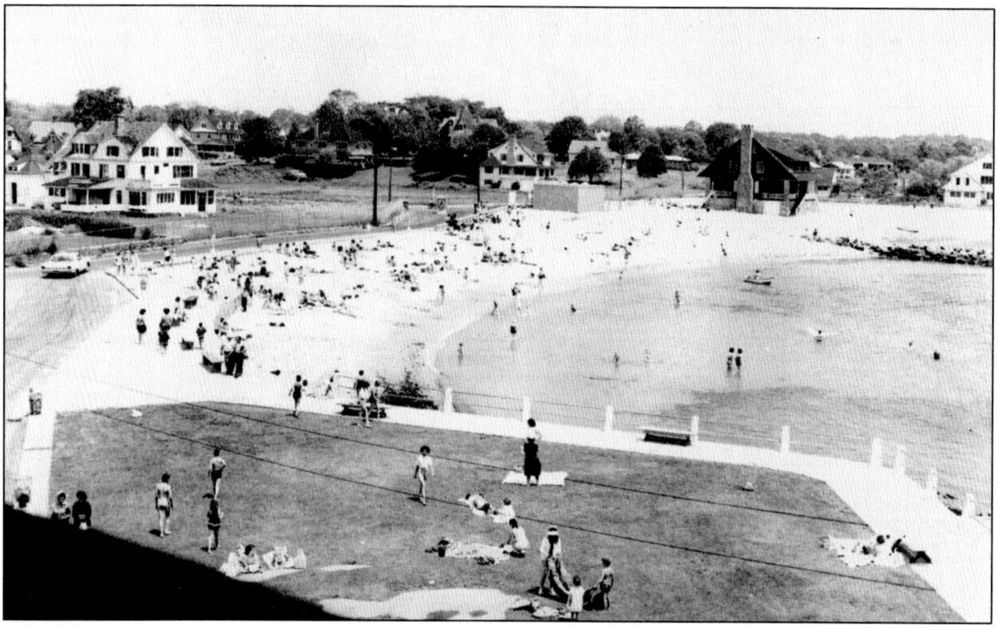

The City of Groton purchased Eastern Point Beach for $40,000 in 1945, and since then the property has been a popular summer destination for the citizens, as this 1960s photograph shows. (Bill Sanford.)

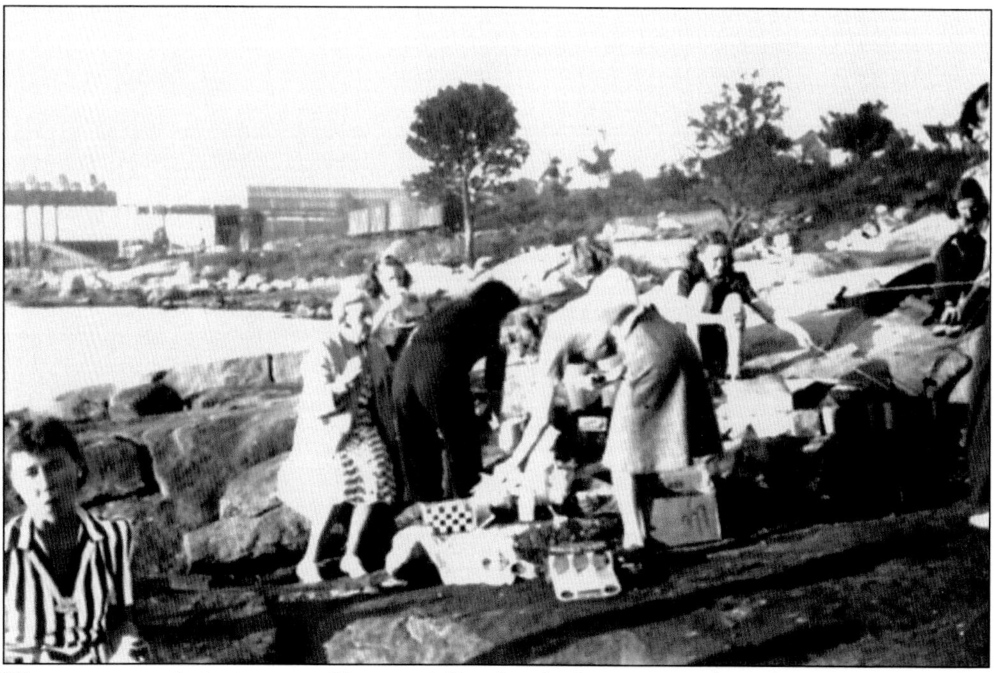

Women get out their picnics at Chapman's Beach, which was a popular swimming and sunning area for residents before the City of Groton purchased Eastern Point Beach in the 1940s. Chapman's Beach was at the south end of the Electric Boat property. (Dorothy Chrissos.)

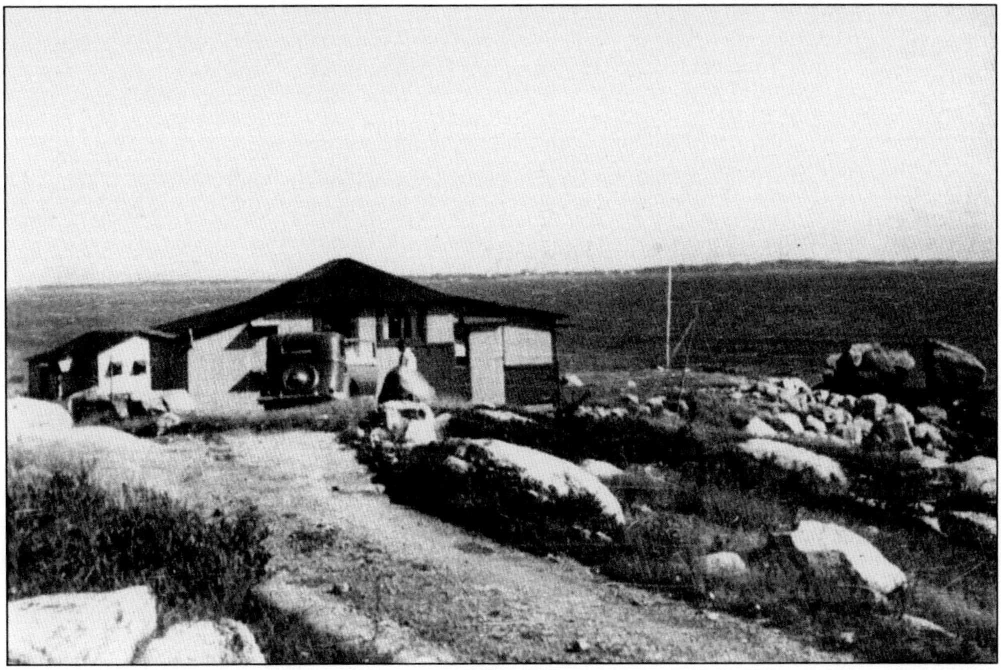

Flagg Cottage sits at the edge of the water at Bluff Point around 1933. The cottage, along with nearly 100 other summerhouses at Bluff Point, was swept away in the 1938 hurricane. The owners were not allowed to rebuild. Today Bluff Point is a coastal reserve owned by the state. (Anne and Alan Bentz.)

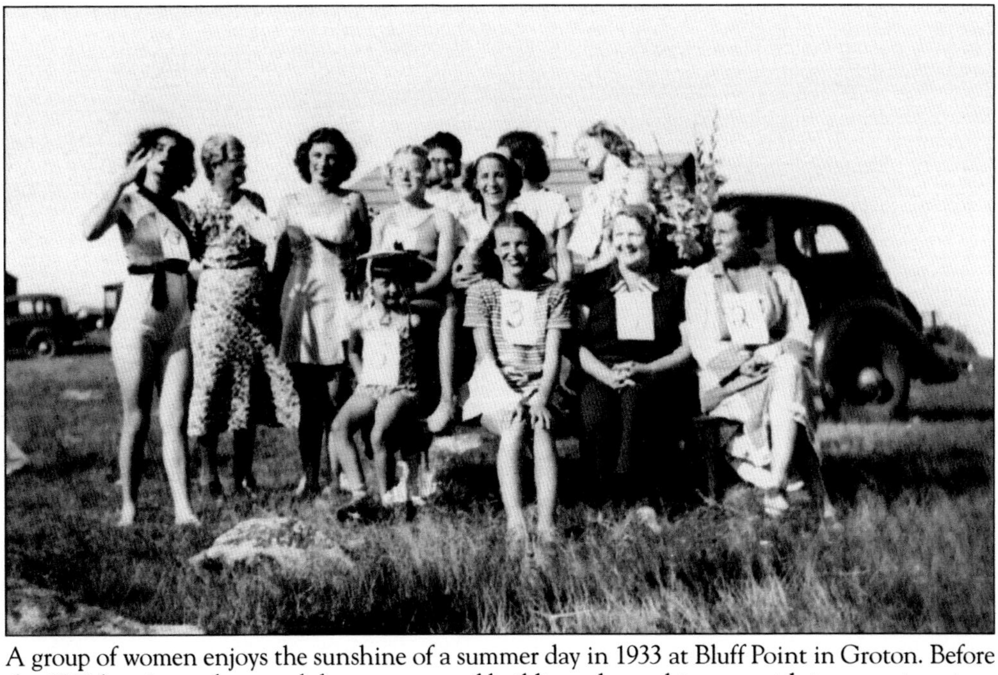

A group of women enjoys the sunshine of a summer day in 1933 at Bluff Point in Groton. Before the 1938 hurricane destroyed the cottages and buildings there, this area, with its sweeping views of Long Island Sound and Fishers Island Sound, was a popular summer enclave. (Anne and Alan Bentz.)

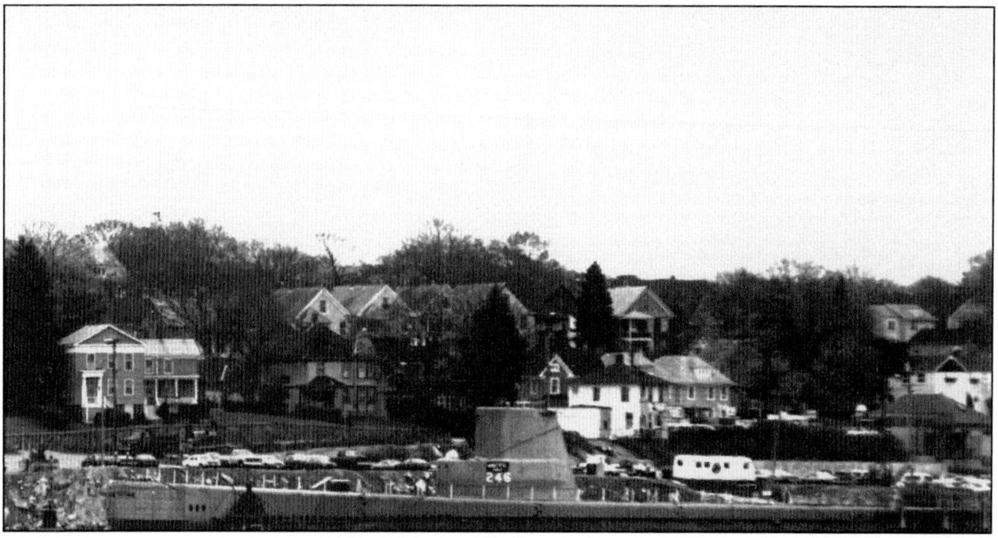

The diesel submarine *Croaker*, built at Electric Boat, was moored off Thames Street from 1976 to 1988, where it was open to the public as the Croaker Memorial. Businessman Frank Scheetz was instrumental in getting *Croaker* transferred to the Submarine Memorial Association so it could be a tourist attraction in town. He also opened a restaurant at the location. *Croaker* was moved to Buffalo in 1988 and is now part of the Naval and Servicemen's Park there. (James L. Streeter.)

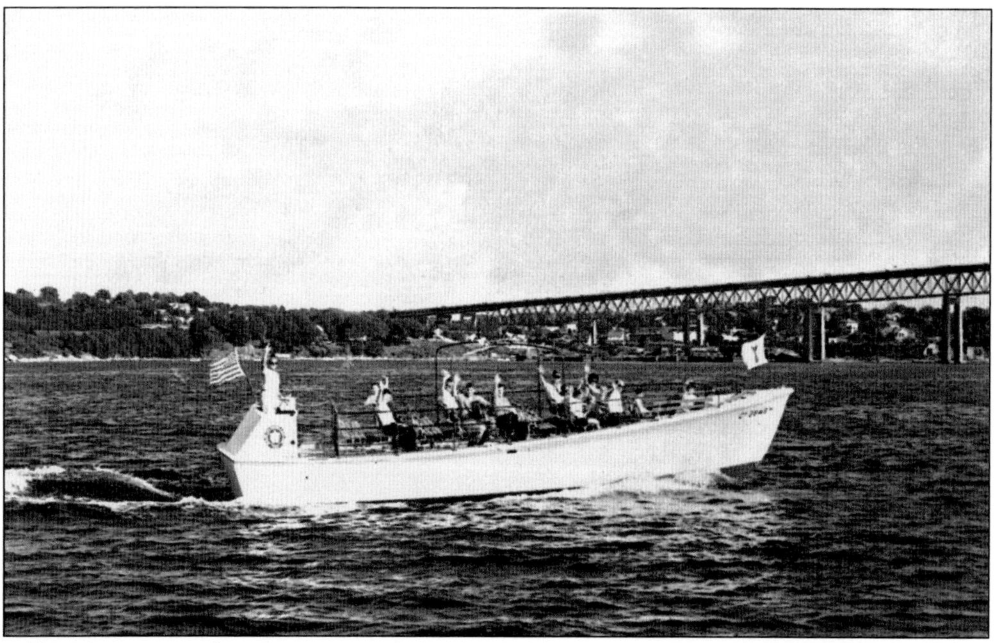

Although Groton is the submarine capital of the world, it was not always easy to see the submarines up close. In the 1970s, Clarence B. Sharp of Whaling City Dredge and Dock started a business called See Submarines by Boat, a launch that sailed up and down the Thames River, allowing passengers to view Electric Boat and the submarine base from the water. (James L. Streeter.)

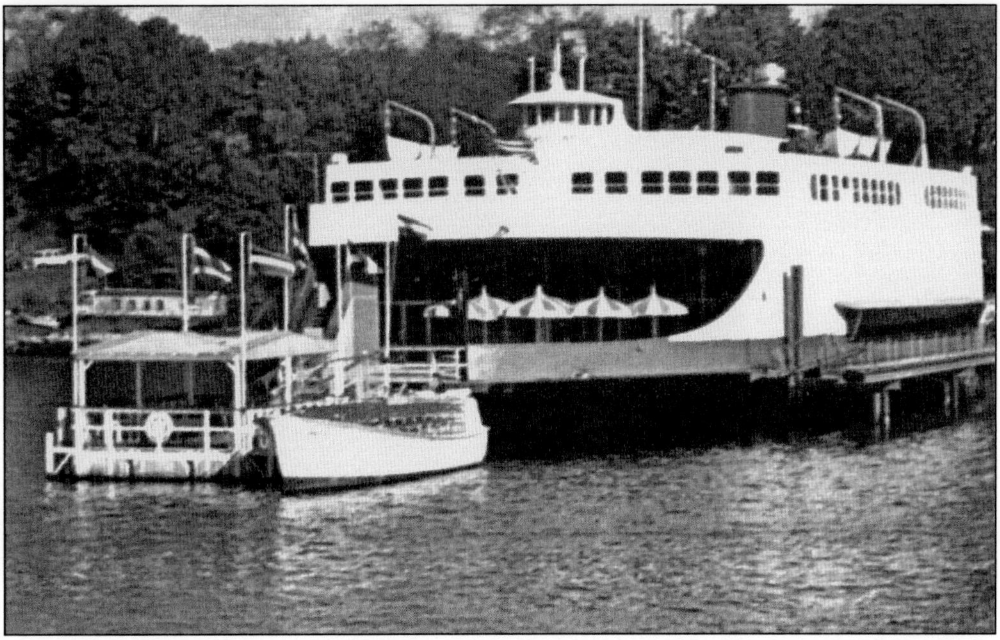

In the 1960s, former Groton mayor Clarence B. Sharp bought the old Jamestown, Rhode Island, ferry and brought it to the Thames River where he converted it to the Ferry Boat Restaurant. The ferry also was used by the See Submarines by Boat business on the Thames River. The restaurant failed after Sharp's death in 1974. (James L. Streeter.)

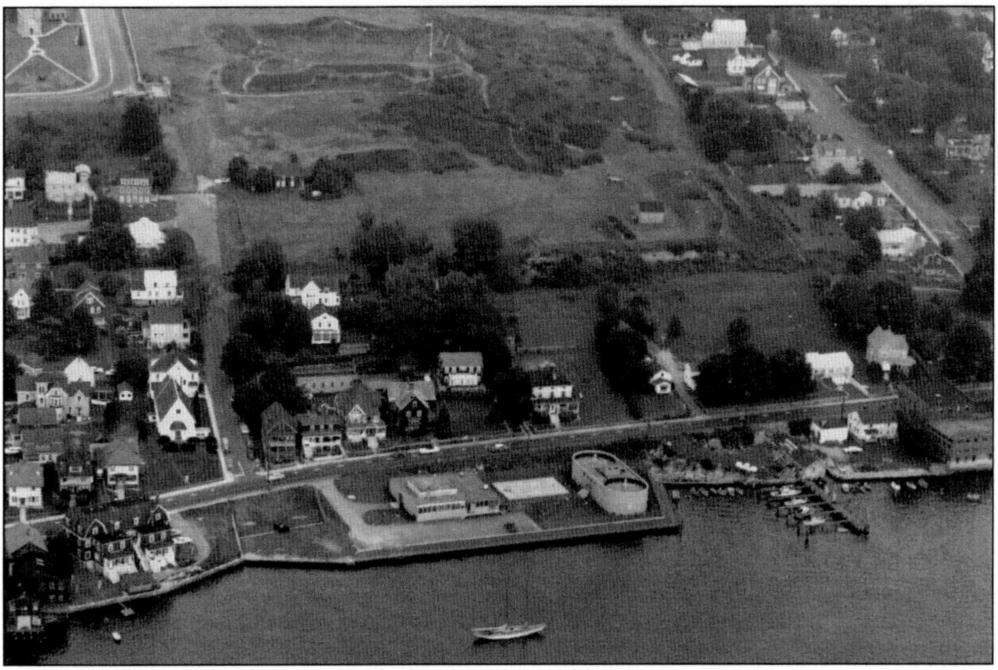

This aerial photograph of the City of Groton Filtration Plant on the Thames River also provides a wonderful view of Fort Griswold Battlefield State Park, where British soldiers, aided by the traitor Benedict Arnold, attacked the fort on September 6, 1781. Fort Griswold is the only intact Revolutionary War battlefield in Connecticut. (Groton Utilities.)

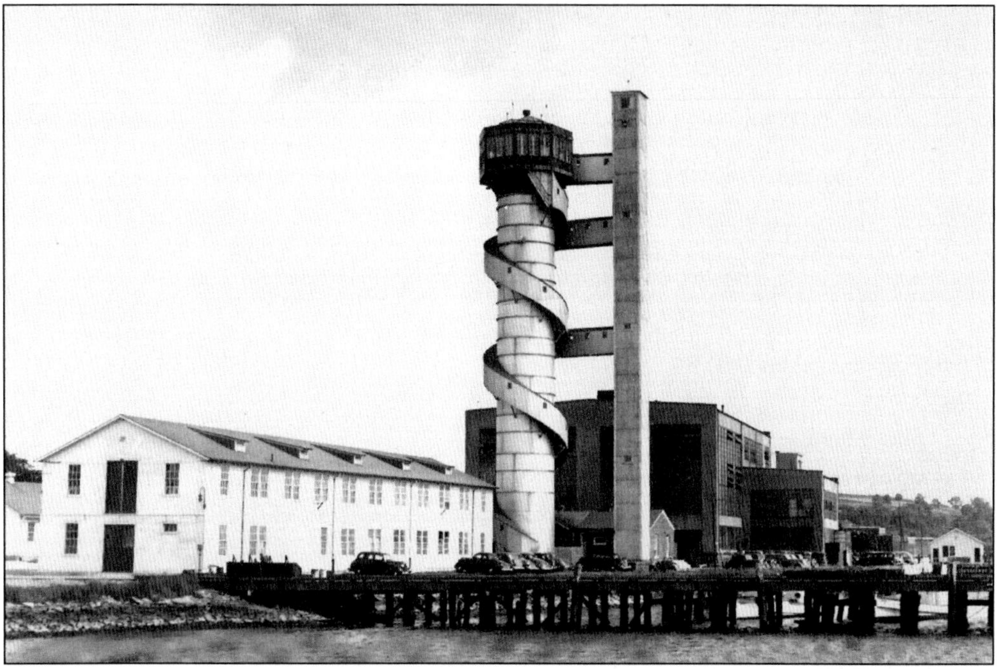

The escape training tower was long a landmark at the naval submarine base. The 120-foot-high steel tower was erected in 1930 after a number of submarine disasters in the 1920s led to the introduction of an escape device known as the Momsen lung. All submariners had to qualify ascending to the surface under pressure. The tower was demolished in 1991. (Sally Allyn Brousseau.)

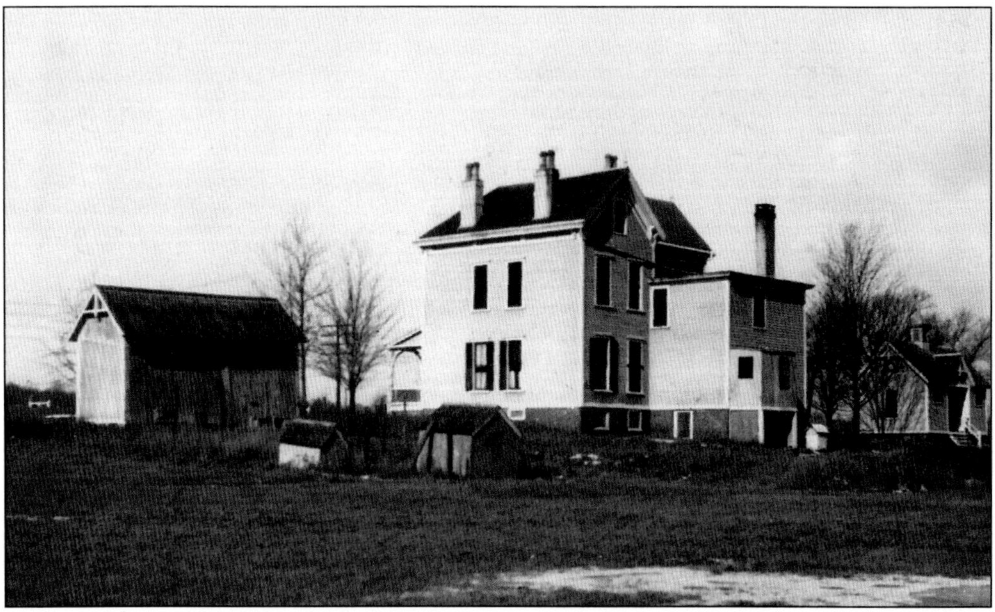

A far cry from the bustling hive of activity that is today's naval submarine base, this 1915 photograph shows the house where the base commandant lived. Just before World War I, the government converted the 1868 navy yard on the Thames River to a submarine base to service the newly created fleet of underwater vessels. (Sally Allyn Brousseau.)

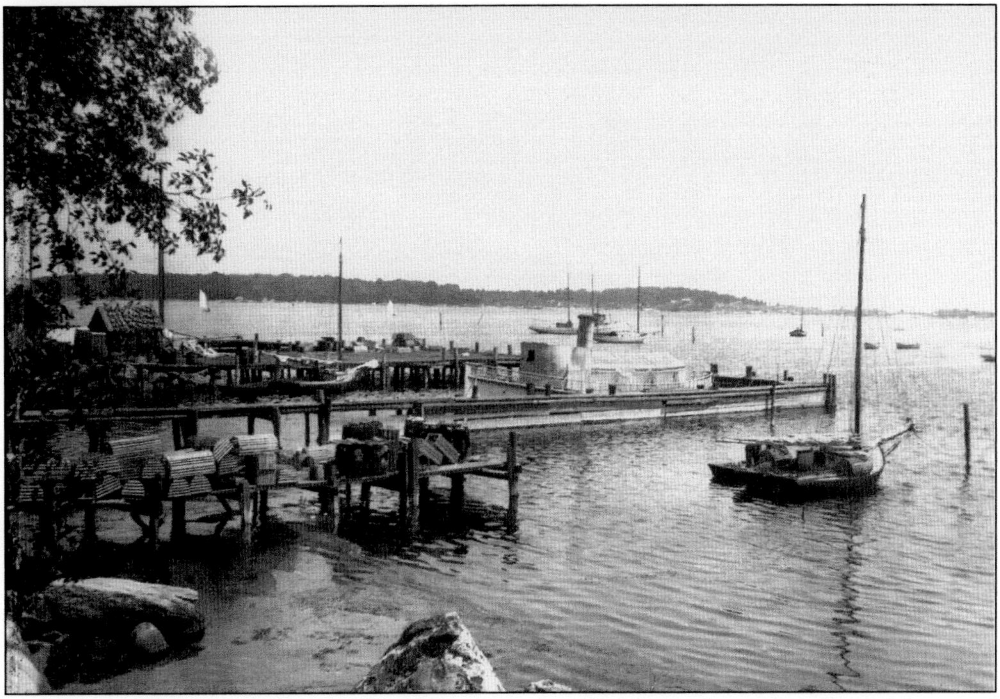

The steamer *Summer Girl* is tied up at dock in Noank in 1901. Noank men have been fishing and lobstering for as long as Groton has been settled. Noank's unique half-rounded lobster pots line the dock in this photograph. Most of the catch was sold in New York. (James L. Streeter.)

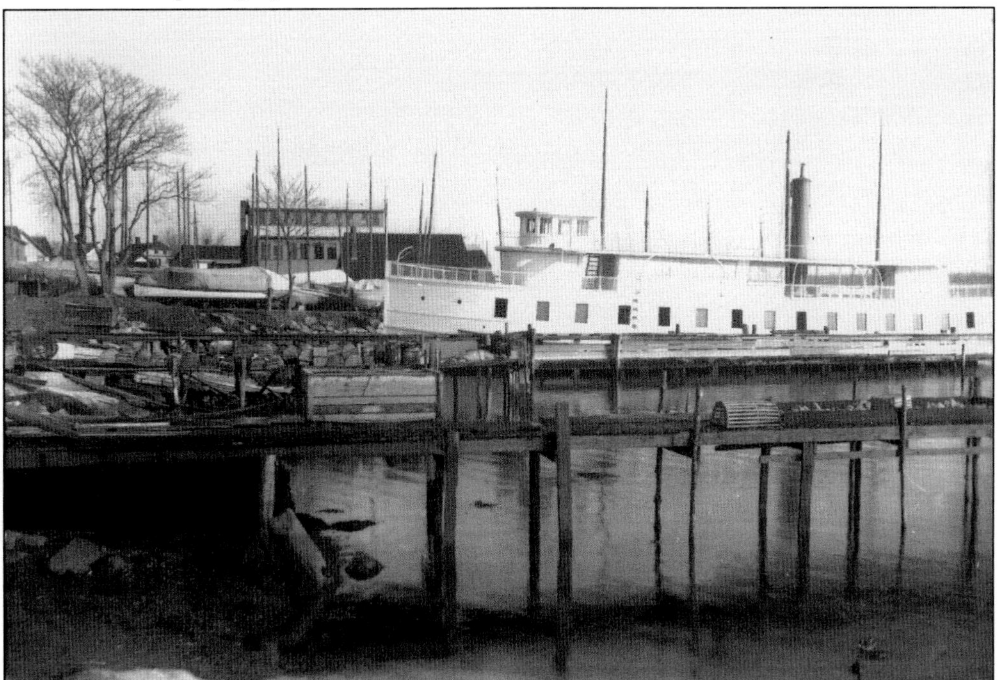

The stock market crash of 1929 cost many people their fortunes and laid up many yachts, like this one tied up at a dock in Noank. (James L. Streeter.)

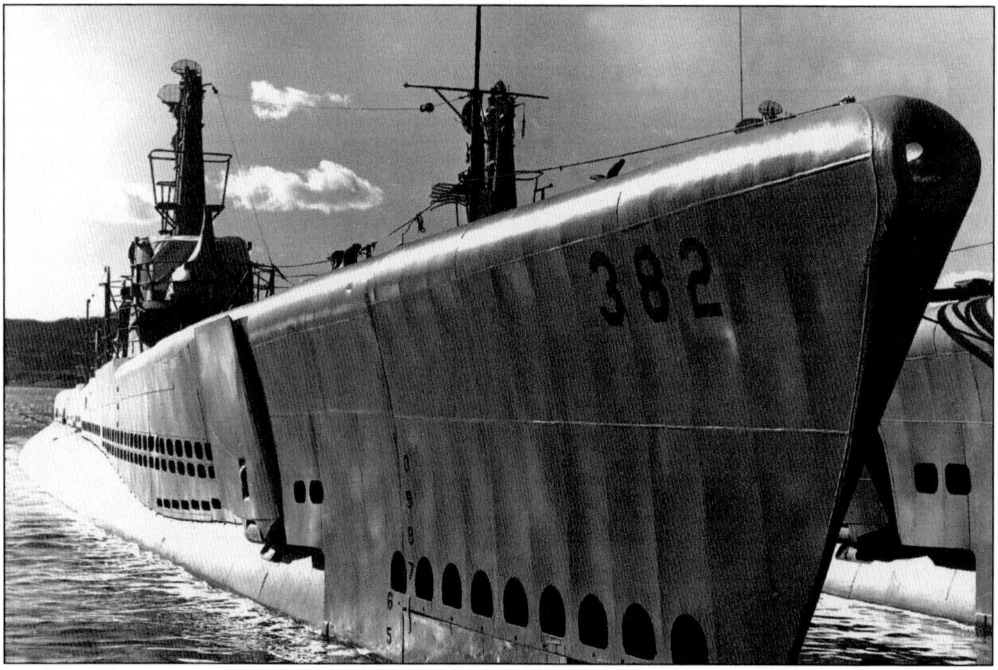

USS *Picuda* (USS 382) was a diesel submarine from World War II named for the giant barracuda of the Caribbean. It was awarded six battle stars for its tours of duty in the Pacific, where it sank a quantity of Japanese ships. After the war, it was assigned as a training ship for the submarine school at the naval submarine base and was a common sight along the Thames River. (George Edwards.)

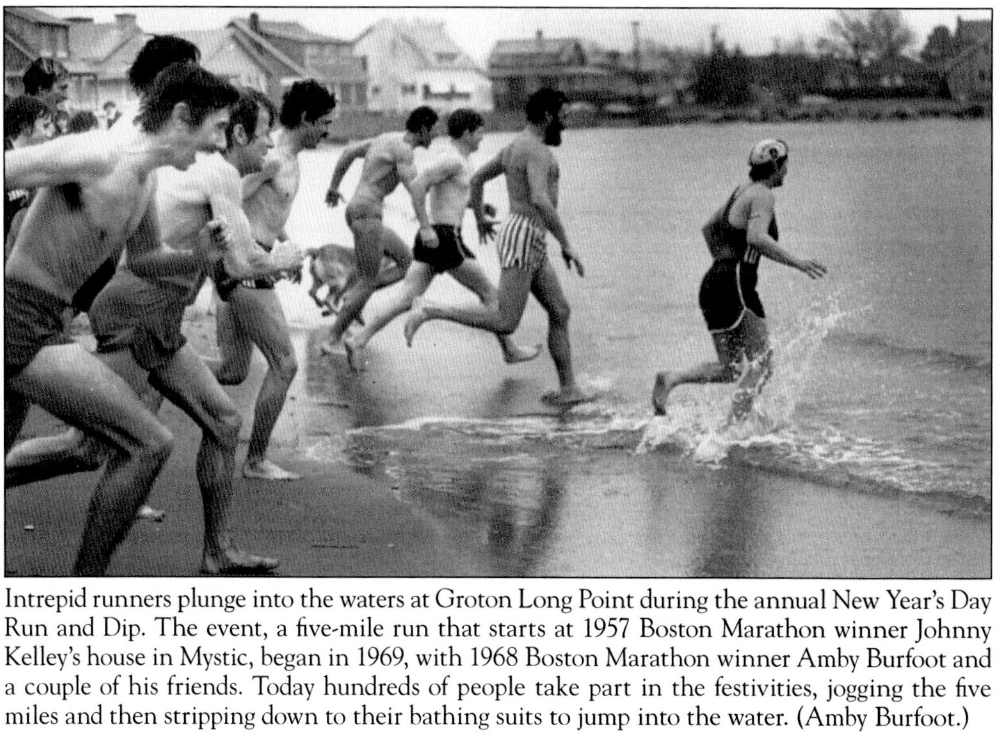

Intrepid runners plunge into the waters at Groton Long Point during the annual New Year's Day Run and Dip. The event, a five-mile run that starts at 1957 Boston Marathon winner Johnny Kelley's house in Mystic, began in 1969, with 1968 Boston Marathon winner Amby Burfoot and a couple of his friends. Today hundreds of people take part in the festivities, jogging the five miles and then stripping down to their bathing suits to jump into the water. (Amby Burfoot.)

Two

People

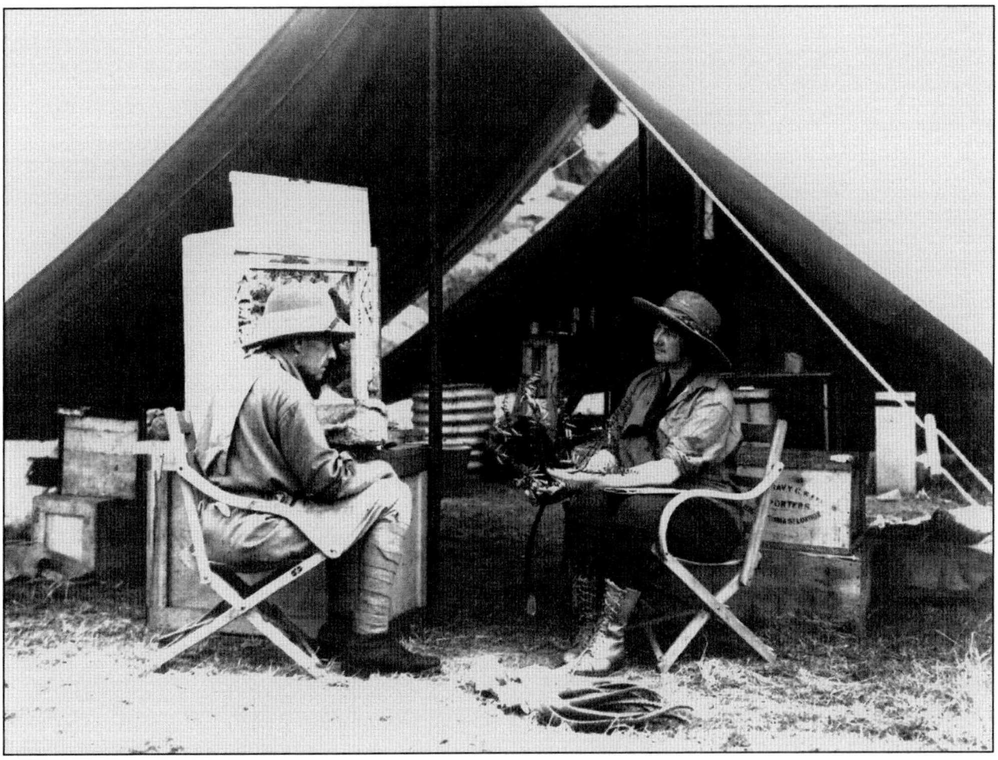

Mary Jobe Akeley lived in Mystic for decades and is best known for the girls' camp she ran from 1916 to 1930 along the Mystic River. She is pictured here with her husband, Carl Akeley, on safari in Africa in 1924, a trip to collect animals for the American Museum of Natural History in New York. Carl died on the trip, and Mary Jobe completed his work. The African hall at the museum is named for her husband. (Carol W. Kimball.)

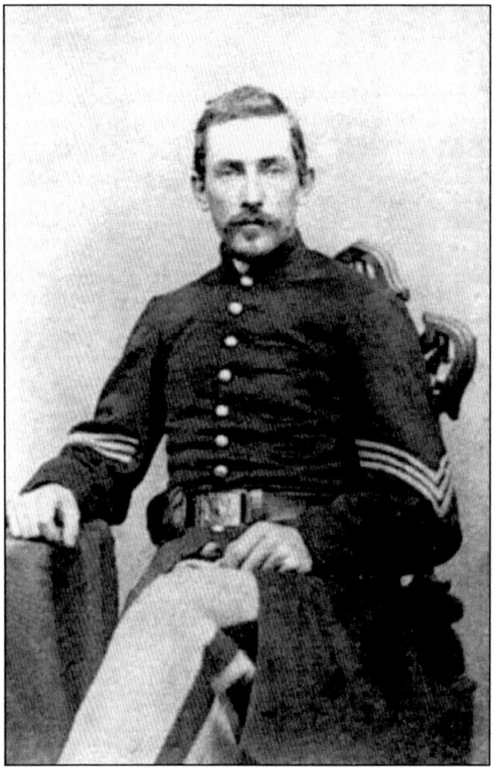

Robert A. Gray, a stonecutter from Groton, earned the Medal of Honor in the Civil War for his action on May 16, 1864, at Drury's Bluff, Virginia. While retreating with his regiment, Connecticut's 21st Regiment, Company C, Gray, a sergeant, voluntarily faced enemy fire to rescue a wounded soldier from his company who could not walk. Gray was mustered out of the army in 1865 and returned to work as a stonecutter. He was in business with Charles Merritt and John Salter, working a quarry on Thames Street. (James L. Streeter.)

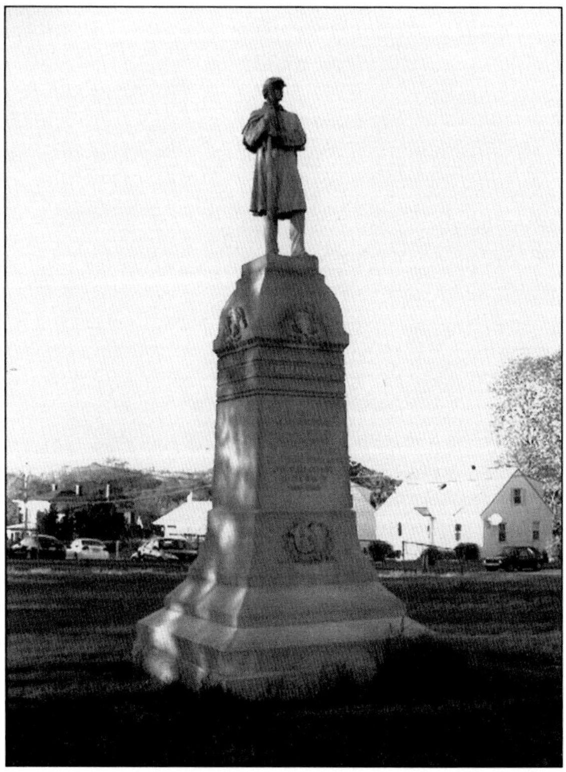

When Medal of Honor winner Gray died, he left money to pay for the Civil War monument that stands east of the Monument House at Fort Griswold. A resident of Ramsdell Street, Gray represented Groton in the state legislature from 1880 to 1881 and also served on the committee to erect a statue at Broad and Hempstead Streets in New London to honor the area's Civil War regiments. That statue was dedicated in 1898. (James L. Streeter.)

Capt. John Knight Bucklyn was a hero of the Civil War and a Medal of Honor recipient for his actions at Chancellorsville on May 5, 1863. A first lieutenant in Battery E, 1st Rhode Island light artillery, Bucklyn, although wounded, fought under fierce fire and managed to save a cannon as the enemy advanced. A Rhode Island native, he settled in Mystic after the war and founded Mystic Valley Institute, a private preparatory school. His mausoleum in Lower Mystic Cemetery carries a plaque noting that he is a Medal of Honor winner. (Jack Bucklyn.)

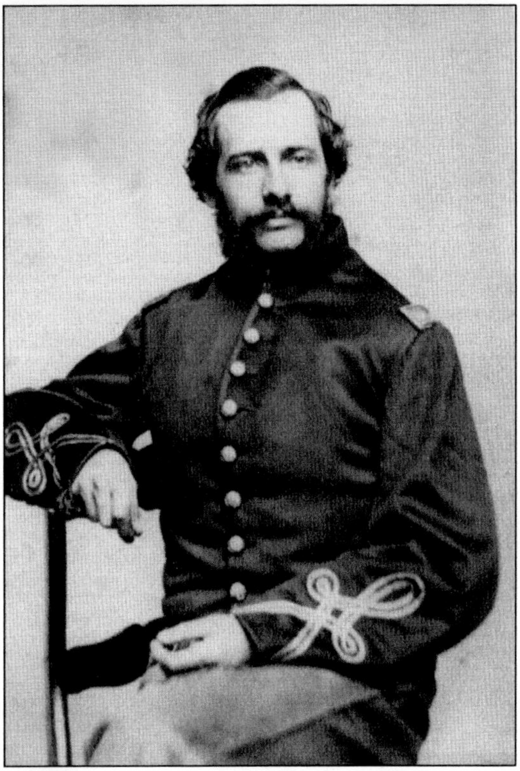

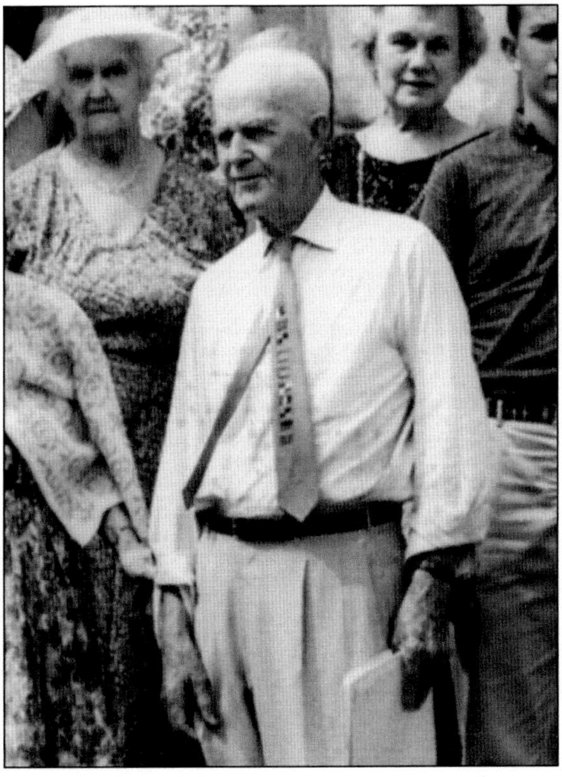

Carl C. Cutler (1878–1966) was a renowned maritime historian and author of *Greyhounds of the Sea: The Story of the American Clipper Ship.* A native of Michigan, Cutler came to Mystic in 1928. He helped found the Mystic Maritime Association, which later became Mystic Seaport Museum, in an effort to preserve America's 19th-century maritime history, especially the wooden vessels he saw being destroyed as iron ships took their place. Cutler was responsible for securing America's last wooden whaling ship, *Charles W. Morgan*, as Mystic Seaport's historic centerpiece. Groton honored Cutler by naming a middle school for him. (Carol W. Kimball.)

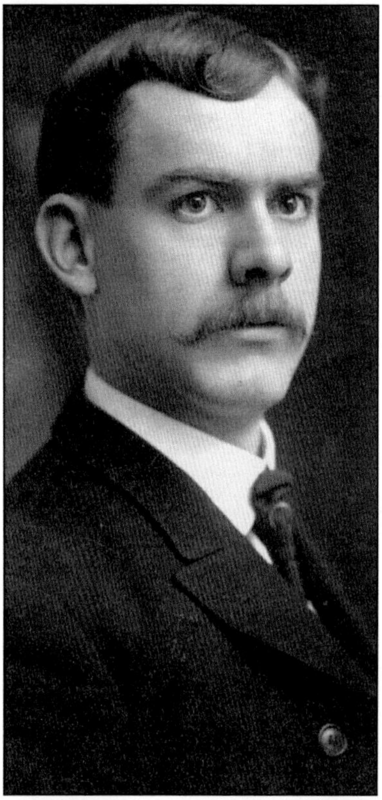

Irving Poppe was the proprietor of the Edgcomb and Poppe men's store on Thames Street. Poppe, who operated the store until it was sold in July 1946, specialized in tailoring. Poppe was involved in town politics for more than 40 years. He was Groton town clerk from 1941 until his death in 1955, at 73. Poppe was active in the Odd Fellows and Masons and was a trustee of the Groton Heights Baptist Church. (Winifred Newbury.)

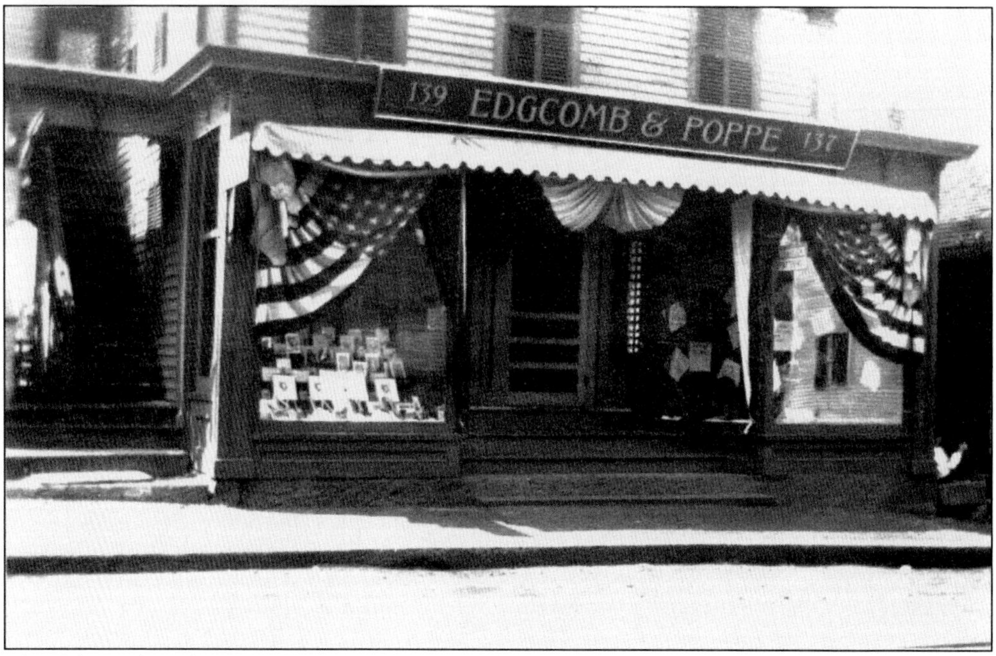

The Edgcomb and Poppe men's store, at 137 Thames Street, was run by Howard A. Edgcomb and Poppe. They specialized in clothing and men's furnishings. Paul's Pasta is in the building today. (James L. Streeter.)

William Seely was Groton's first casualty in World War II. At 18 years old, Seely was aboard the USS *Arizona* at Pearl Harbor on December 7, 1941. He had finished high school just six months earlier. Seely's last name is misspelled on the Arizona Memorial at Pearl Harbor. (James L. Streeter.)

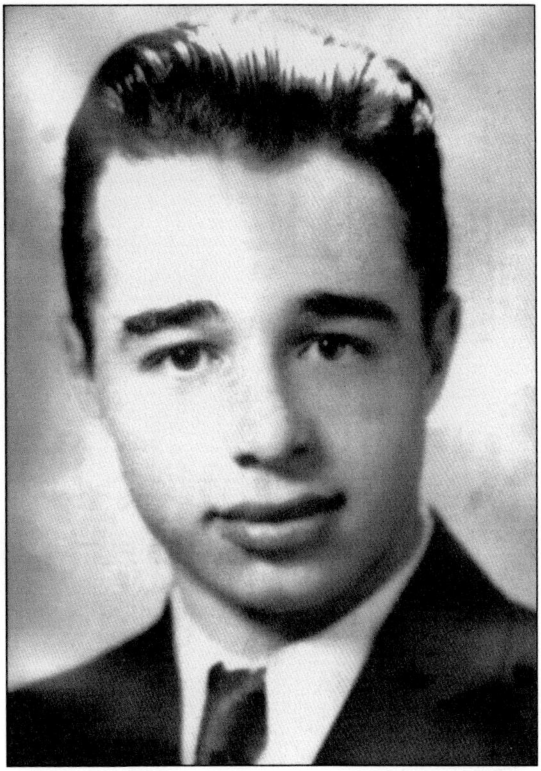

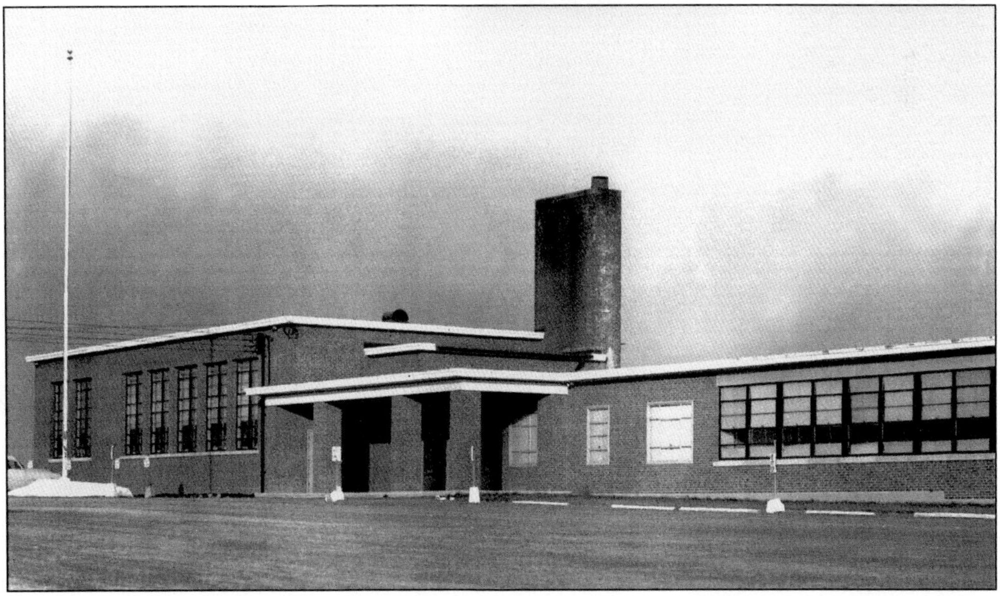

In 1956, Groton named the new school it built to accommodate navy families for the neighborhood boy Seely, who died at Pearl Harbor. A photograph of Seely hung in the school, and each year on December 7, a special ceremony was held to remember him. The school closed in 2003 and is now used by the town recreation department. A flag that had flown over the USS *Arizona* was given to the school and is now in the office of the superintendent of schools. (James L. Streeter.)

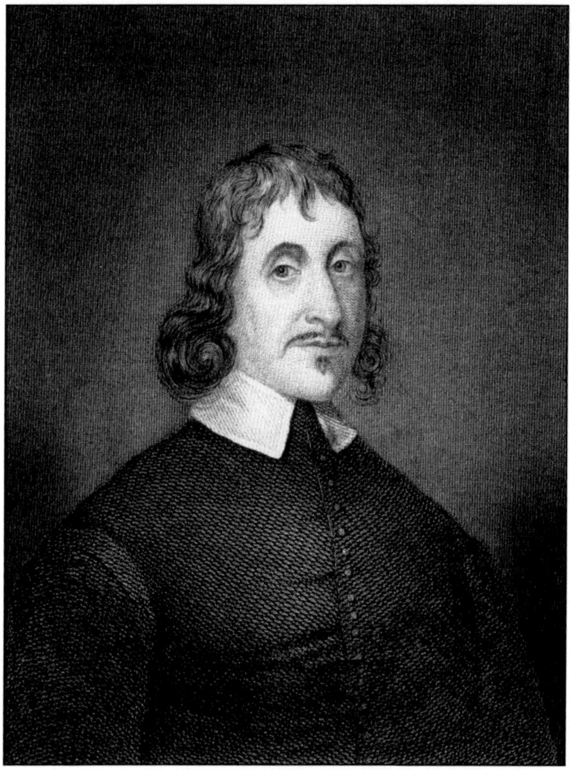

John Winthrop Jr. was Groton's founder and the eldest son of John Winthrop, who led the settlement of Massachusetts Bay Colony. In 1645, he came to southeastern Connecticut, where he established Pequot Plantation, encompassing what today is New London, Groton, Ledyard, and Montville. He was granted land that included Bluff Point, Mumford Cove, and Groton Long Point, although he never lived there. Groton takes its name from Winthrop's ancestral estate in England. Winthrop later served 18 years as Connecticut's governor. (Carol W. Kimball.)

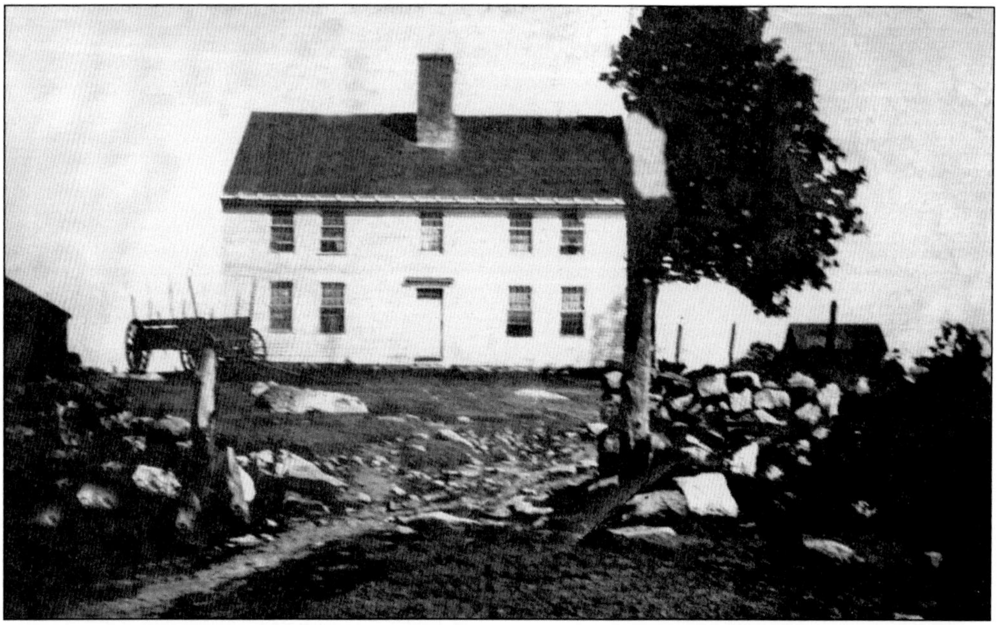

The Winthrop House at Bluff Point was built about 1712 by Edward Yeomans on the Winthrop farm, which was leased from the Winthrop family. This photograph was taken in the early 1900s, when John Abbott Ackley and his family occupied the house. The structure burned on September 14, 1962, leaving nothing but the chimney standing. Today only traces of the foundation can be found at Bluff Point Coastal Reserve. (Carol W. Kimball.)

John Abbott Ackley, called "Jack" by his friends, was Groton's potato king. In 1907, he leased Poquonnock Farm, 1,135 acres that encompassed Bluff Point and stretched north to Fort Hill, where Poquonnock Plains Park is today. In 1914, he planted his first potato crop. At the height of his prosperity, Ackley hired 100 youths from the surrounding area to handpick his harvest, at 7¢ per bushel. (Ackley family.)

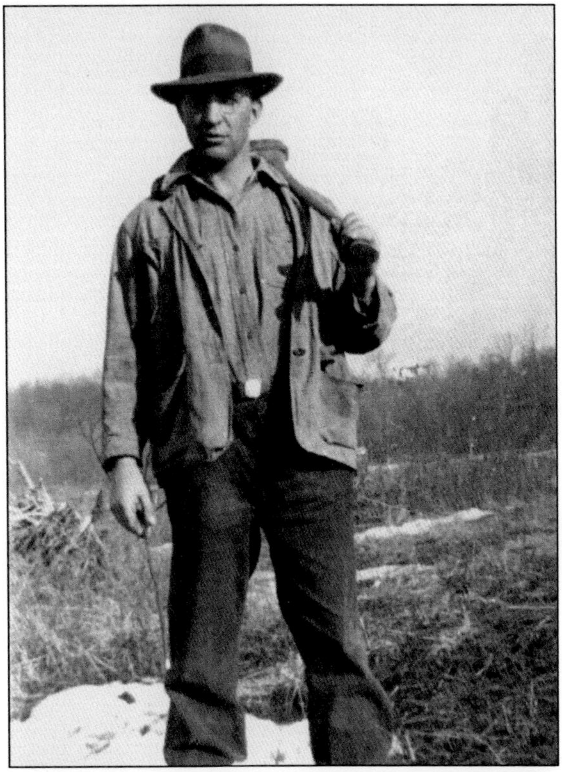

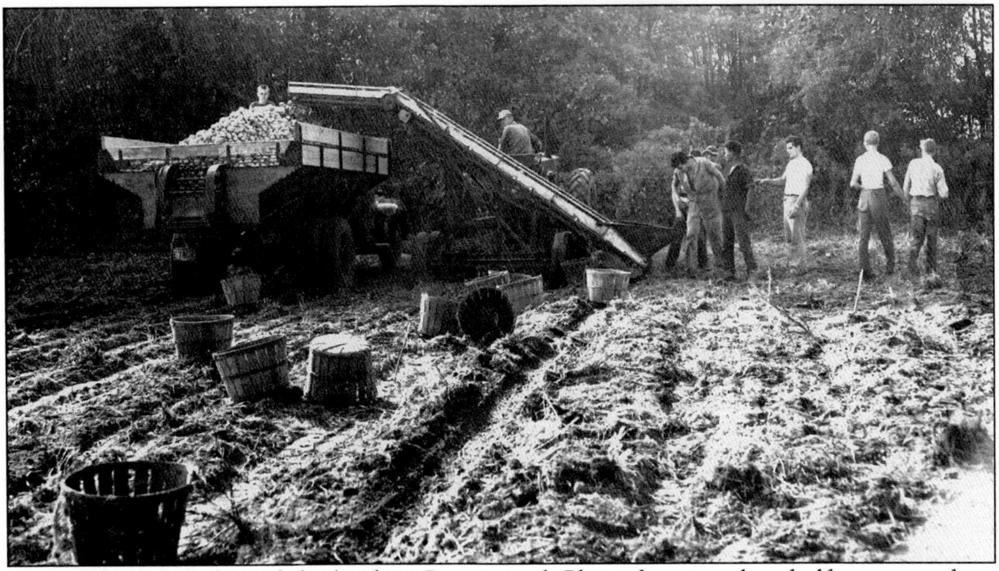

The Ackley family farmed the lands in Poquonnock Plains for more than half a century, from the early 1900s through the 1950s. They owned potato fields all over southeastern Connecticut and Rhode Island. Their most productive fields, however, were 300 acres near Groton Town Hall, now Fort Hill Homes. The federal government took the land in 1942 to build "temporary housing for the duration of World War II" for workers building submarines for the war effort at Electric Boat. It spelled the beginning of the end for potato fields in Poquonnock Plains. (Ackley family.)

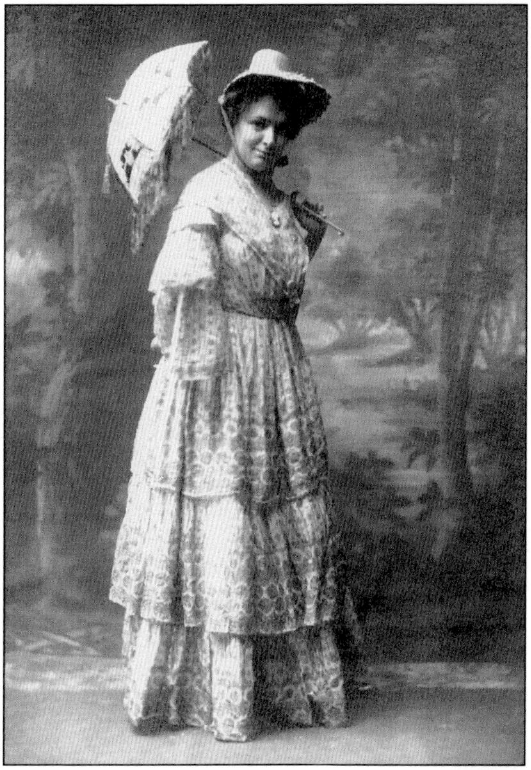

Juliet Haley (1892–1977) was the granddaughter of Groton native Caleb Haley, who made his fortune in the Fulton Fish Market in New York City and later bought the 428-acre Haley Farm in Groton, now part of the town's green space. Her father was Samuel Haley and her mother Juliette Gates, daughter of Capt. George W. Gates of Mystic. Juliet never married and, in later years, lived in her great-grandfather Horatio Nelson Fish's house on High Street in Mystic. (Fish family.)

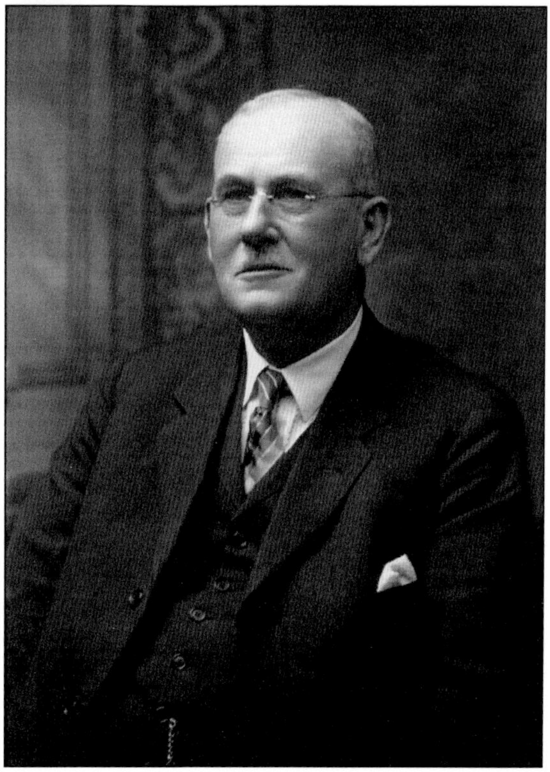

Henry L. Bailey served as Groton town clerk for 34 years, from his election in 1907 to 1941. He was the first clerk to serve in the new town hall, built as a gift by Morton F. Plant in 1908. Bailey, who lived at 60 Ramsdell Street with his wife, Louisa, also was an insurance agent at H. L. Bailey and Son at 174 Thames Street and a partner in Coe and Bailey General Store at 241 Thames Street. (Bea Thomson.)

Edward Randall Welles was born at Old Mystic on February 23, 1900, the son of William P. and Isabella Dean Welles. He worked as a machine engineer at Lathrop Engine Company in Mystic from 1916 to 1954, traveling the East Coast as the company's salesman and troubleshooter. In 1954, he opened Welles Marine Service in Old Mystic. His memoirs were the subject of *Recollections of a Small Town Yankee Mechanic*, published in 1987 by the Groton Public Library. Welles died on September 23, 1988. This portrait is by George E. Tingley, a noted local photographer. (Carol W. Kimball.)

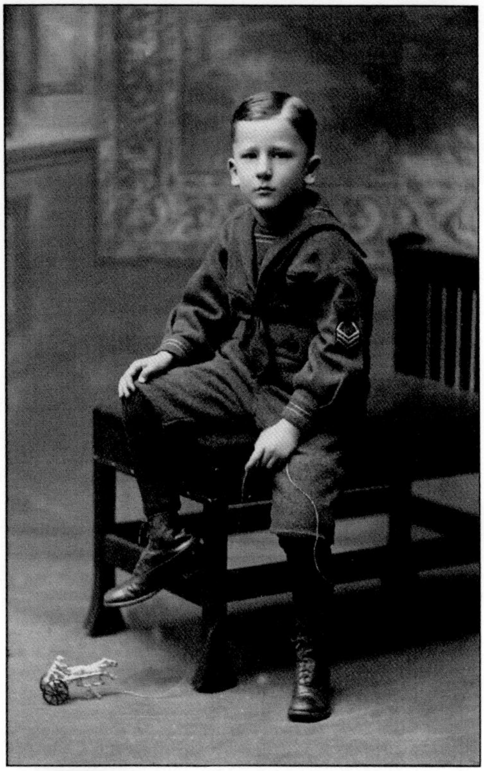

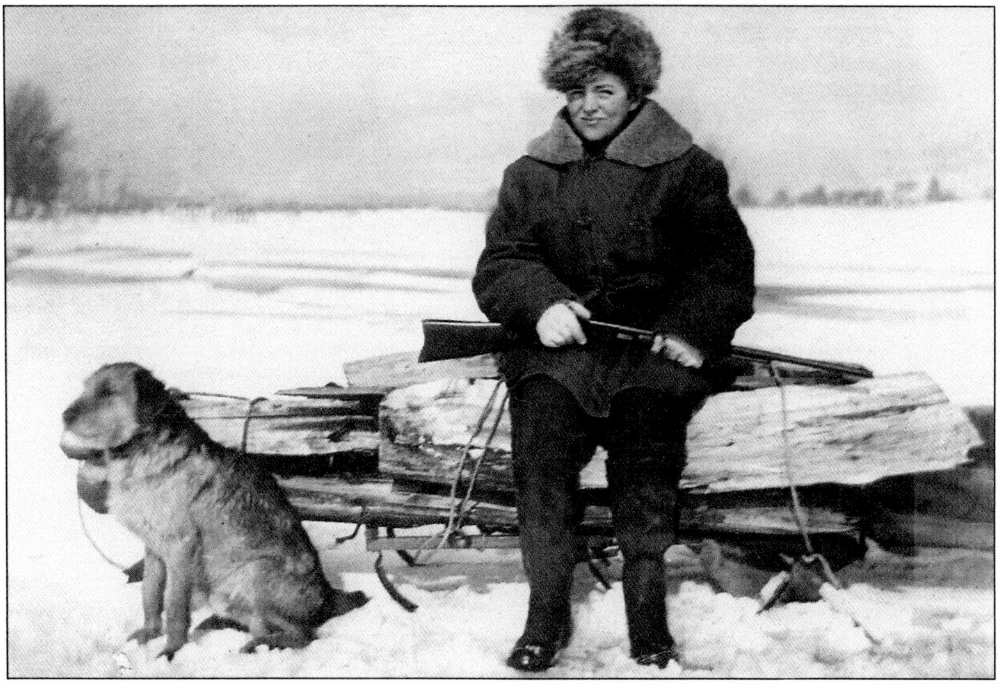

Well-known Groton architect Sanford Brown Meech was born in Groton on December 18, 1903. He was a 1924 graduate of Yale University. Here Meech, at age 14, stands on the ice at Pine Island Bay during the cold winter of 1917–1918 with his gun, dog, and sled. (Larry Jacobsen.)

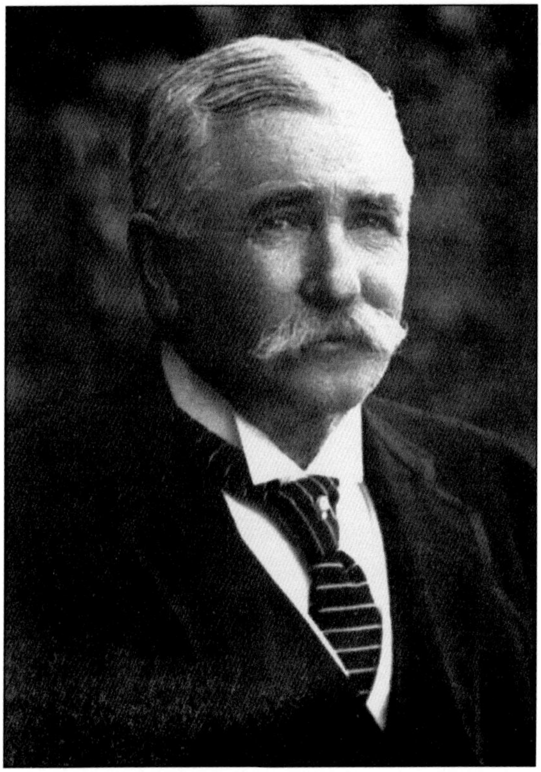

Millionaire Morton F. Plant was one of Groton's greatest benefactors. Plant, whose father made the family fortune in southern hotels and railroads, came to Groton in 1902 to build his summer home, Branford House, overlooking Fishers Island Sound. In 1908, Plant presented the town with a $25,000 town hall. For all his publicity, Plant rarely was photographed. (James L. Streeter.)

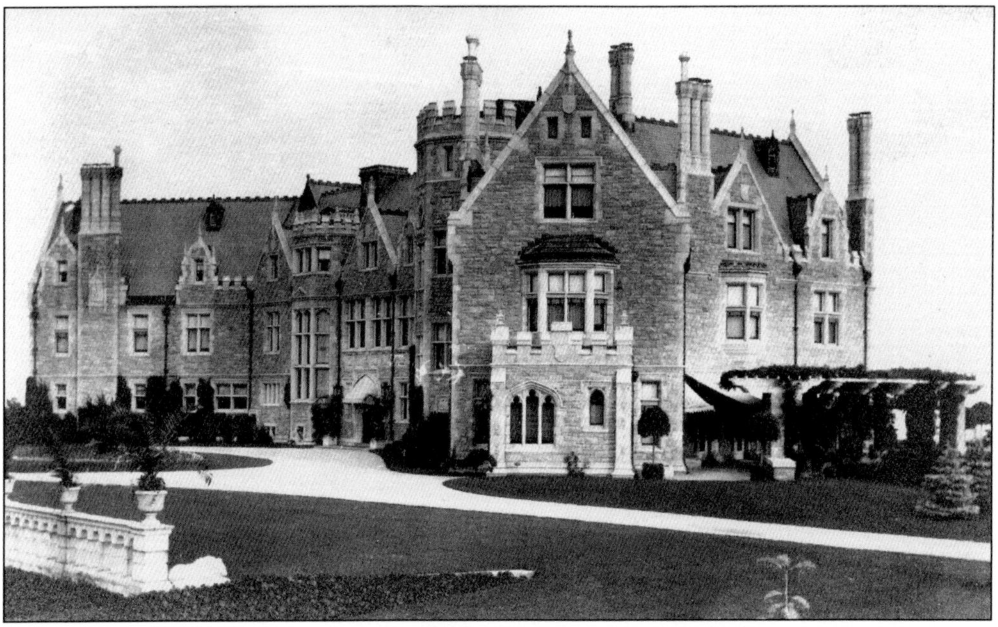

Branford House, now on the grounds at the University of Connecticut at Avery Point, was Morton F. Plant's summer home, named for the town in Connecticut where he was born. After moving into the home, Plant was unhappy with the shabby summer hotel nearby, the Fort Griswold House. He bought it, tore it down, and replaced it with the Griswold, which became the most stylish resort on the Connecticut coast. (James L. Streeter.)

Today Clarence B. Sharp is best known for the Groton highway that bears his name. The Ohio-born Sharp came to Groton in the early 1940s as superintendent of construction for the Gold Star Memorial Bridge. In 1944, he joined Whaling City Dock and Dredge, later becoming its president and then buying the company in 1958. Sharp was elected mayor of the city of Groton in 1966. He considered his greatest achievements installing sewers and constructing the city municipal building. The Defense Access Highway was renamed for him after he died in 1974. (James L. Streeter.)

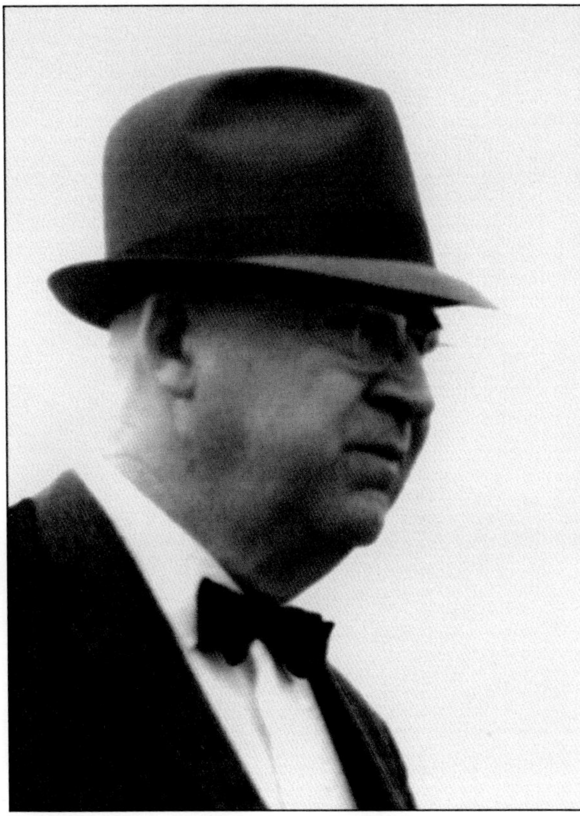

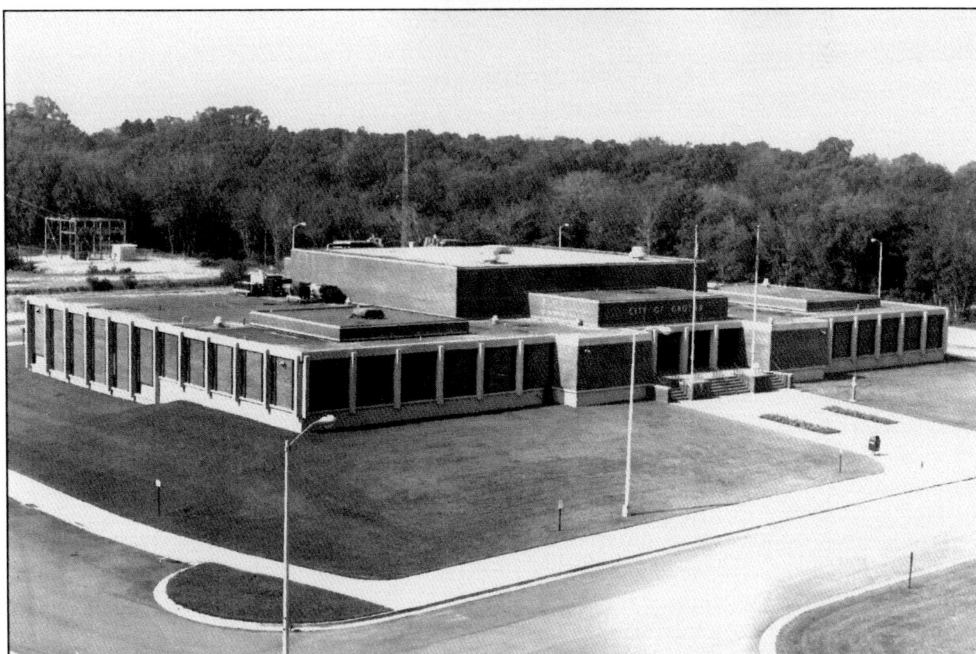

The City of Groton Municipal Building on Meridian Street was built in the late 1960s, when Sharp was city mayor. (City of Groton.)

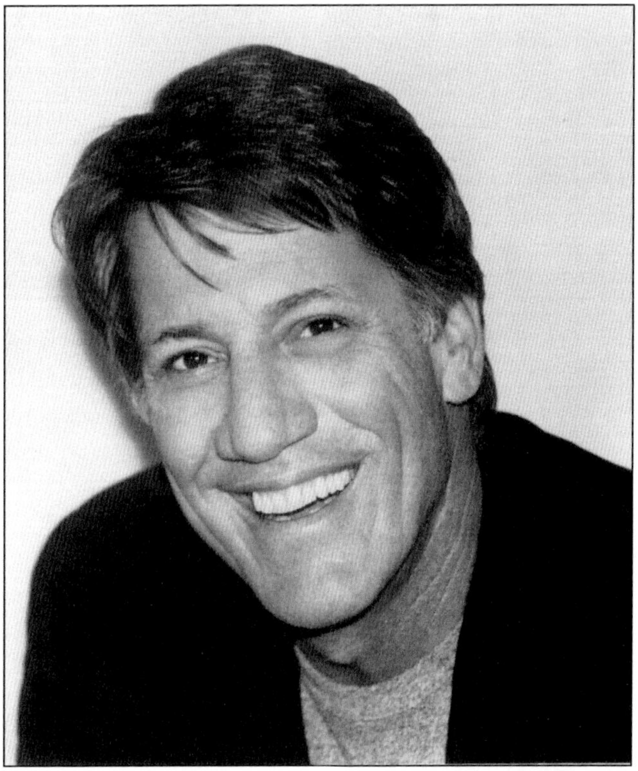

Stephen Macht has been a television actor for many years, appearing on such shows as *Cagney and Lacey*, *Star Trek: Deep Space Nine*, and *Murder She Wrote*. Born in Philadelphia, Macht moved to Mystic at age 9, with his mother and older brother, to live with his maternal grandparents on Pearl Street. His grandfather ran a clothing store in Mystic. Macht is a 1959 graduate of Fitch High School and a graduate of Dartmouth College in New Hampshire. His son Gabriel Macht is also an actor. (Carol W. Kimball.)

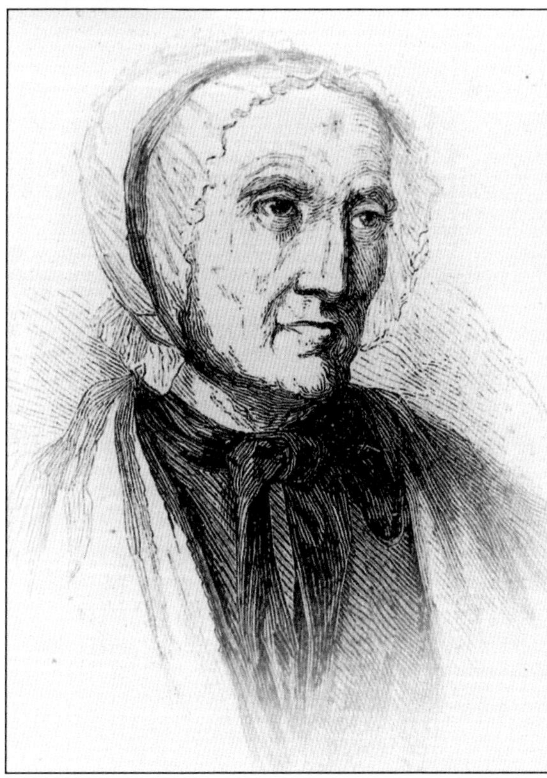

Anna Warner Bailey, known as "Mother Bailey," was one of the first women to approach Fort Griswold after the Battle of Groton Heights, September 6, 1781. Bailey became nationally famous during the War of 1812 by donating her petticoat for wadding at Fort Griswold. The local chapter of the Daughters of the American Revolution is named for her. This portrait was drawn from life by Bensen J. Lessing in 1848. (Carol W. Kimball.)

Capt. Silas Beebe came to Groton from Waterford around 1808. His homestead was on Beebe Cove in West Mystic at Devil's Foot Hill. He was master of the sloops *Nancy* and *Ranger*, and the schooner *LaGrange*, among other vessels. He became a whaling agent with his partner, Jedediah Randall, and sent out several Mystic whaling vessels. Beebe had three wives, Hannah Rathbun, Nancy Breed, and Prudence Morgan. He died in 1863 at 82 and is buried in Lower Mystic Cemetery. (Fish family.)

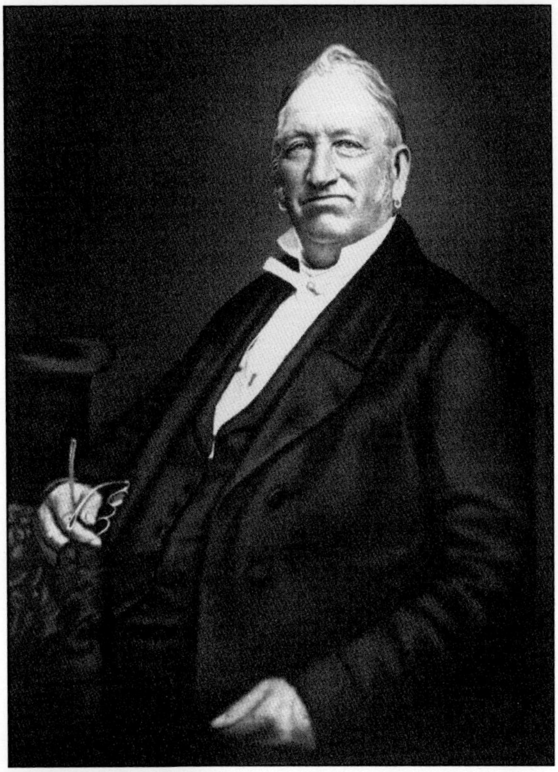

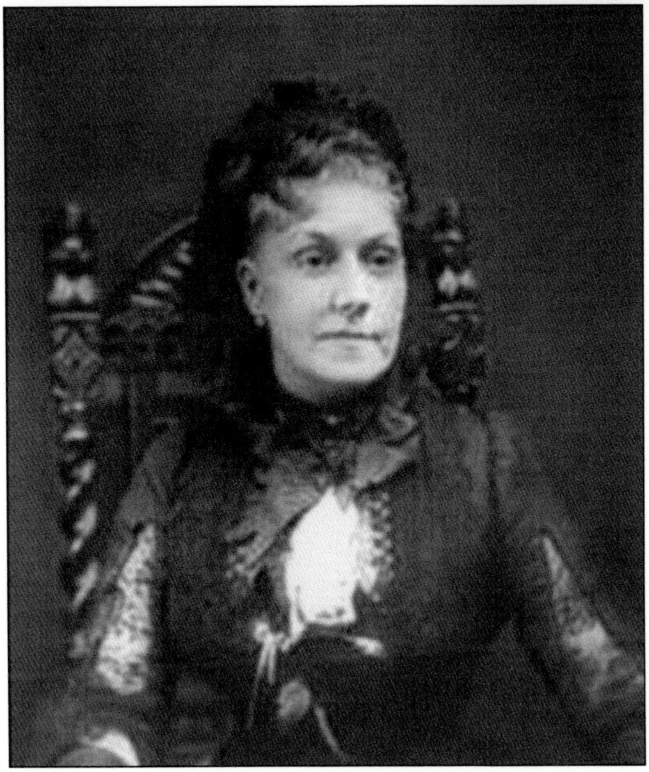

The town and the state owe a debt of gratitude to New Orleans native Abby Day Slocomb, who played a major role in preserving local history. In 1888, she bought the house across the street from Fort Griswold. During the 18 years she lived there, she convinced the government to preserve the Revolutionary War fort, established a museum near the monument, and organized the Groton chapter of the Daughters of the American Revolution. She also designed the Connecticut state flag. (Wally Troland.)

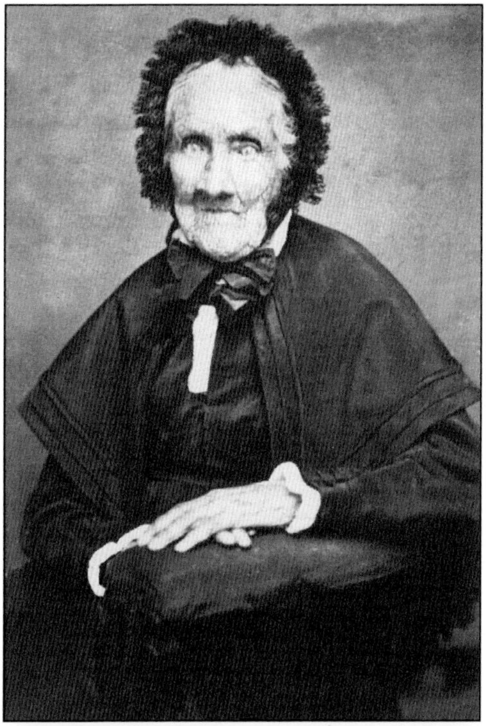

Mary Goodale was born in Groton in 1775 and lived in Poquonnock by the river in the old house called the Beehive. In August 1876, when she was 101, her grandchildren took her to New London, dressed in her best, to have her picture taken. These photographs were sent to the Centennial Exposition in Philadelphia, a fitting representation from Poquonnock. The village annually marked her birthday until her death in March 1879, at 103 years, 9 months. (William N. Peterson.)

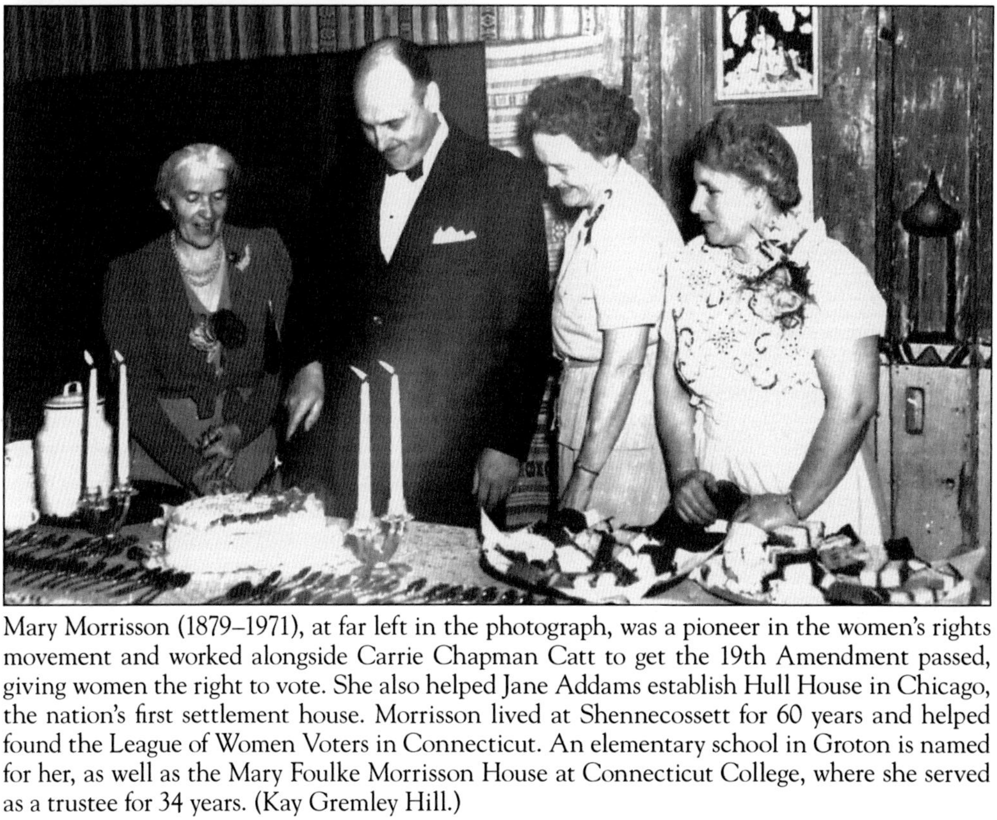

Mary Morrisson (1879–1971), at far left in the photograph, was a pioneer in the women's rights movement and worked alongside Carrie Chapman Catt to get the 19th Amendment passed, giving women the right to vote. She also helped Jane Addams establish Hull House in Chicago, the nation's first settlement house. Morrisson lived at Shennecossett for 60 years and helped found the League of Women Voters in Connecticut. An elementary school in Groton is named for her, as well as the Mary Foulke Morrisson House at Connecticut College, where she served as a trustee for 34 years. (Kay Gremley Hill.)

George E. Tingley's photographs help Mystic appreciate its past. The award-winning photographer, who worked in the same studio on West Main Street for 55 years, once said his ambition was "to bring to the attention of the public the loveliness of the Mystic scene." In 1884, Tingley apprenticed to Mystic photographer Everett E. Scholfield, becoming his partner two years later. He took hundreds of portraits and landscapes, signed neatly in pencil in the corner. From 1894 to 1939, he worked alone. Tingley died at 94 on January 15, 1956. He is buried in Elm Grove Cemetery. (Carol W. Kimball.)

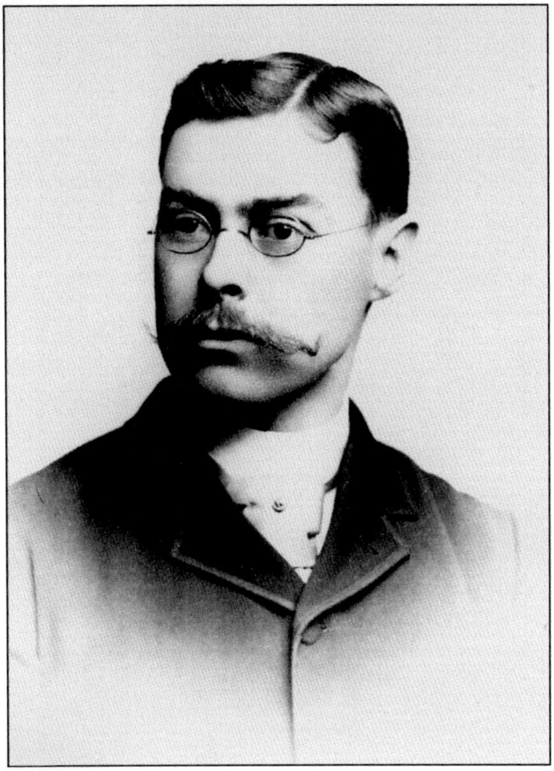

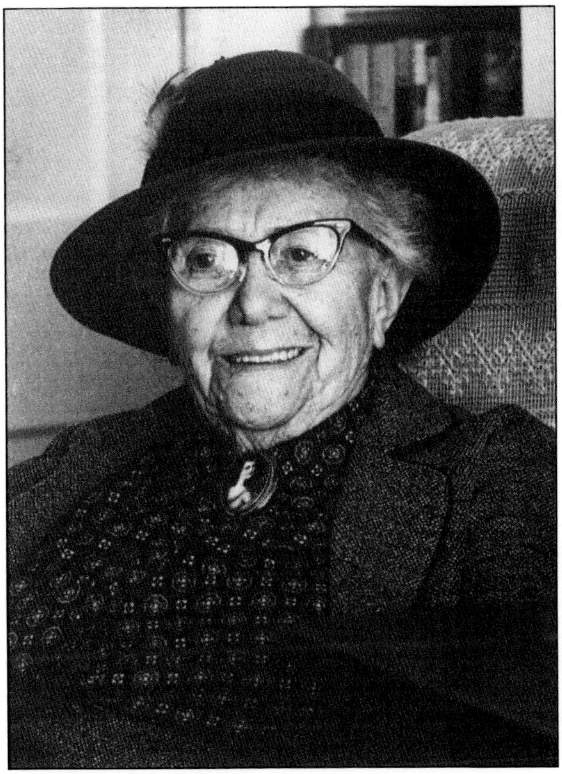

Mary Virginia Goodman, affectionately known as the "Duchess of Noank," was a Groton schoolteacher by profession and a historian and columnist by choice. She grew up in Poquonnock Bridge in the shadow of town hall, where her grandfather was town clerk. She spent her adult years in Noank, teaching at Noank School and also at Groton Heights. Known for her flamboyant hats and pithy remarks, Goodman was married three times. In later years, she was a popular lecturer on local history and wrote a column called "Noank Notes" that appeared regularly in the *Groton News* and later in the *Norwich Bulletin*. (Carol W. Kimball.)

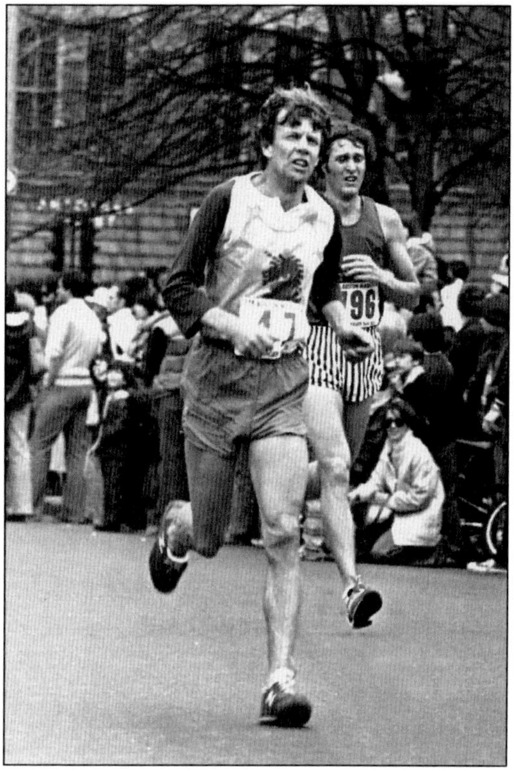

Groton is home to two winners of the Boston Marathon. Johnny Kelley, the younger, pictured here, won the Boston Marathon in 1957. Kelley taught English at Robert E. Fitch High School for decades and was coach of the school's cross-country team. One of his cross-country team members, Amby Burfoot, was the 1968 Boston Marathon winner. (Amby Burfoot.)

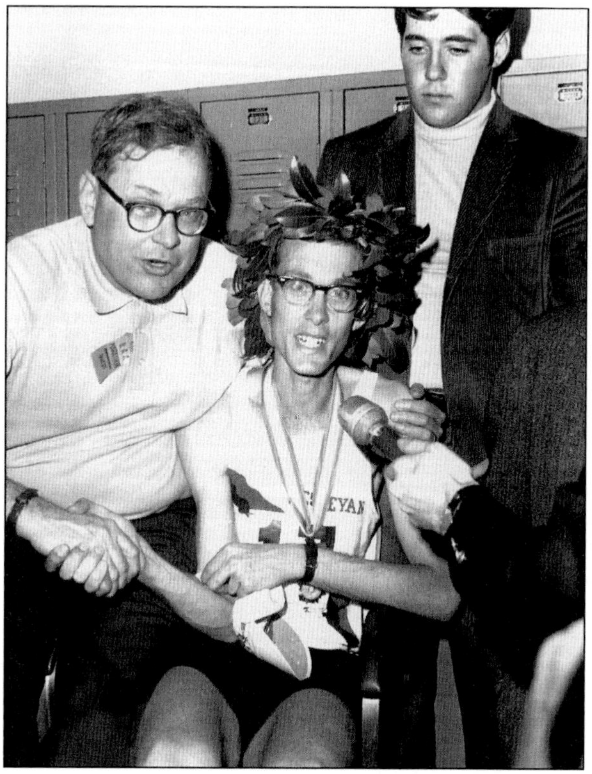

Amby Burfoot, a 1964 graduate of Robert E. Fitch High School, is congratulated by his father, Amby Burfoot Sr., after winning the 1968 Boston Marathon. At Fitch, Burfoot was a member of the cross-country team coached by Johnny Kelley, the 1957 Boston Marathon winner. Burfoot is a graduate of Wesleyan University and today is editor of *Runner's World* magazine. (Amby Burfoot.)

Three

School Days

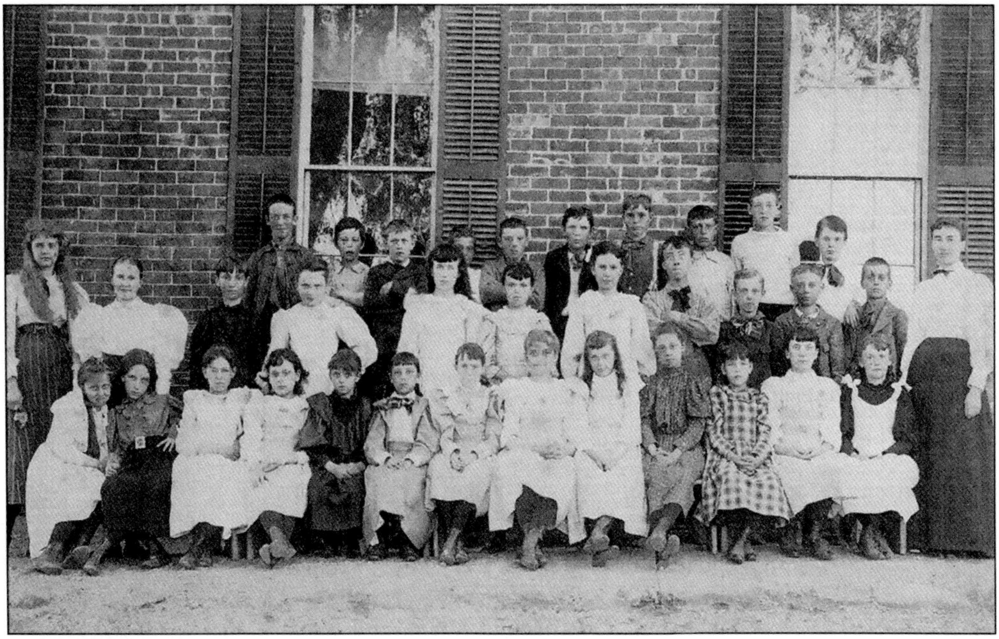

In this 1894 photograph, students sit outside the original Mystic Academy building on Academy Lane in Mystic. The building was replaced in 1910 with a more modern school, which was used by the town until it was closed in 1990. (Robert Bankel.)

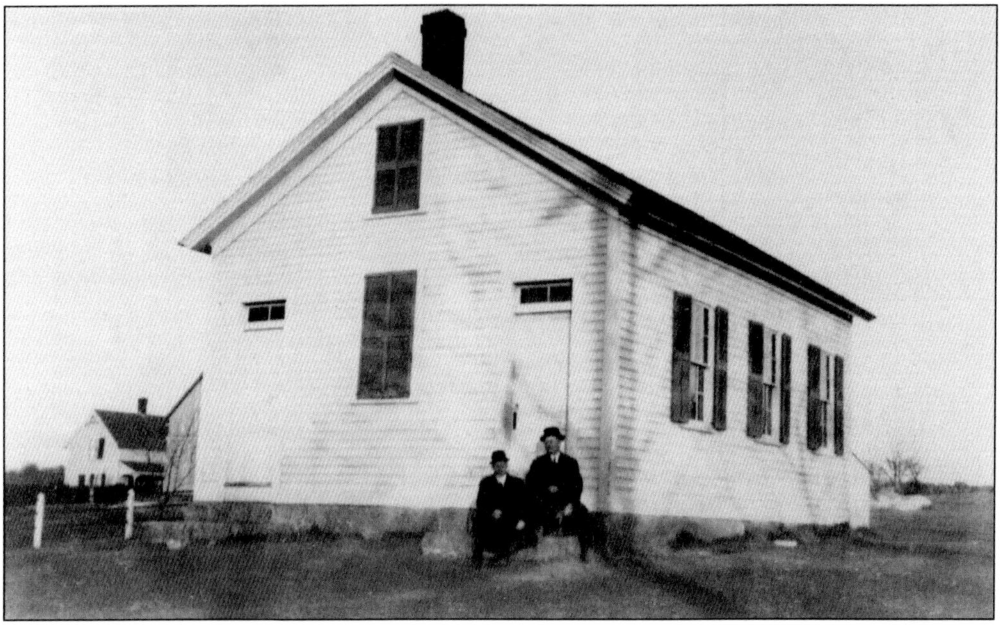

Two men sit on the steps of the old Eastern Point School. The one-room school served Groton's Eighth District schoolchildren until 1920, when it was replaced by a four-room structure that was the nucleus of today's Eastern Point School. (James L. Streeter.)

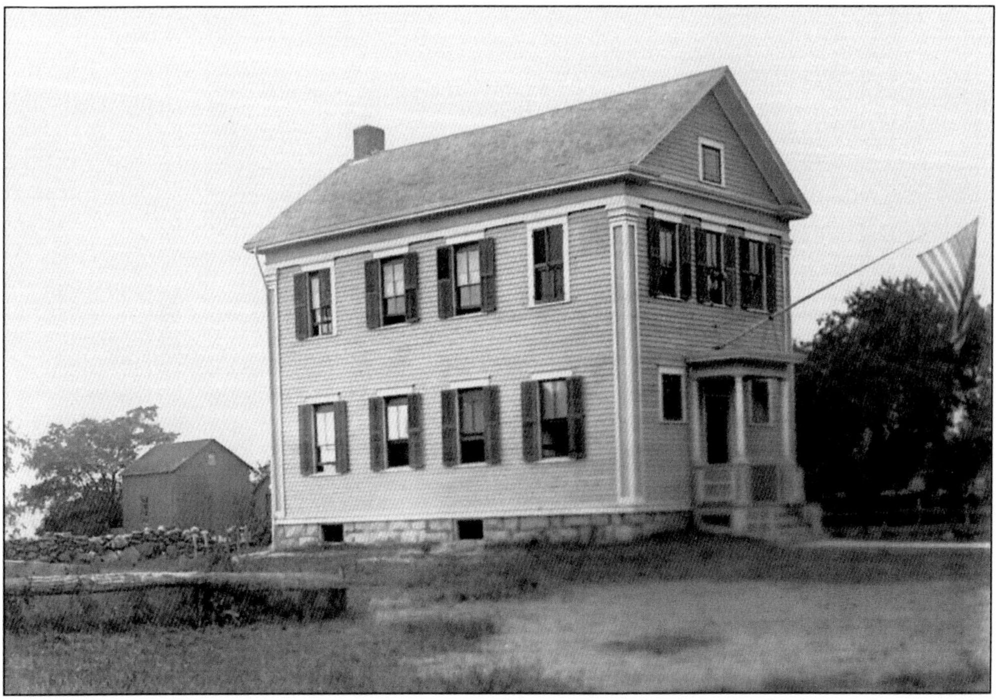

Groton's first kindergarten was housed on Ramsdell Street in this house, which was destroyed by fire about 1906. In his writings, Groton draggerman Ellery Thompson (1899–1986) recalled "the Ramsdell Street one-grade school, which I attended at the age of six in 1905. But fire destroyed the school as I finished first grade." (James L. Streeter.)

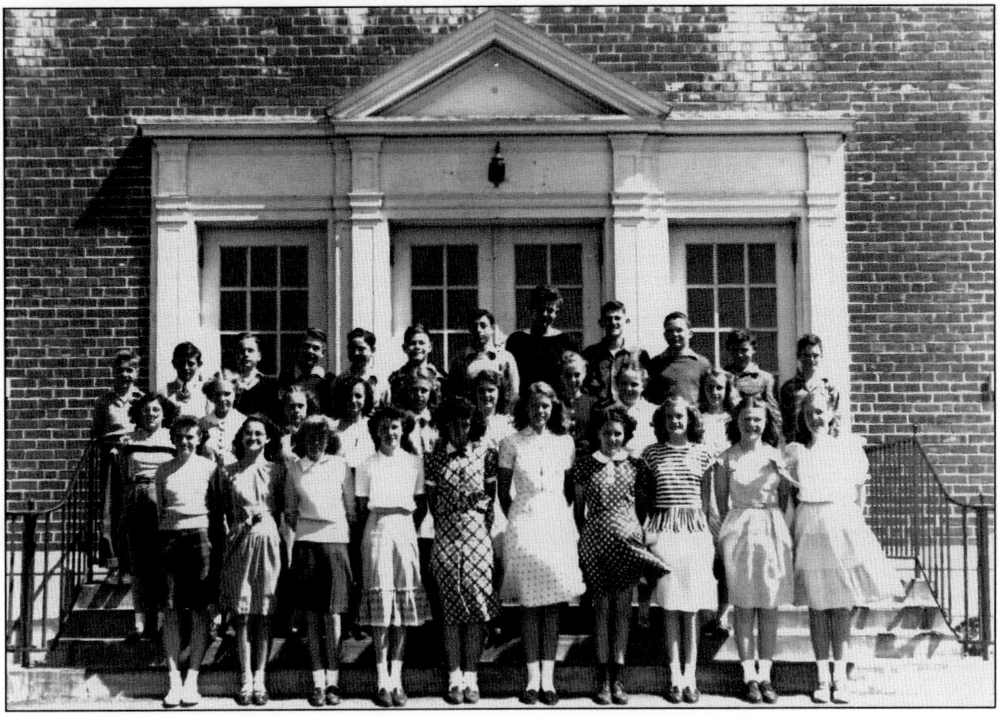

In this 1948 photograph, the seventh grade at Eastern Point School poses outside the doors to the gymnasium, an addition to the original school. (LaRoue family.)

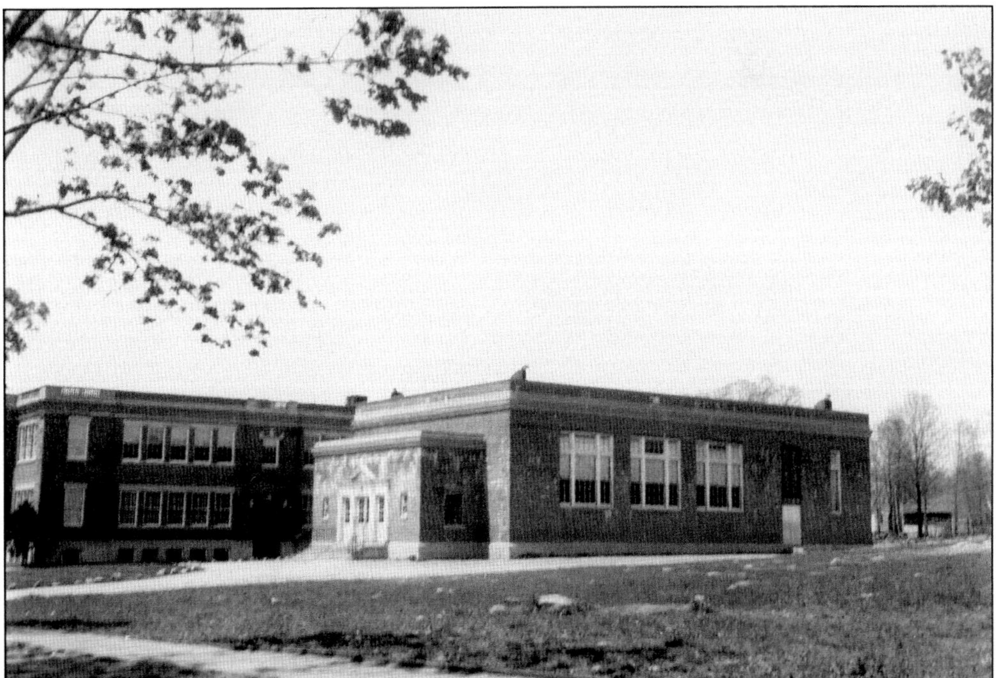

This 1956 photograph of Eastern Point School shows the new gymnasium. The school is scheduled to close in 2007 as a result of the town's school construction program. (James L. Streeter.)

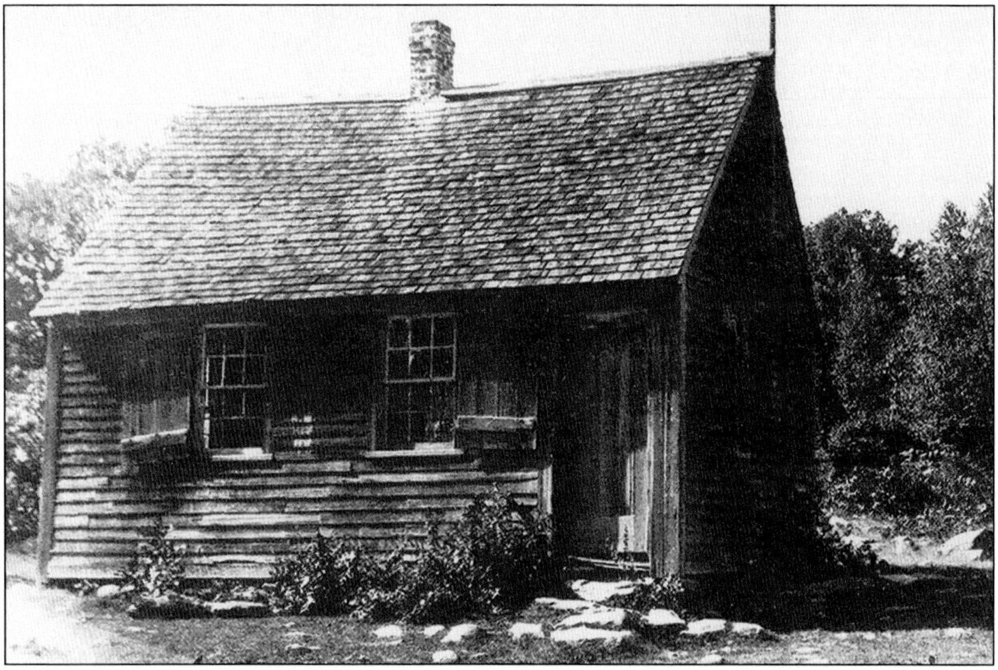

The Fishtown School, officially listed in town records as Flanders School District 9, served as the schoolhouse for the Fishtown section of Mystic from the early part of the 19th century into the early 20th century. It was off Noank Ledyard Road. (Robert Bankel.)

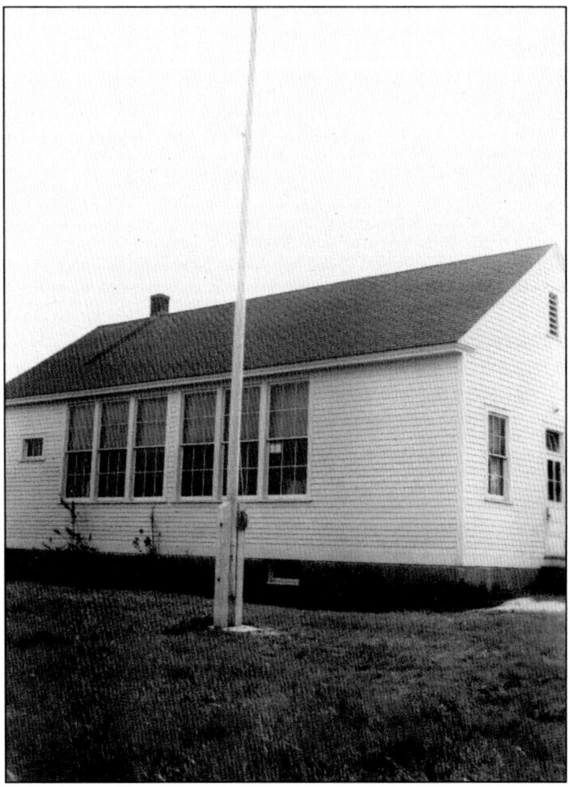

This photograph of the Old Mystic School on Welles Road was taken in 1950. The one-room schoolhouse was used by the town until 1960; its last year was as a kindergarten. (James L. Streeter.)

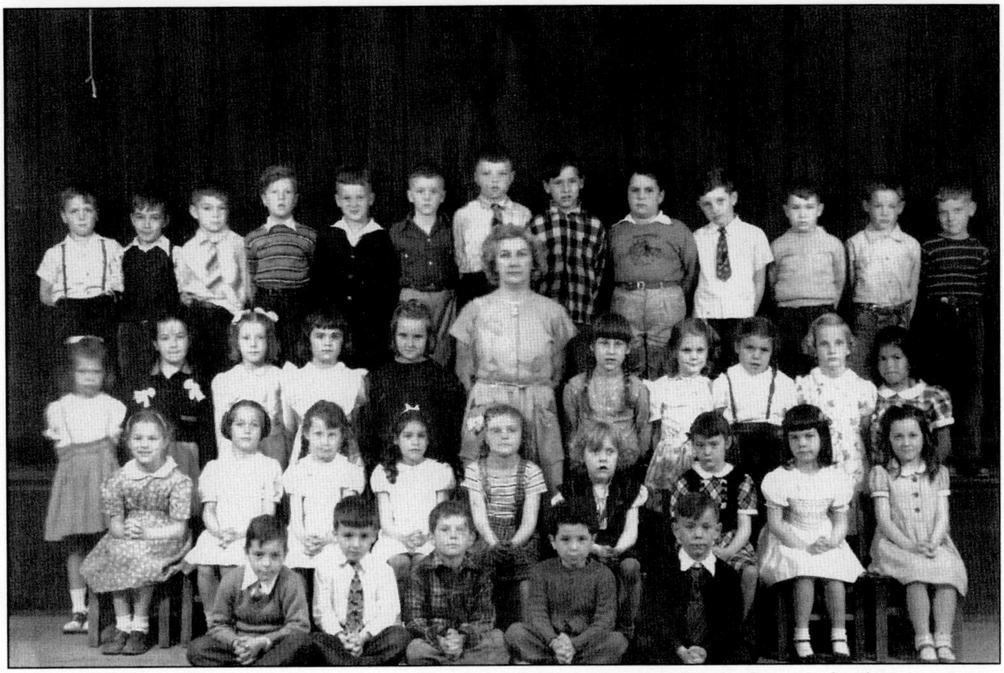

Teacher Madge Albro stands at the center of this 1948 photograph of a first-grade class at Mystic Academy. The academy opened in 1849 in a wooden building on Academy Lane in Mystic. It was replaced with a brick building in 1910 and served as a public school until 1990. Today it is Academy Point, an assisted living facility for the elderly. (Marilyn J. Comrie.)

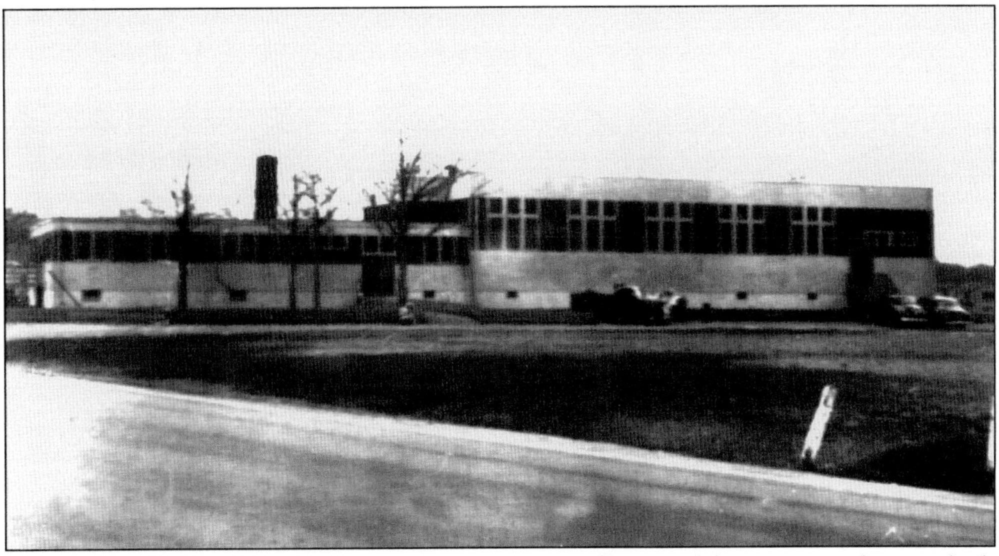

The Fort Hill School and Community House was originally part of the emergency housing built in Poquonnock Bridge for World War II. The L-shaped building was 170 feet long and contained an auditorium, stage, kitchen, management offices, and nursery school for war workers' children. As Groton schools bulged with postwar baby boomers, the building became classroom space to supplement the Fort Hill School across the street. The building later became headquarters for school administrators. It was destroyed by fire in the 1980s. (Town of Groton Department of Public Works.)

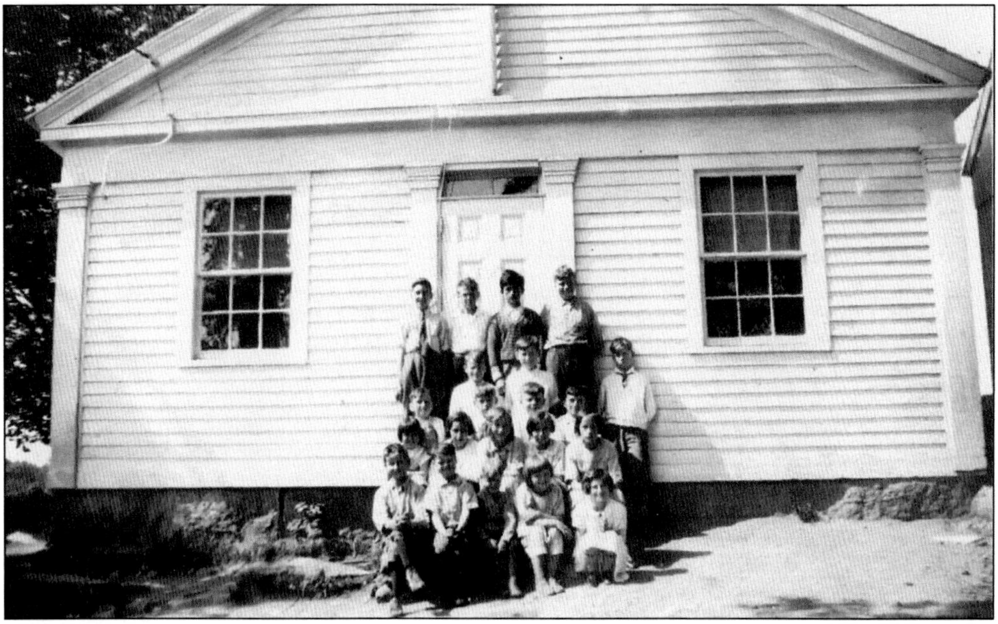

Students pose outside Pleasant Valley School in 1927. The school, with its utility shed containing the privy, stood at Route 12 and Gungywamp Road, also known as Skunk Lane. (LaRoue family.)

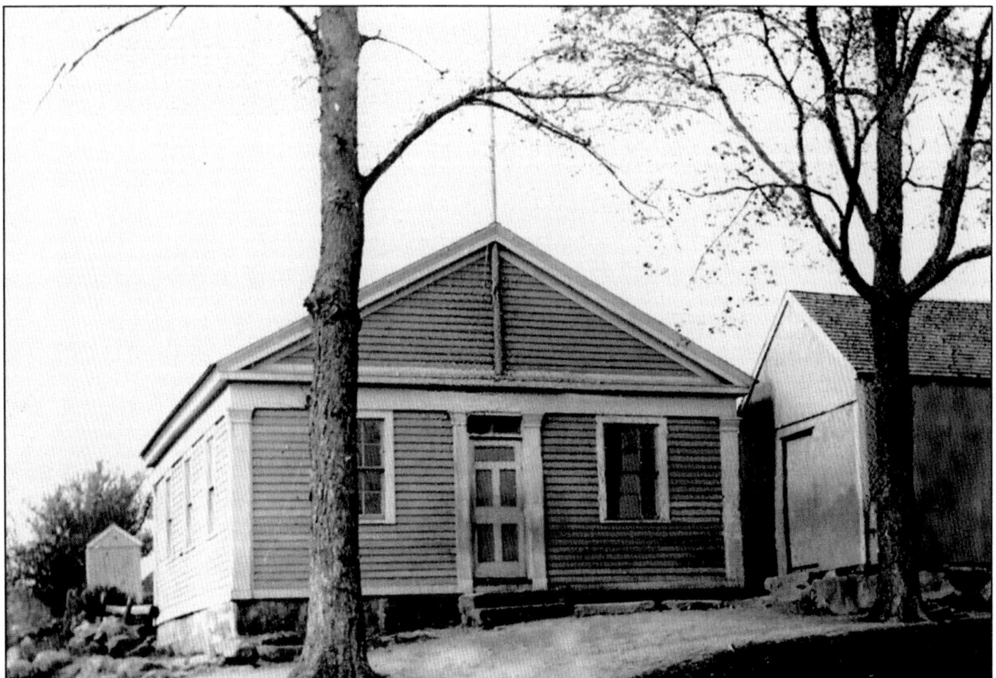

Pleasant Valley School was among the many one-room schools across the town in the 19th and early 20th centuries. With the advent of World War II, it was replaced in 1944 by a seven-room wooden structure on Pleasant Valley Road. (James L. Streeter.)

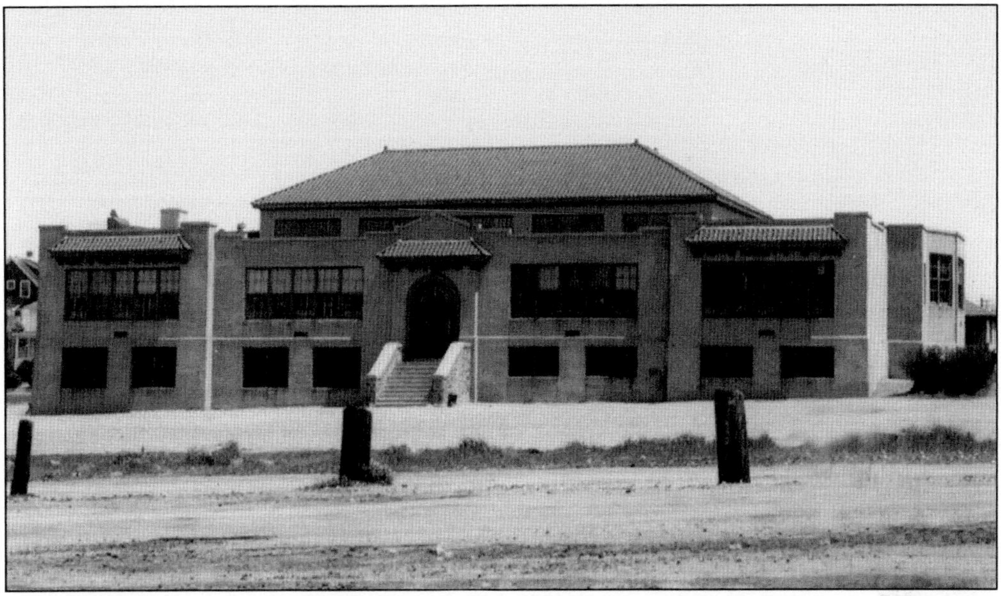

The old Colonel Ledyard School at 61 Chicago Avenue housed kindergarten through eighth grade. It was named for Col. William Ledyard, who was killed at Fort Griswold during the Battle of Groton Heights on September 6, 1781. (James L. Streeter.)

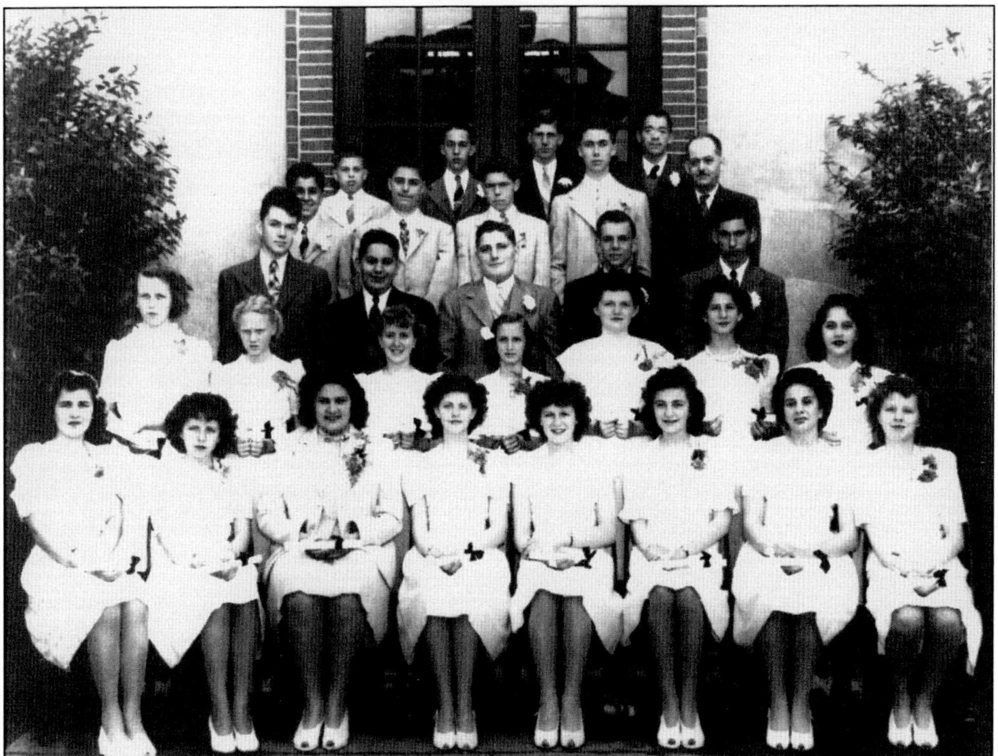

The eighth-grade class at Colonel Ledyard School in Groton poses for its graduation photograph in 1945. The original Colonel Ledyard School was at 61 Chicago Avenue. It eventually was sold to Electric Boat, and a new school was built at 120 West Street in 1963. (Sal Giordano.)

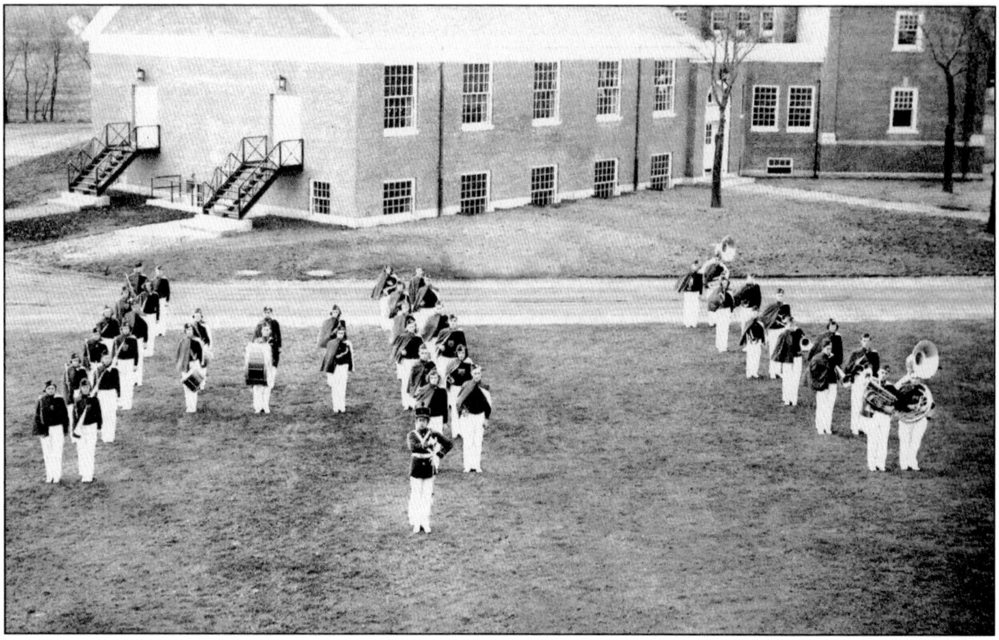

The Robert E. Fitch High School marching band practices in the field next to the school in 1937. The band played for the dedication of the addition to the town hall that year. Albert I. Dorr was the director of the band from 1935 to 1947, and the band won many competitions across New England under his leadership. Dorr was killed on a band trip to Montreal in 1947, when he was struck by a car while crossing the street. The football field at the high school is named for him. (Larry Jacobsen.)

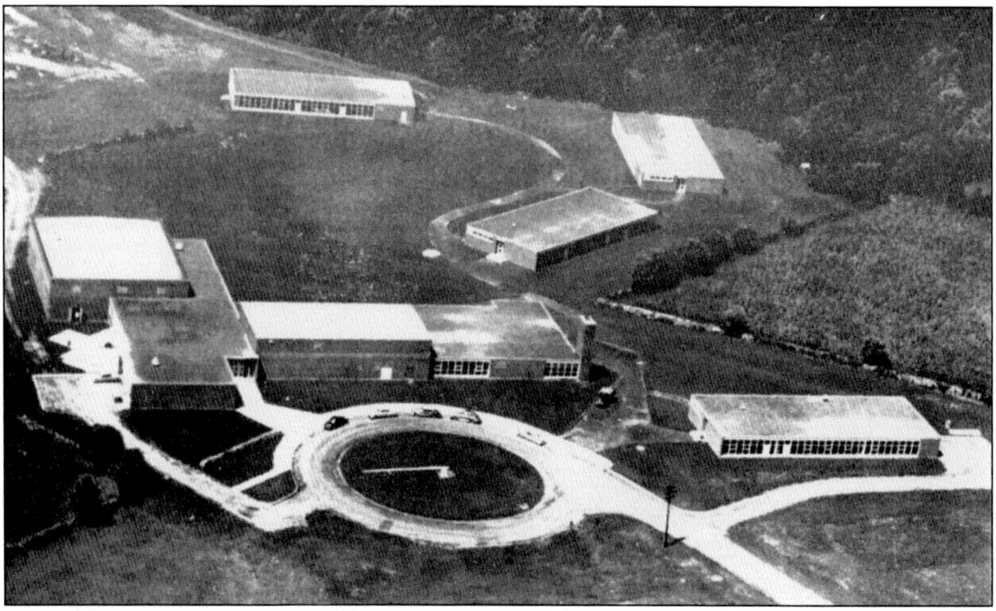

This 1955 aerial photograph of Robert E. Fitch Senior High School shows the campus just before the new high school opened. It replaced the original Fitch High School, next to town hall in Poquonnock Bridge. The open campus with several unconnected buildings was an unusual design for a New England school. (James L. Streeter.)

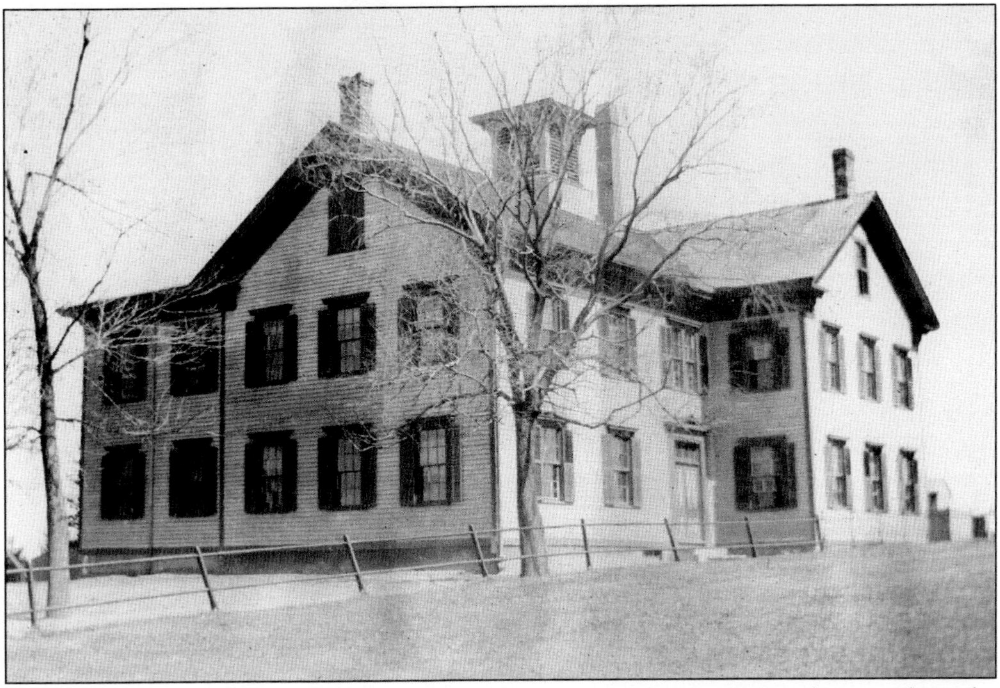

The first Groton Heights Elementary School was a wooden structure that stood in the shadow of the Fort Griswold monument. It was replaced in 1912 by a modern brick school. (James L. Streeter.)

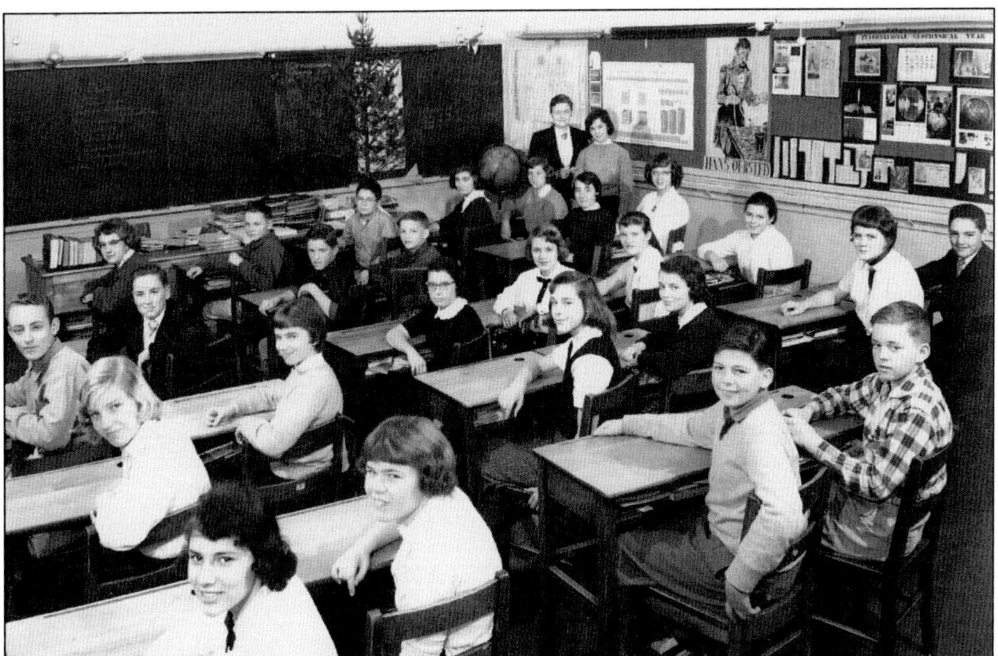

Bessie LaRoue's eighth-grade class of 1957–1958 at Robert E. Fitch Junior High School smiles for a class photograph. LaRoue taught science and mathematics, which explains the bulletin board displays on the wall. (LaRoue family.)

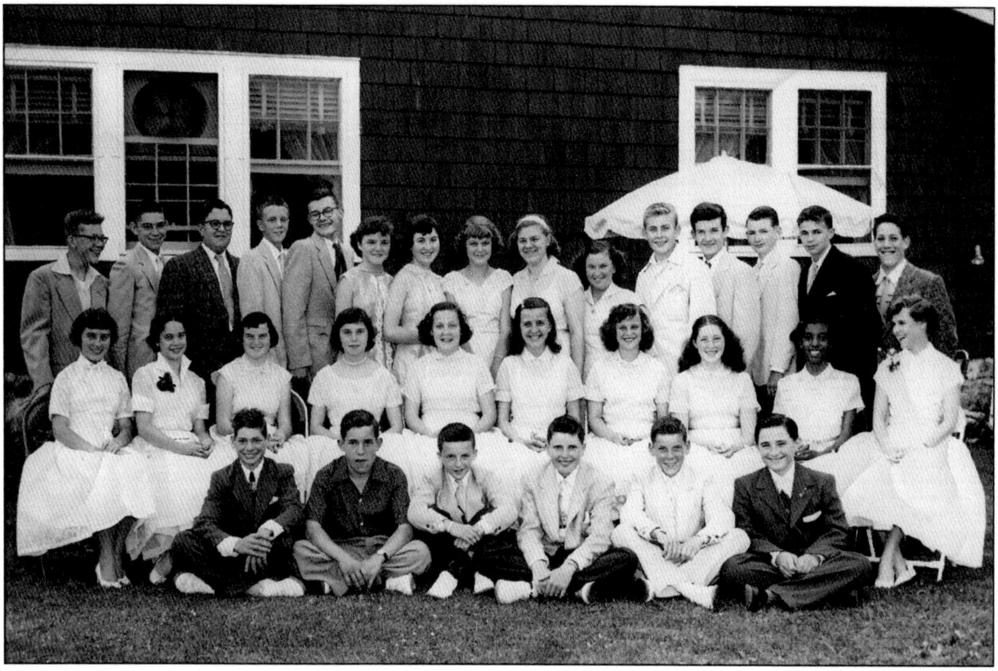

The class of 1955 was the last eighth-grade class to graduate from Mystic Academy. The Town of Groton switched to a junior high system after that. Pictured are, from left to right, (first row) David Stiles, Ken Sylvia, Richard Joseph, Art Geyer, Steve Friedlander, and Peter Reinke; (second row) Pamela Richardson, Frances Menzie, Sandra Beauchamp, Shirley Findleyson, Janice Plouffe, Phyllis Bailey, Justine Fowler, Ruth Watrous, Gloria Wilson, and Rowena Jones; (third row) Gene Pender, Bobby Wheeler, Ed Comrie Jr., Bruce Burrows, Paul Mason, Ann Whittle, Carrie Saunders, Janice Wolff, Gloria Smith, Beverly Robinson, George Anderson, Gary Effman, James Munro, Ralph Godfrey, and Stephen Macht. (Marilyn J. Comrie.)

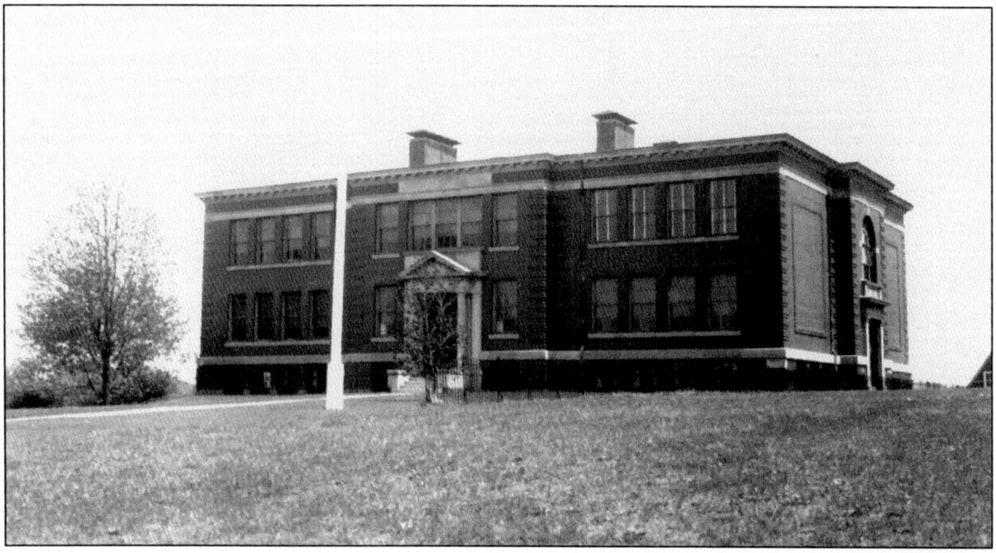

The second Groton Heights School also stands in the shadow of Fort Griswold monument. The 1912 structure, built and presented to the town by philanthropist Frederic Bill, is scheduled to be closed late in 2007 with the opening of the Catherine Kolnaski School. (James L. Streeter.)

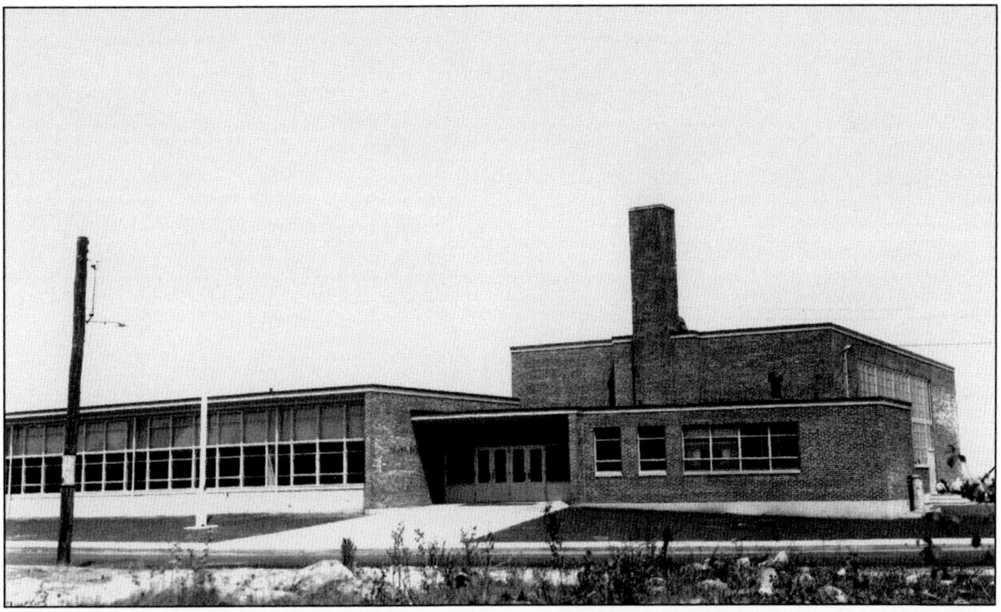

This 1950 photograph shows the Noank Elementary School, which was built in 1949. This neighborhood school is slated to close when the current school reconsolidation and building program is completed. (James L. Streeter.)

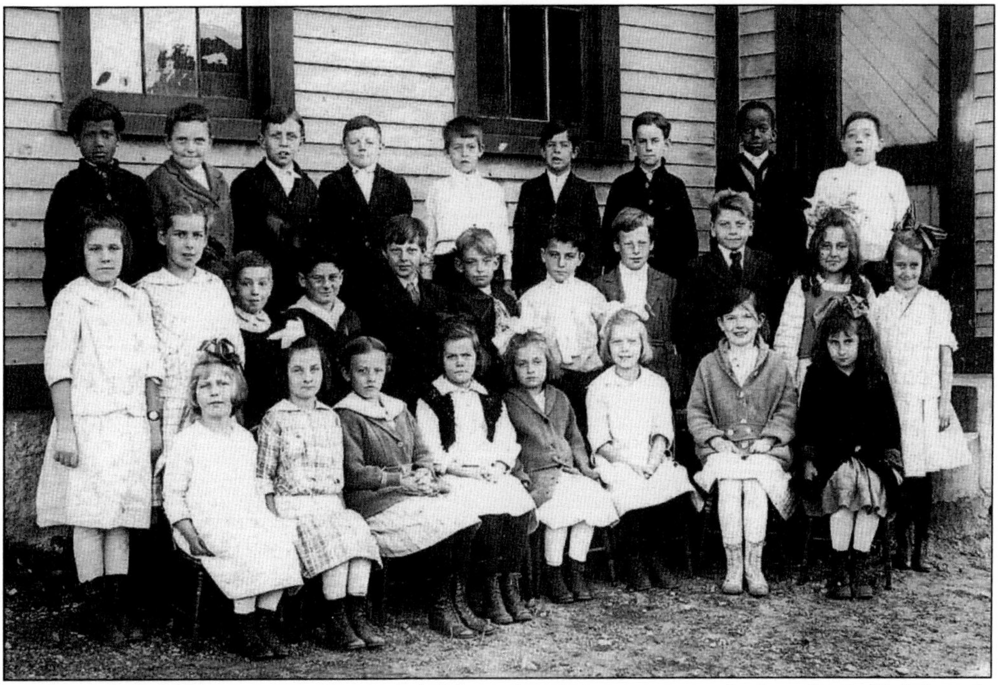

A class at Noank Elementary School, probably in the 1920s, poses outside the school. (Bob Irons.)

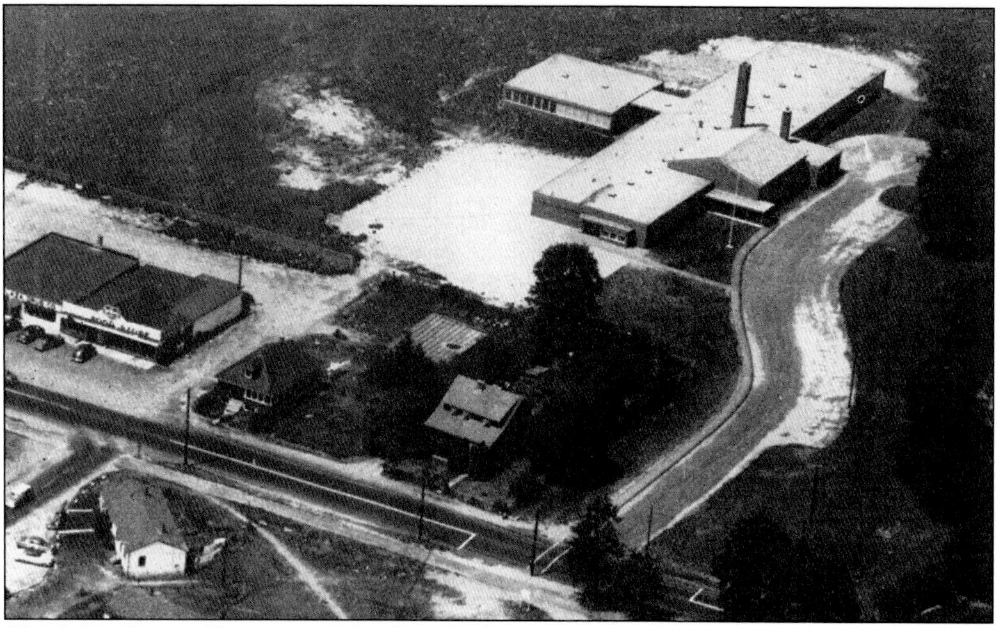

Claude M. Chester Elementary School was built in 1953, one of several new schools constructed to accommodate the post–World War II baby boom. The school, on Route 1 in Poquonnock Bridge, was named for Claude Milton Chester, a member of the board of education and an undertaker from Noank. (James L. Streeter.)

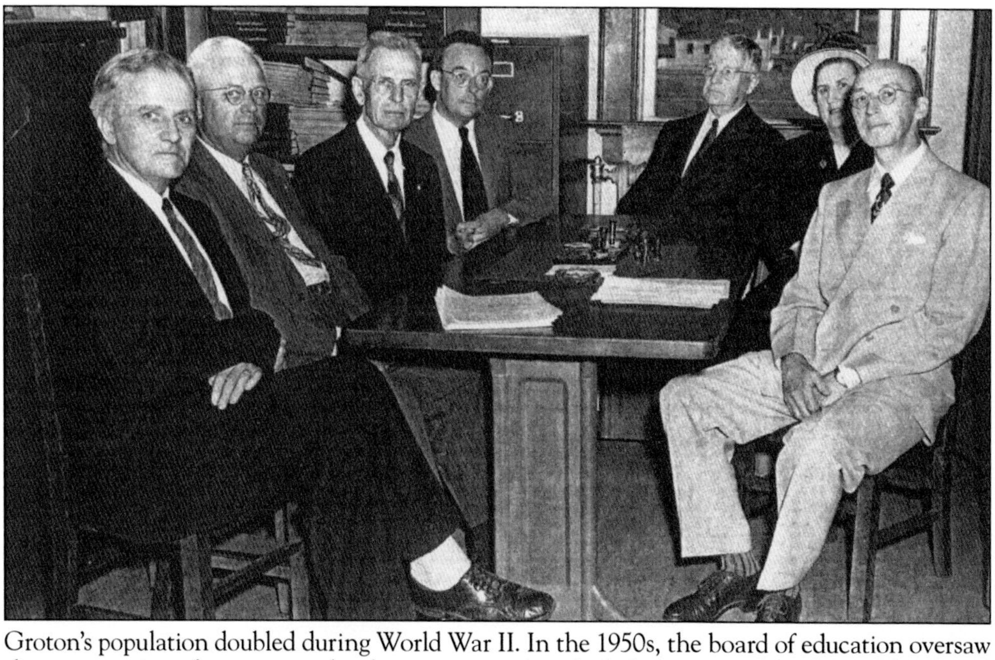

Groton's population doubled during World War II. In the 1950s, the board of education oversaw the construction of many new schools to accommodate the baby boomers. Members of that board were, from left to right, superintendent of schools Sylvester B. Butler, A. T. Avery, D. Palmer Brown, town attorney J. Rodney Smith (likely at the meeting to give legal advice), Claude M. Chester, Jessie Plumstead, and William A. Hall. Two of the new schools were named for Butler and Chester. (Robert Bankel.)

Four

BRIDGES

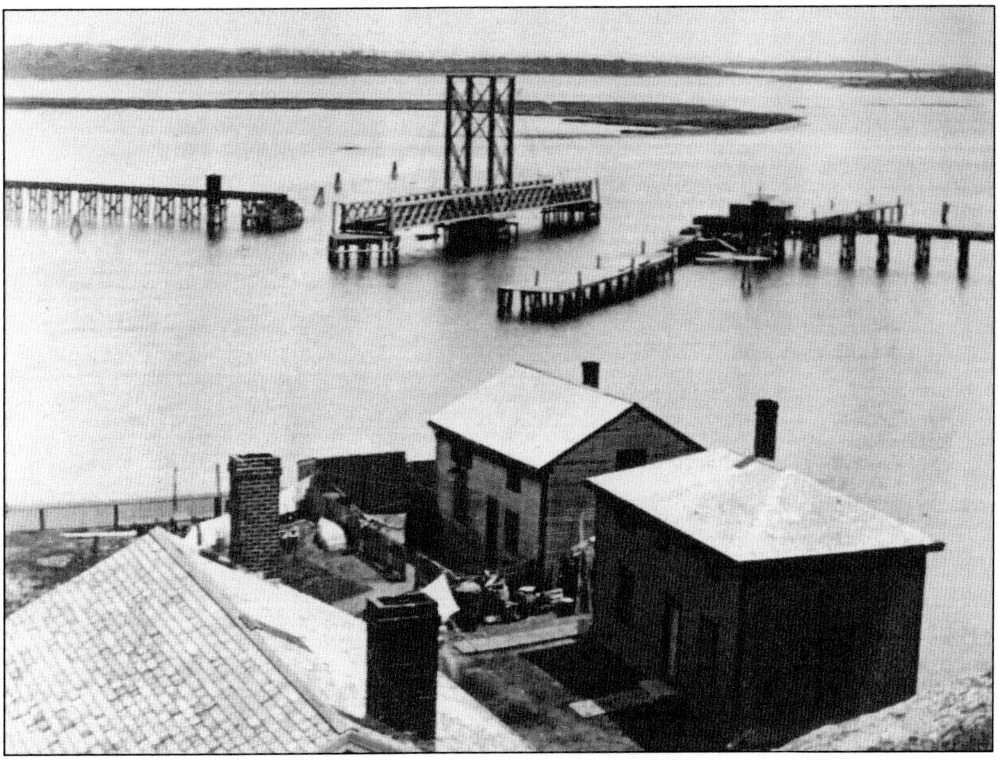

This is the original railroad bridge across the Mystic River for the Shoreline Railroad's Groton extension (from Stonington to the Thames River), which went into operation on November 12, 1858. This stereoscopic view dates from July 23, 1875, and was taken from Fort Rachel. (Carol W. Kimball.)

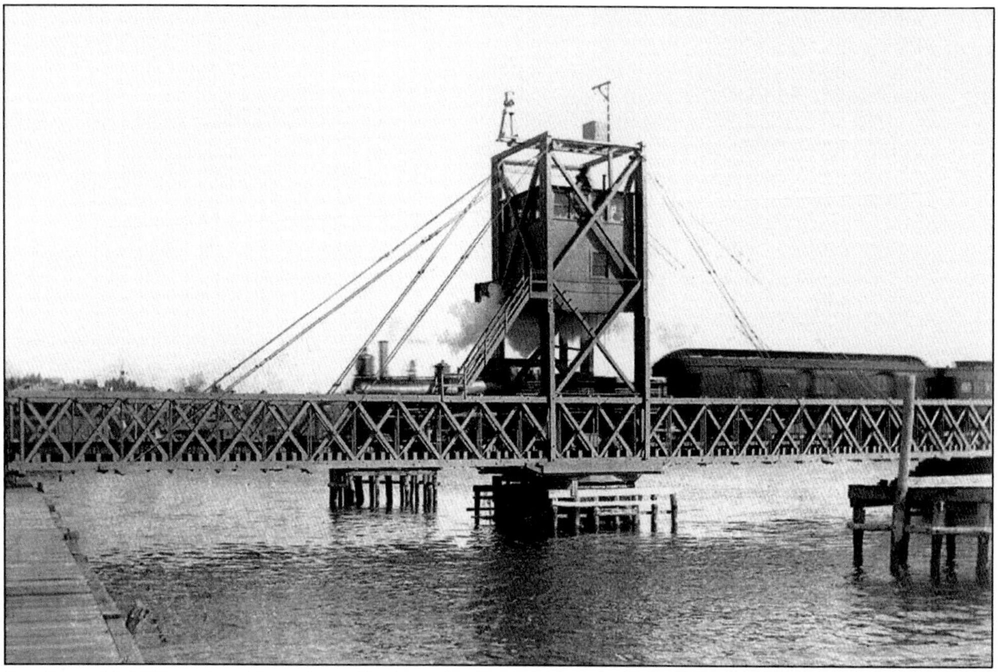

In the mid-1880s, the Shoreline Railroad was double-tracked except for the Mystic railroad bridge. An interlocking plant was installed in the elevated house over the tracks. It controlled the switches and signals. The cranklike gearing was extended to the tower and reached by a catwalk visible in the picture. (Bob Irons.)

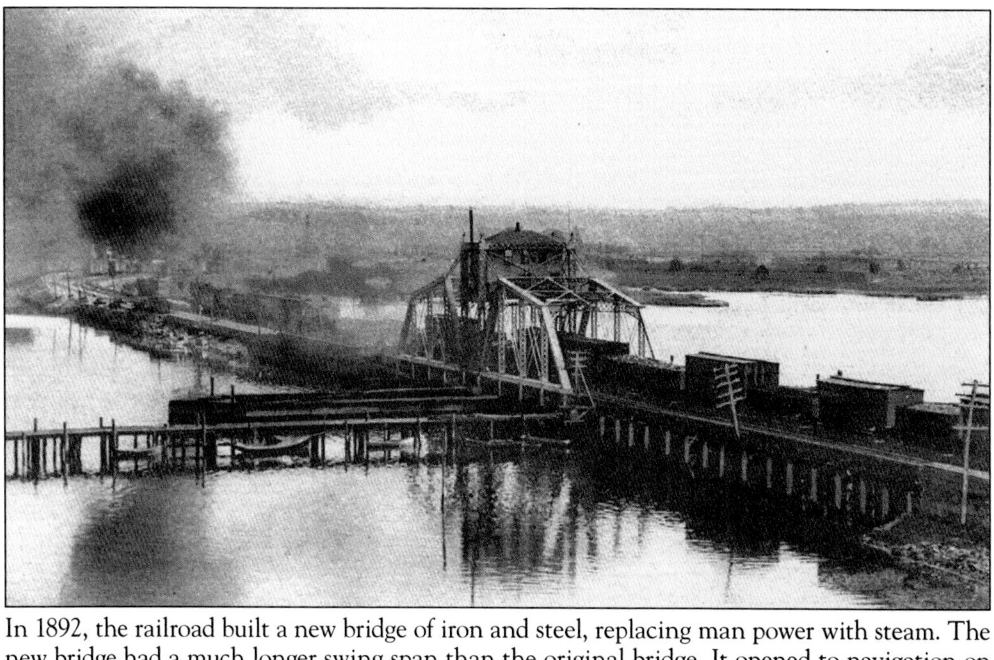

In 1892, the railroad built a new bridge of iron and steel, replacing man power with steam. The new bridge had a much longer swing span than the original bridge. It opened to navigation on April 2, 1892, when the sloop *Red Rover* passed through. (James L. Streeter.)

One reason the Yale-Harvard Regatta Committee chose the Thames River in 1878 as the home for its annual collegiate rowing competition was that the waterway had a straight four-mile stretch with no impediments. That changed in 1889, when the New York, New Haven and Hartford Railroad built the first bridge across the river. Here divers prepare to work on construction of the span. (Bill Memorial Library.)

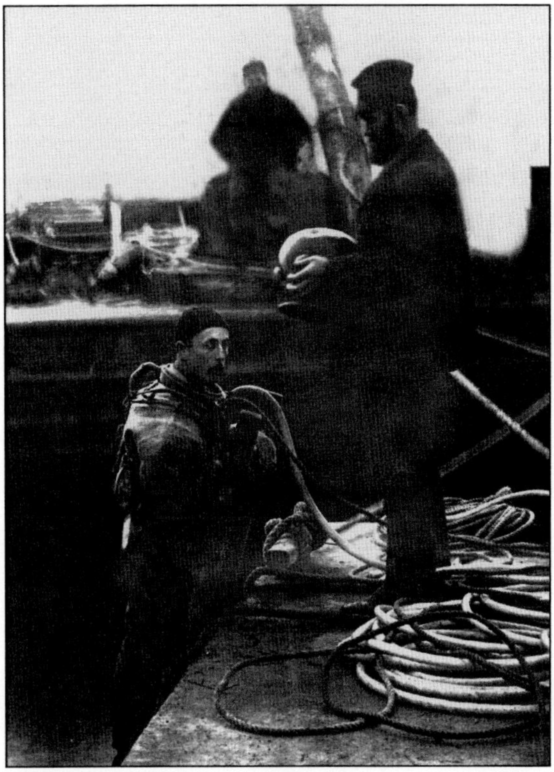

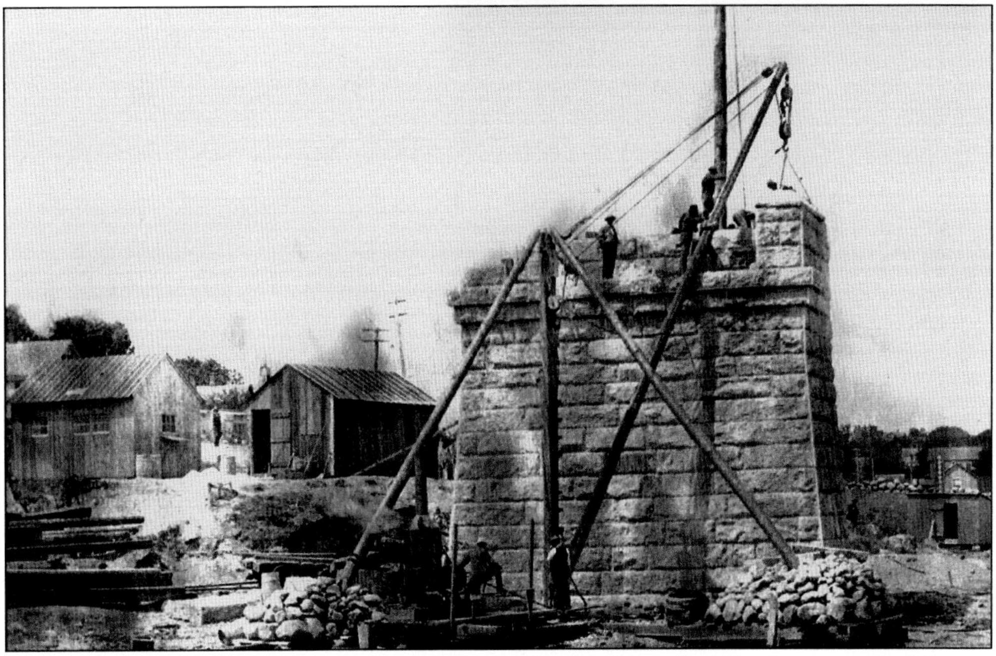

Workers lift stone into place, creating an abutment for the first railroad bridge across the Thames River. The railroad swing bridge later would be converted into the first motor vehicle bridge across the Thames River. The structure was taken down for scrap metal in September 1943, after the Gold Star Memorial Bridge opened. (Bill Memorial Library.)

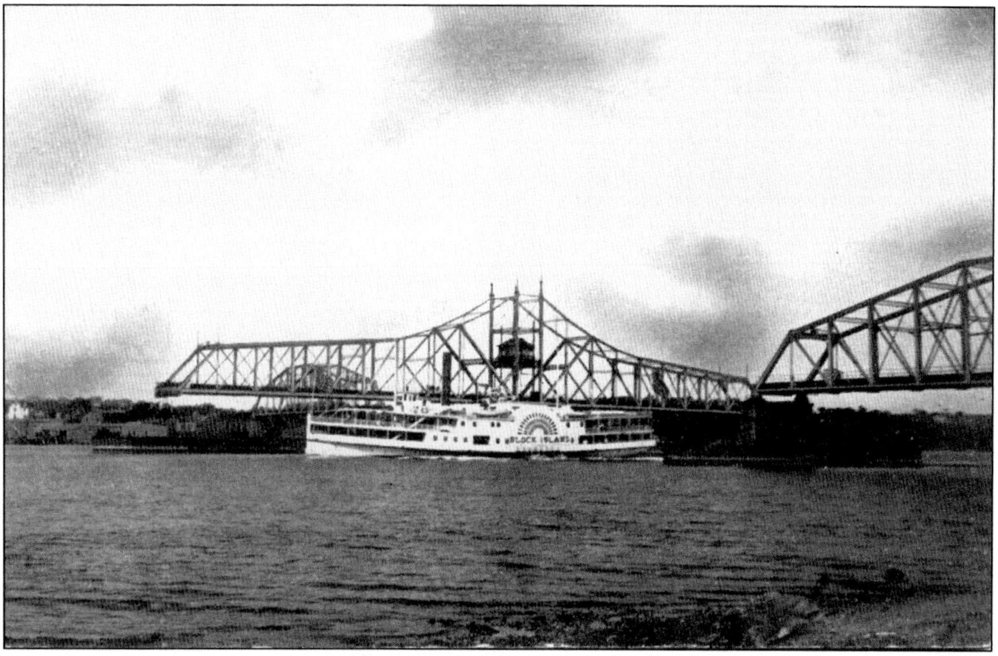

When the New York, New Haven and Hartford Railroad opened its bridge across the Thames River in 1889, it was billed as the longest span in the world. In this photograph, the swing span of the bridge is open to allow the side-wheel steamer *Block Island* to pass upriver. (James L. Streeter.)

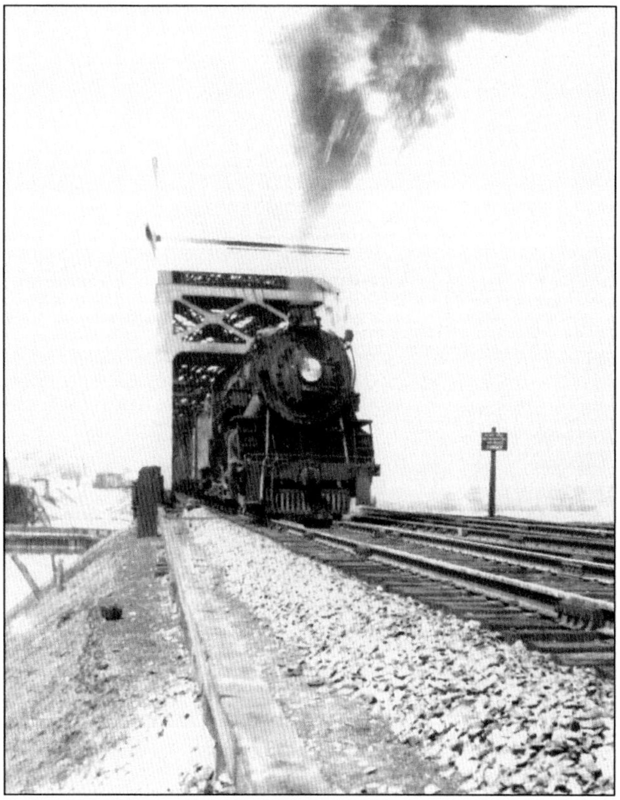

A train crosses the first railroad bridge over the Thames River. The bridge represented modern technology at its best. Before it was built, the railroad used ferries to carry trains between Groton and New London. (James L. Streeter.)

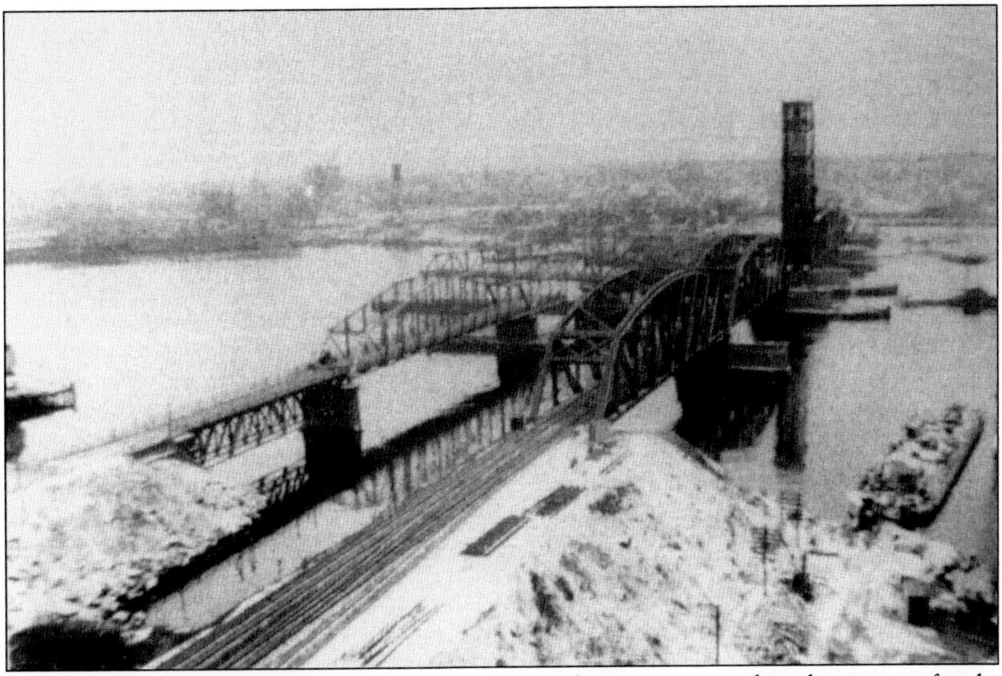

By World War I, the original railroad bridge could no longer accommodate the growing freight loads the railroad carried. In 1916, a new bridge was built alongside the original bridge. The new bridge had a section that lifted rather than swung to allow boat traffic to pass. The draw is open in this photograph. (James L. Streeter.)

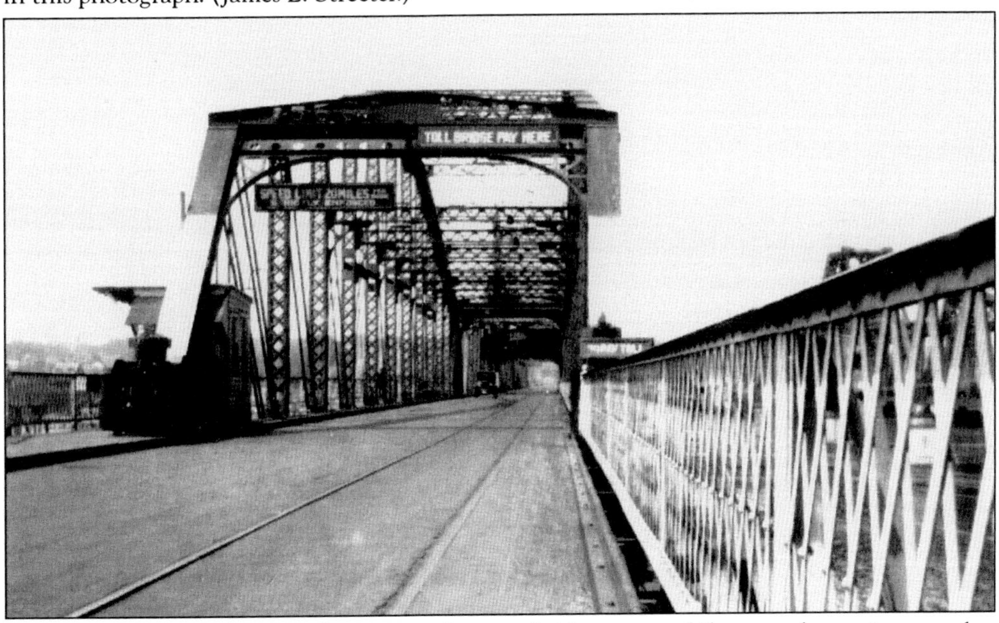

When the railroad abandoned its original swing bridge, automobiles were becoming popular. The State of Connecticut converted the bridge for motor vehicle traffic, opening it to traffic in 1919. There were problems in the conversion, however. The railroad had built its new bridge so close to the old one that the swing span could not open all the way. Half of the span had to be shortened, costing more money for the conversion. (James L. Streeter.)

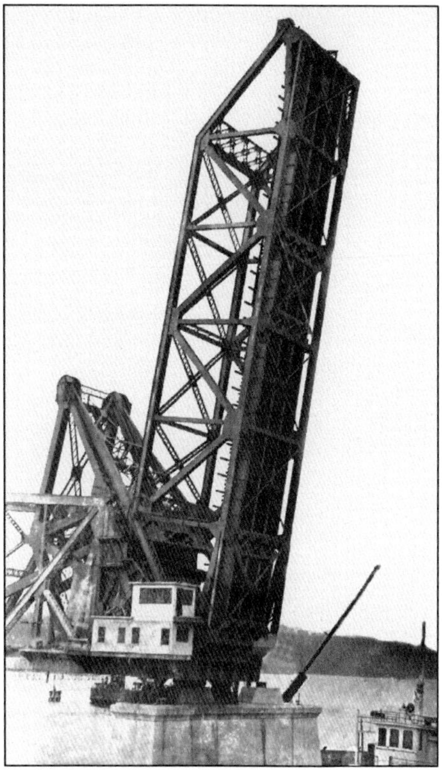

The second railroad bridge over the Thames River opens to allow boat traffic to pass. (James L. Streeter.)

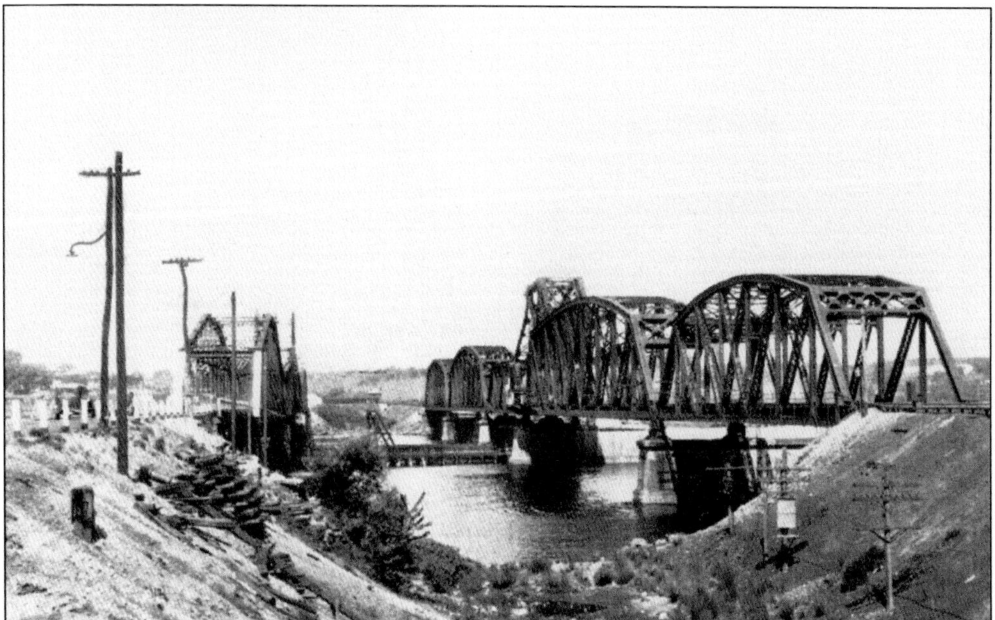

The Thames River railroad and motor vehicle bridges sit side by side. Within three years of its opening, the converted motor vehicle bridge was obsolete. Boat traffic on the river and additional motor vehicle traffic from workers at Electric Boat caused gridlock on the bridge as it swung open regularly to allow boats to pass on the river. (James L. Streeter.)

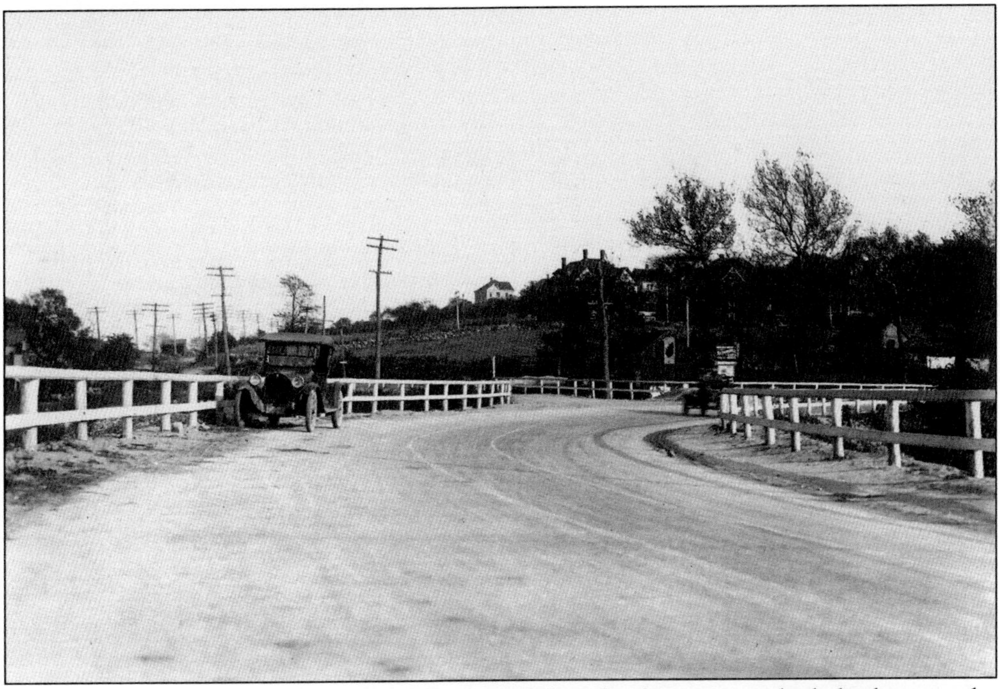

A vehicle, on the Groton side of the river, approaches the first motor vehicle bridge over the Thames River. (Connecticut Department of Transportation.)

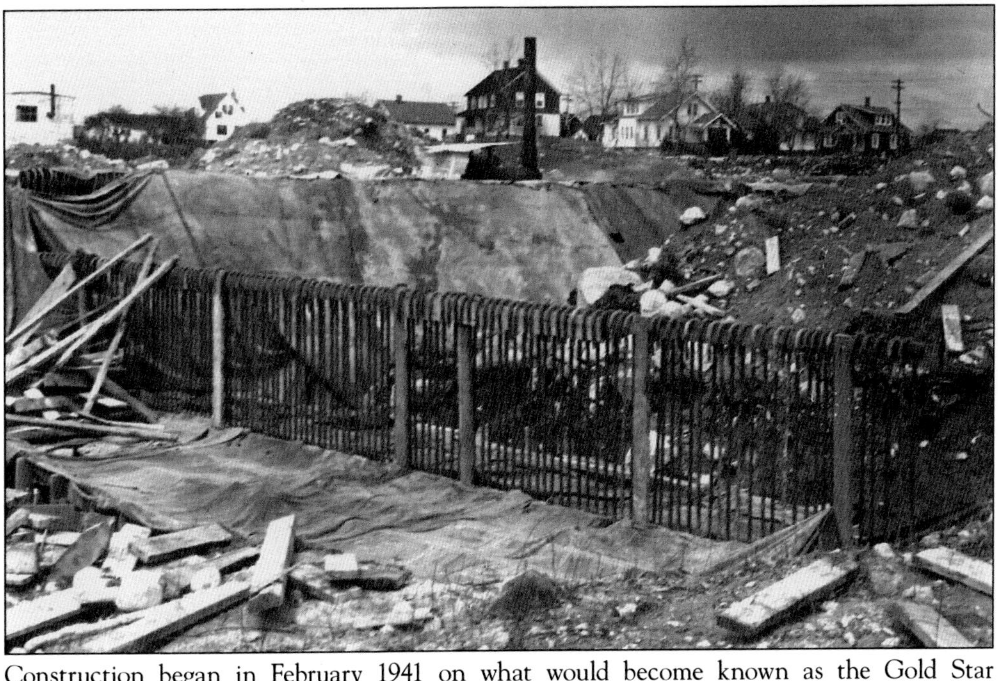

Construction began in February 1941 on what would become known as the Gold Star Memorial Bridge. As early as 1927, local legislators had begun lobbying Hartford for a cantilever bridge over the Thames River. In 1939, the Connecticut General Assembly finally approved a toll bridge initially called the Thames River Highway Bridge. (Connecticut Department of Transportation.)

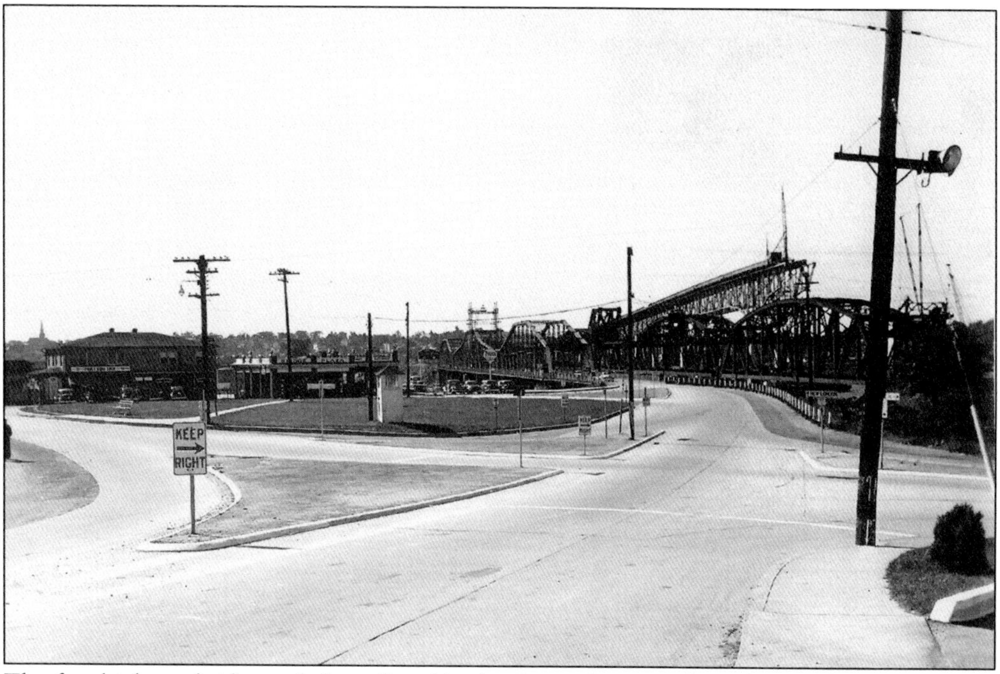

The first highway bridge and the railroad bridge keep silent watch as the Gold Star Memorial Bridge begins to rise over the Thames River in this 1941 photograph. Five workers died in the construction of the bridge, which took nearly two years to complete. (Connecticut Department of Transportation.)

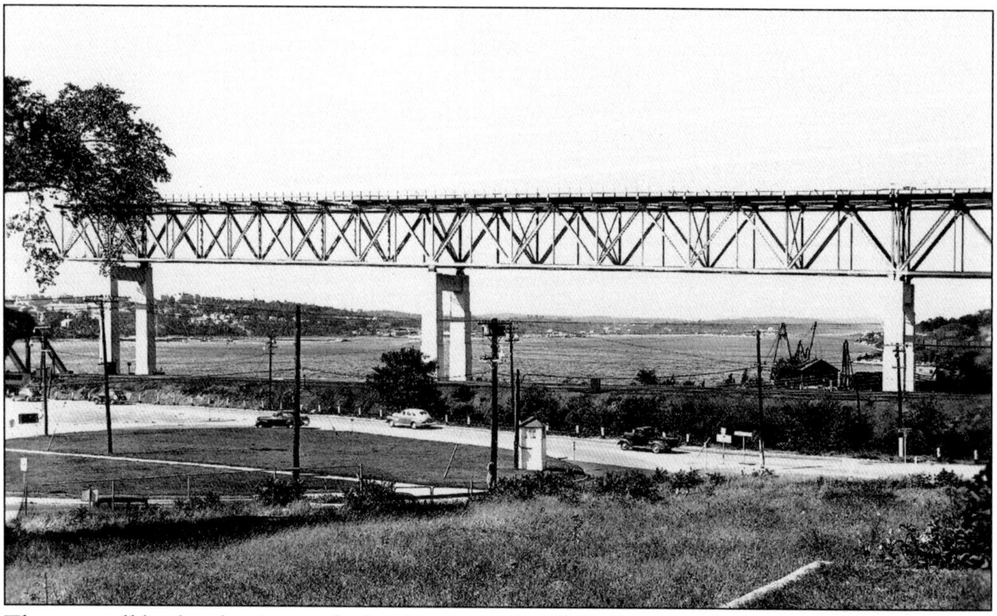

The new toll bridge dominates the landscape in this 1942 photograph. Construction was nearly halted when World War II broke out and the federal government stopped all nonessential construction to divert steel to the war effort. Electric Boat was building submarines to fight the Japanese, and Groton convinced Washington the bridge was vital for Electric Boat workers to get to work on time. So construction went forward. (Connecticut Department of Transportation.)

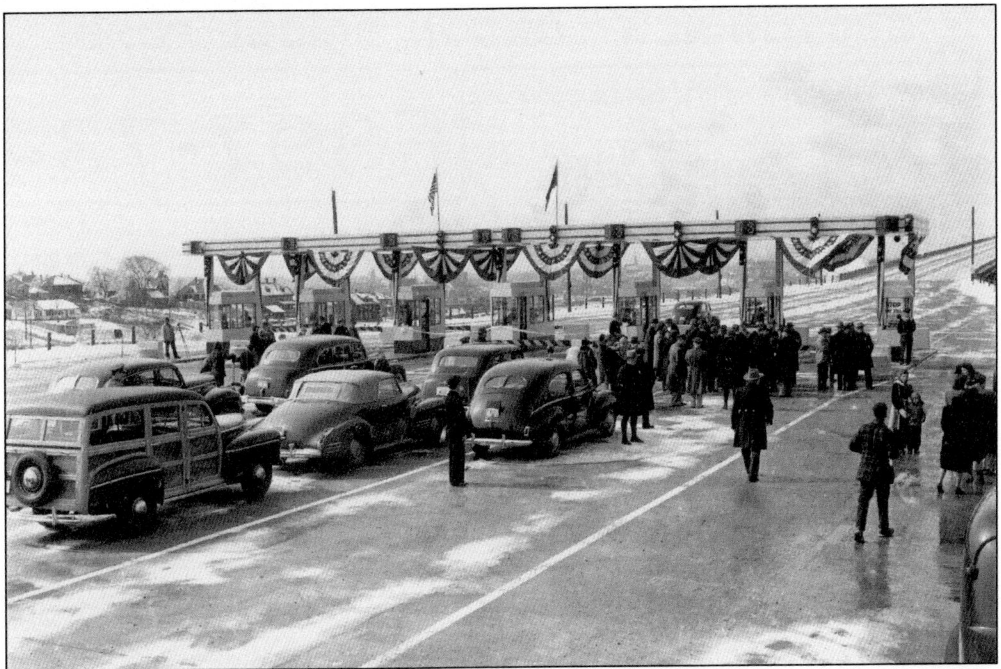

On February 27, 1943, Gov. Raymond Baldwin led a group of 20 dignitaries who cut the ribbon officially opening the Thames River Highway Bridge. The guest list originally included 700, but two months earlier, the federal government instituted gas rationing for the duration of World War II, which forced the state to scale back the festivities considerably. Here the dignitaries gather at the toll booths on the Groton side of the river. (Marty Artale.)

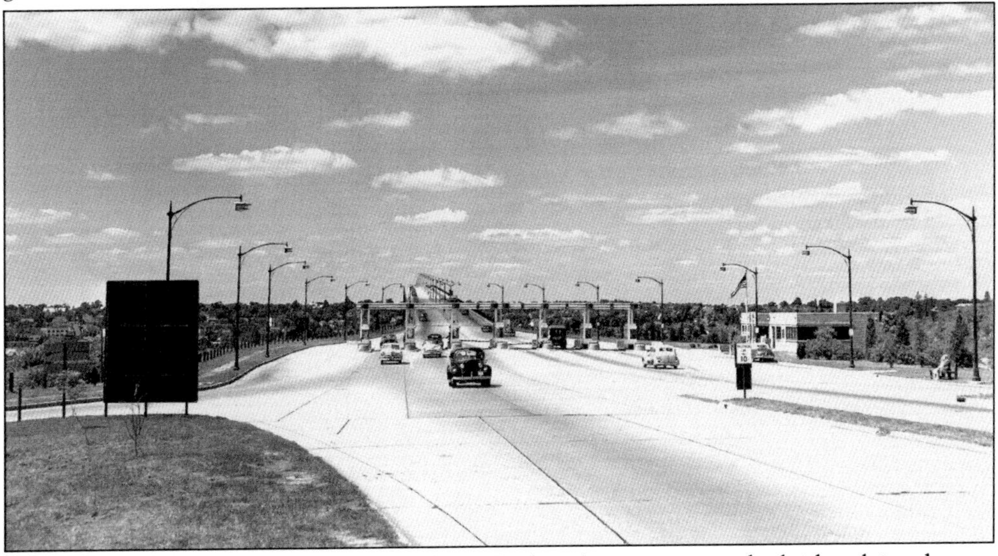

Cars travel across the Thames River Highway Bridge. At its opening, the bridge claimed many New England architectural and engineering records. At $6 million, it was the most costly; at 5,925 feet, it had the longest cantilever span; and at 540 feet, it was the second-largest channel span. Mount Hope Bridge in Rhode Island was first. The state renamed the span the Gold Star Memorial Bridge in 1951, in honor of Connecticut citizens killed in World War II. (James L. Streeter.)

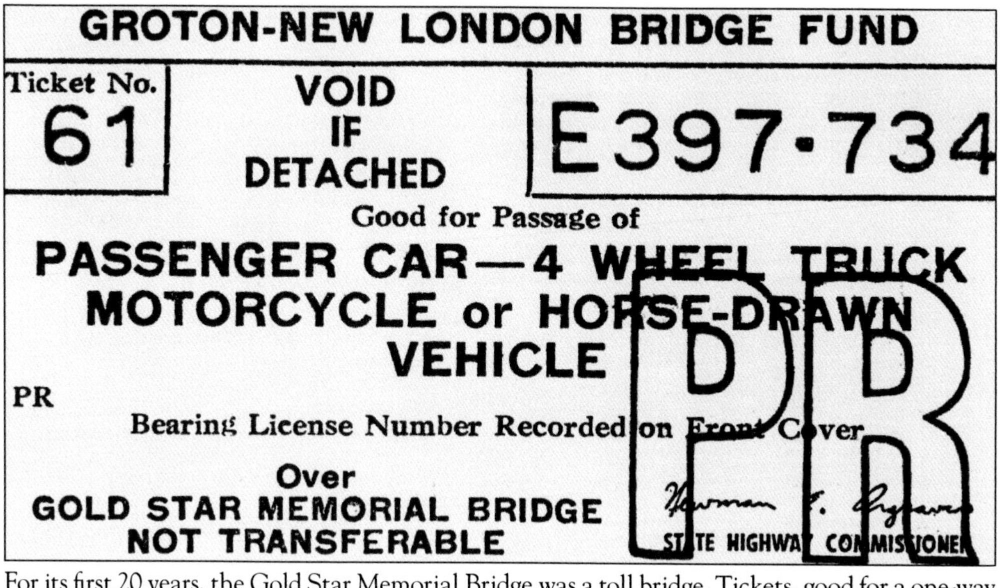

GROTON-NEW LONDON BRIDGE FUND

Ticket No. 61

VOID IF DETACHED

E397•734

Good for Passage of

PASSENGER CAR—4 WHEEL TRUCK MOTORCYCLE or HORSE-DRAWN VEHICLE

PR

Bearing License Number Recorded on Front Cover

Over

GOLD STAR MEMORIAL BRIDGE

NOT TRANSFERABLE

STATE HIGHWAY COMMISSIONER

For its first 20 years, the Gold Star Memorial Bridge was a toll bridge. Tickets, good for a one-way crossing, were sold in books of 100, for $2.50 a book. The only way local legislators could convince the state to build a cantilever bridge over the Thames River was to lobby for a toll bridge. Residents protested loudly, but to no avail. Tolls remained in effect until 1963, when the Gold Star Memorial Bridge became part of the Interstate 95 corridor. (James L. Streeter.)

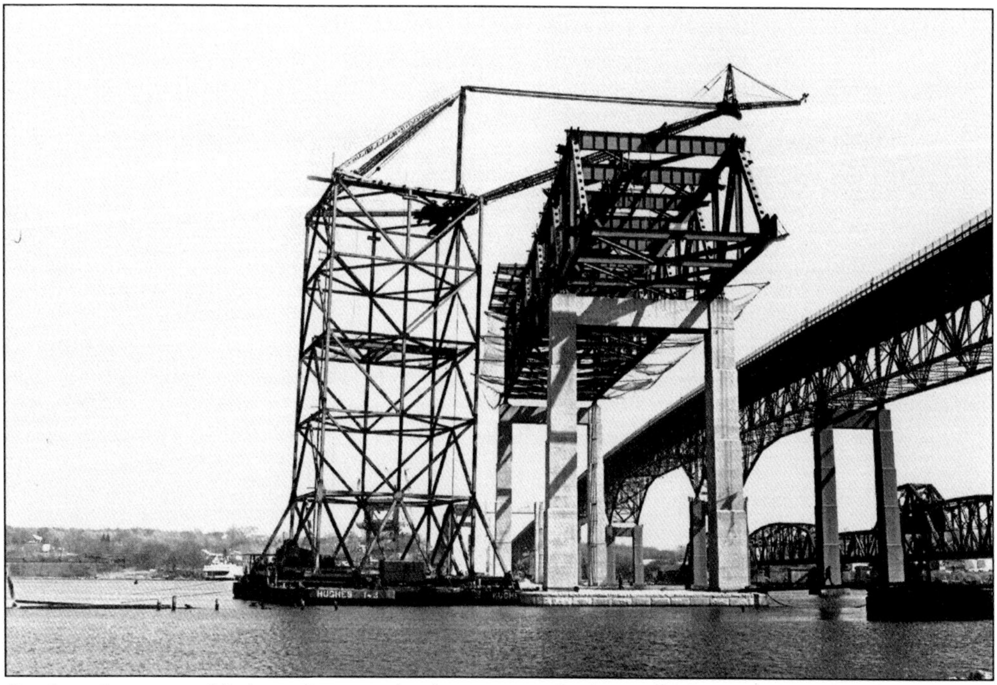

Steel girders are added to the new bridge span, which would become what today are the southbound lanes of Interstate 95 over the Thames River. The original bridge comprises the northbound lanes of Interstate 95. (Connecticut Department of Transportation.)

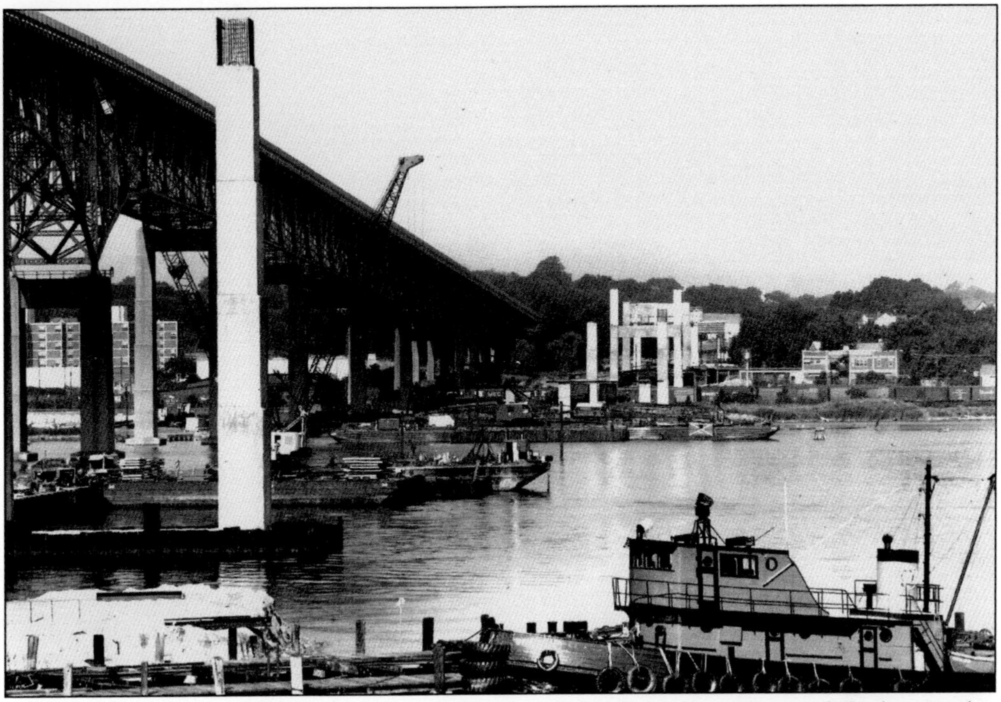

In 1969, construction began on the second span of the Gold Star Memorial Bridge. In this photograph, taken from the Groton side of the river looking toward New London, the concrete supports for the new span are being put into place. (Connecticut Department of Transportation.)

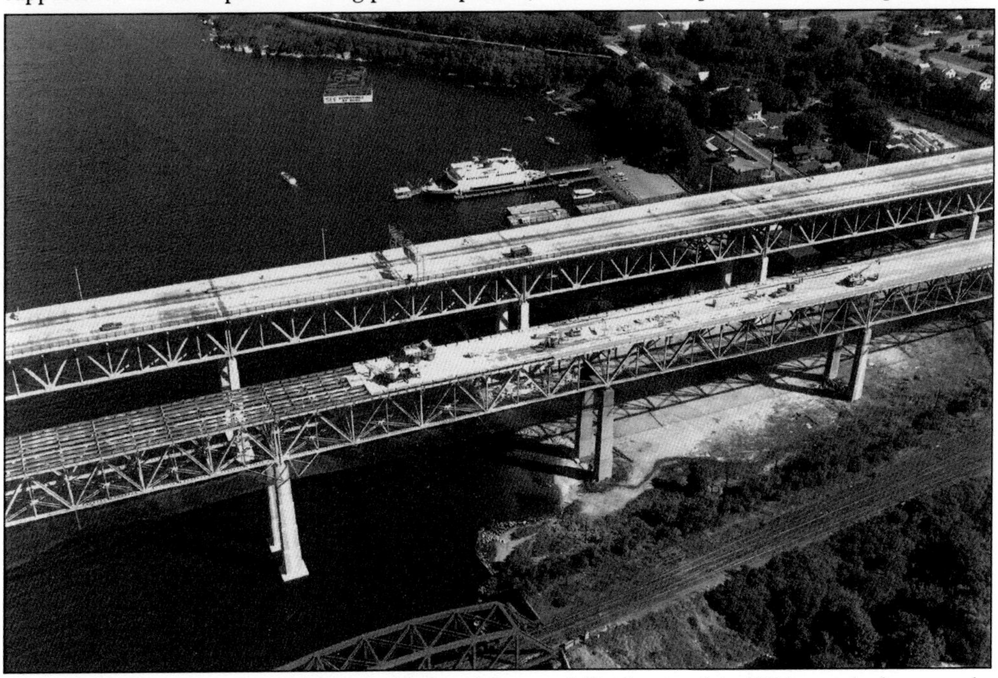

Cars travel the new span of the Gold Star Memorial Bridge in this 1974 aerial photograph, while the original bridge is refitted to become a five-lane span to carry the northbound traffic on Interstate 95. (Connecticut Department of Transportation.)

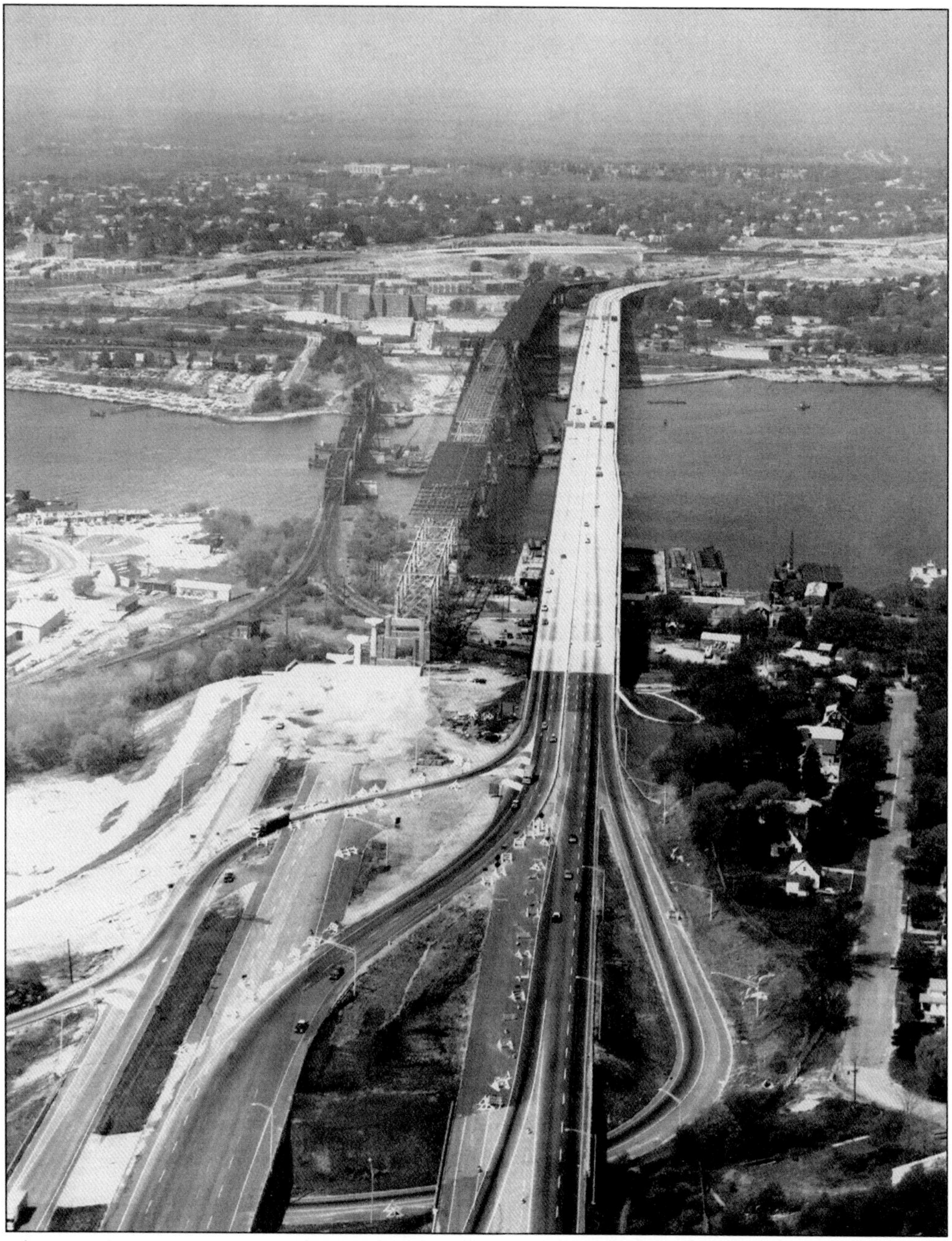

This aerial photograph shows the second span of the Gold Star Memorial Bridge, which opened on June 13, 1973. It took four years and $40 million to complete and was part of a $91 million project to create two five-lane bridges across the Thames River to eliminate any major traffic flow problems on Interstate 95, which runs from Maine to Florida. (Connecticut Department of Transportation.)

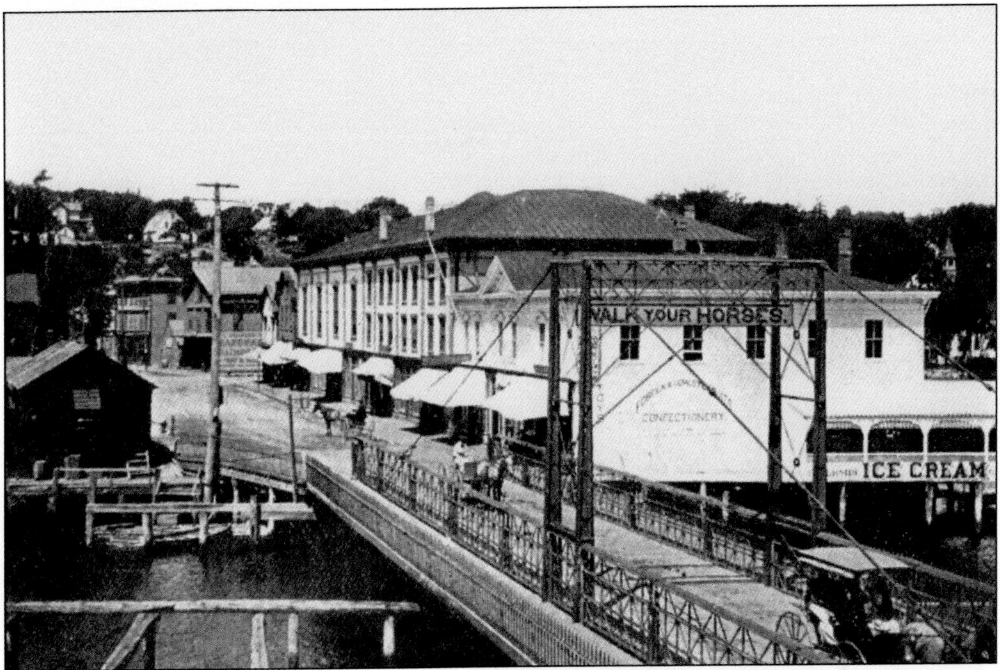

Traffic crosses the Mystic drawbridge in this late-19th-century photograph. The bridge, made of iron, was built in 1866. An early sign hung on the structure, advising travelers to "Trot Not on This Bridge." This later was replaced by one stating "Walk Your Horses." (Carol W. Kimball.)

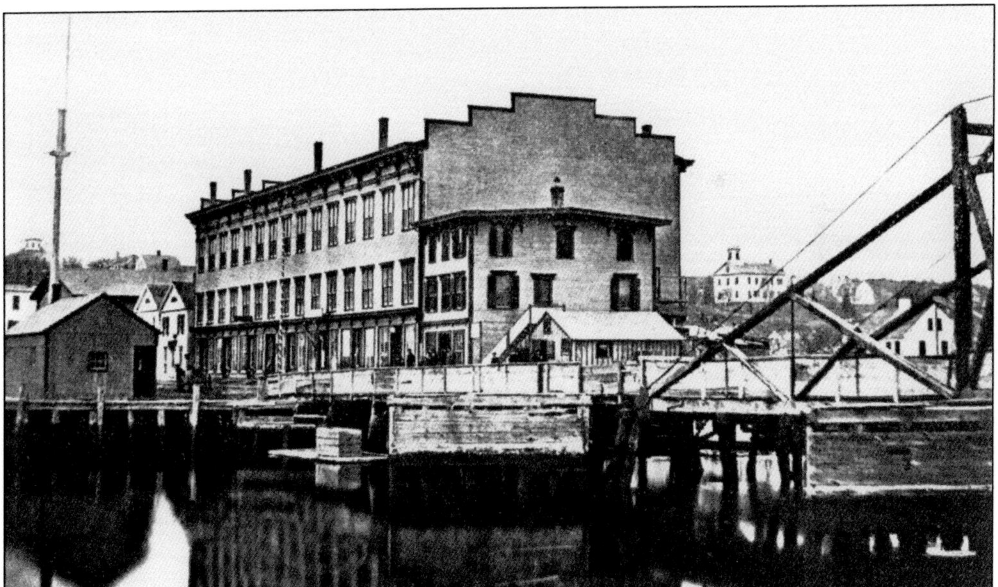

Mystic's last old wooden highway bridge was built in 1854 by Henry Latham. The construction of the bridge marked the end of tolls to cross the river and the beginning of ownership and maintenance of the bridge by the towns of Groton and Stonington. It was replaced by the iron bridge in 1866. The original wooden Mystic Academy building is visible on the hill above the bridge. (James L. Streeter.)

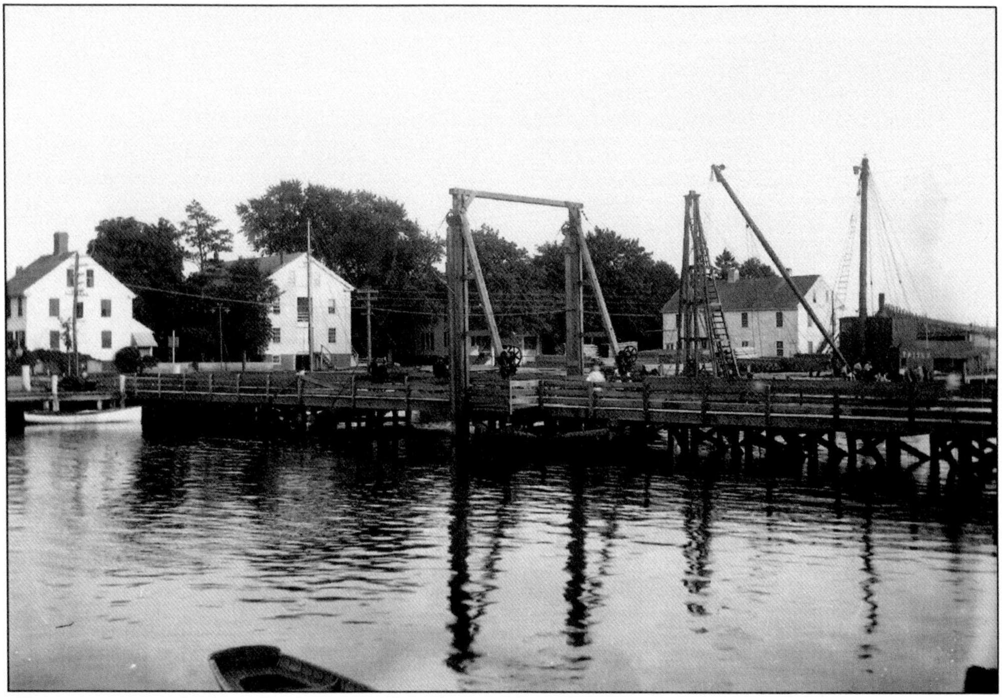

This temporary bridge, for horse and pedestrian traffic, was erected in 1904 just south of the Mystic drawbridge and was used from June to September while the new steel bridge was being constructed. The new bridge opened on September 21, 1904, and this bridge was dismantled. (Indian and Colonial Research Center.)

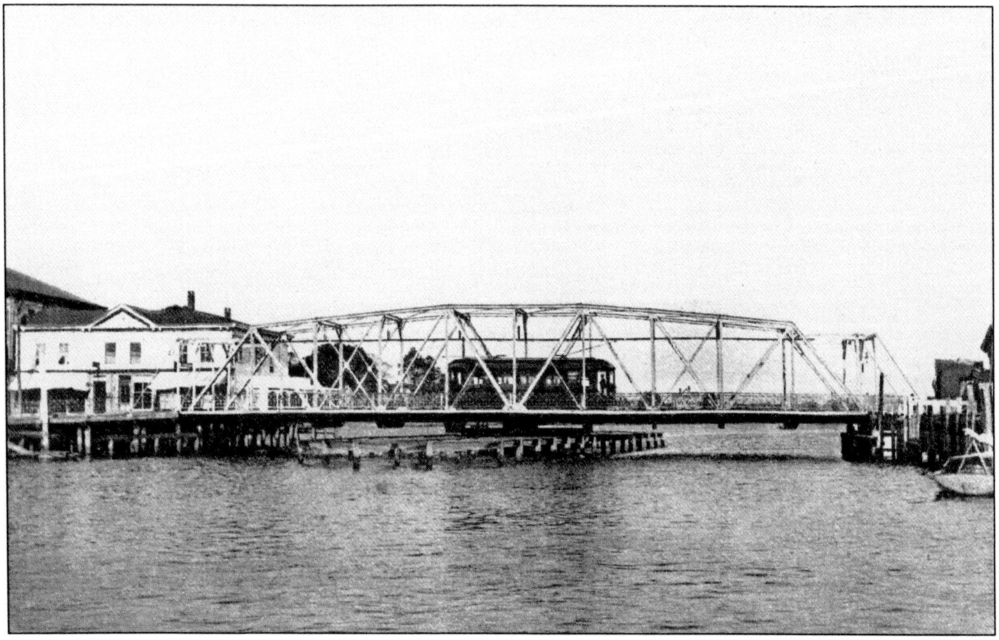

This 1904 photograph shows the new steel Mystic highway bridge with a trolley passing over it. The heavy traffic over the bridge caused it to settle unevenly, and the swing portion often would get stuck open, leaving vexed travelers waiting for hours to cross the span. (James L. Streeter.)

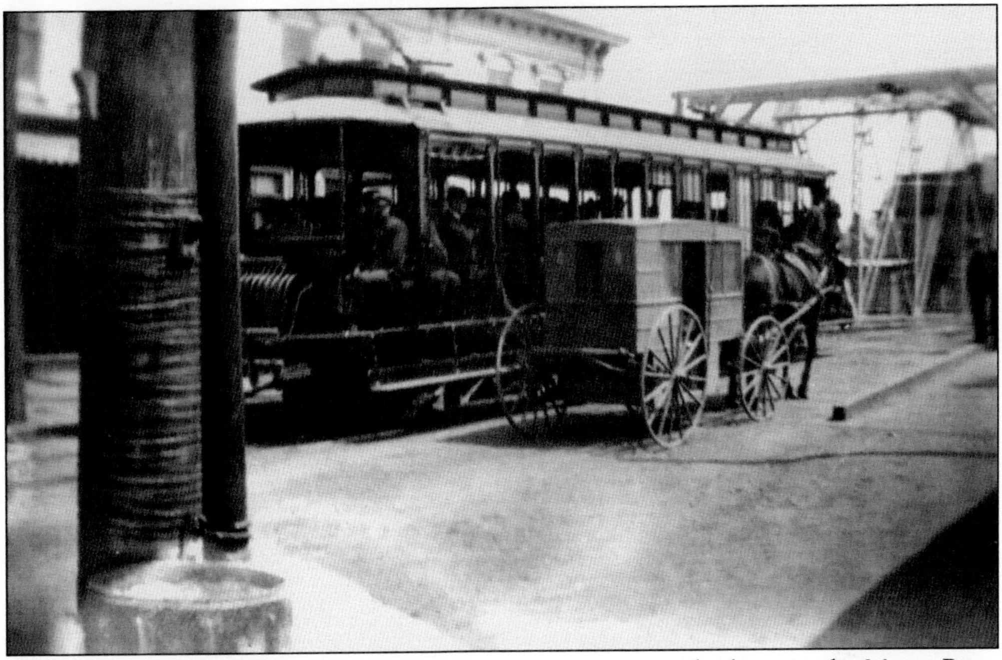

The 20th century brought new inventions, so a newer, stronger bridge over the Mystic River was needed to support trolley tracks and trolleys. In September 1904, a new steel bridge opened. This photograph shows a crowded trolley and a horse and wagon approaching the bridge. (Janet Crossman.)

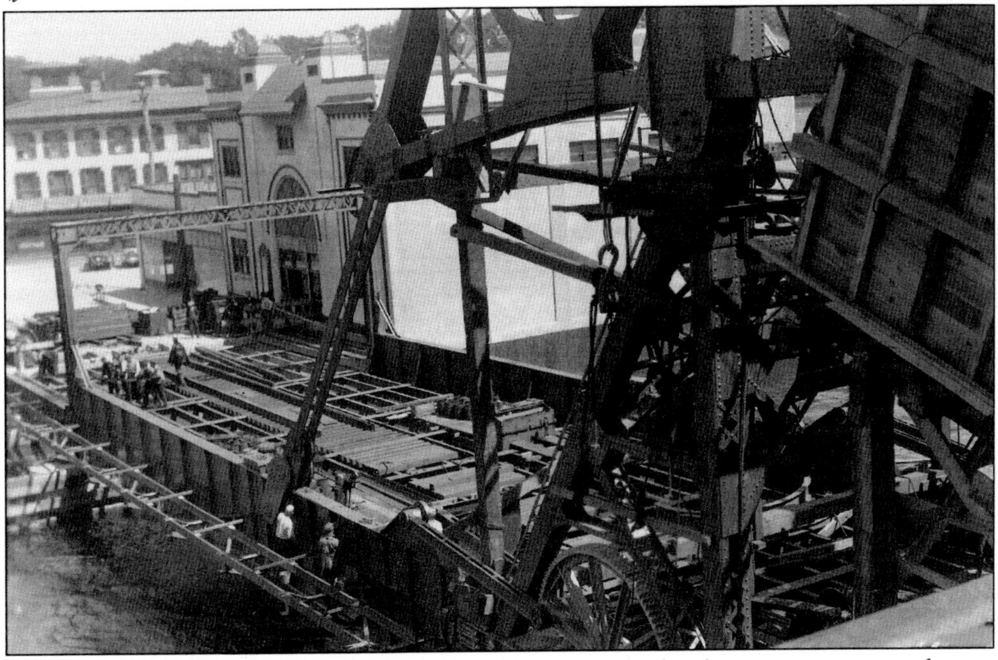

With the automobile becoming more popular and the 1904 bridge showing major signs of stress, Groton and Stonington made plans for a new bridge. Construction began in 1922. Workers cleared pilings and old piers from the river and laid a solid foundation for the bridge. (Connecticut Department of Transportation.)

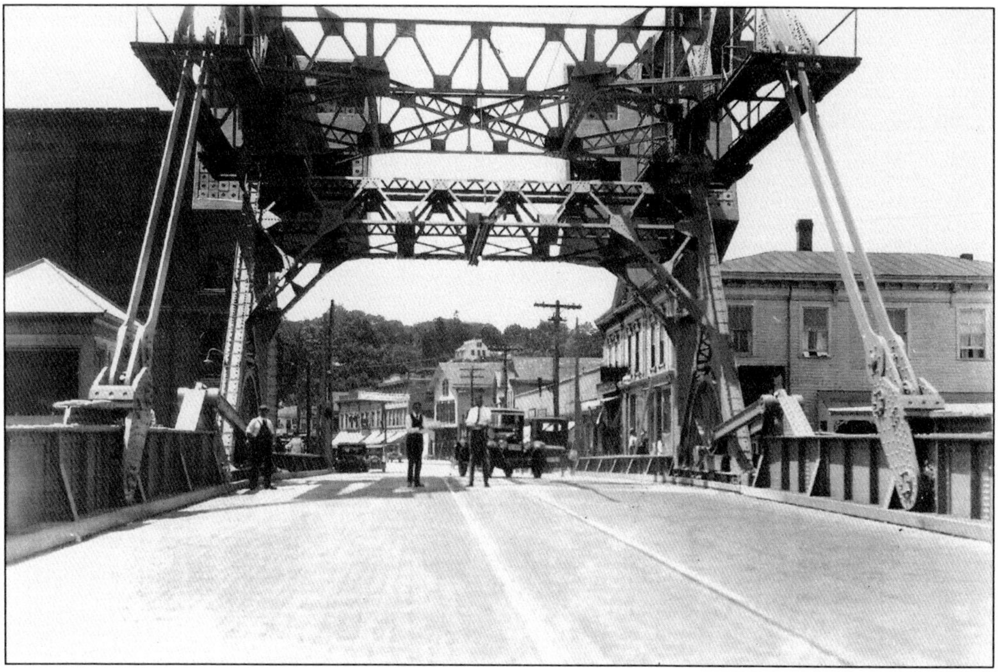

Mystic's bascule bridge was the first of its kind in the country. To open the 88-foot lift, counterweights were designed and finely balanced so two 36-horsepower motors could raise the bridge in 35 seconds. On July 10, 1922, the first automobile crossed the new bridge. The structure remains today one of Mystic's major tourist attractions. (Connecticut Department of Transportation.)

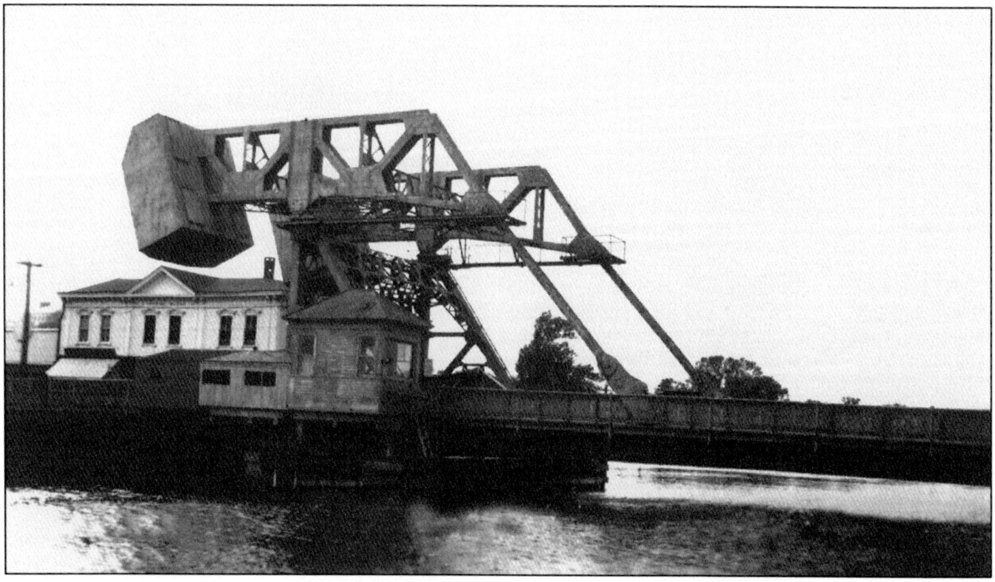

This stark photograph shows the new Mystic drawbridge looking from Cottrell Street toward the Groton side of the river. The bridge cost $254,000 to construct. Groton paid $63,000, Stonington paid $53,000 and the state paid the balance. The bridge has been part of the Mystic landscape for 85 years. The state recently announced major repairs to the structure, slated over the next two winters, so the summer tourism trade is not interrupted. (James L. Streeter.)

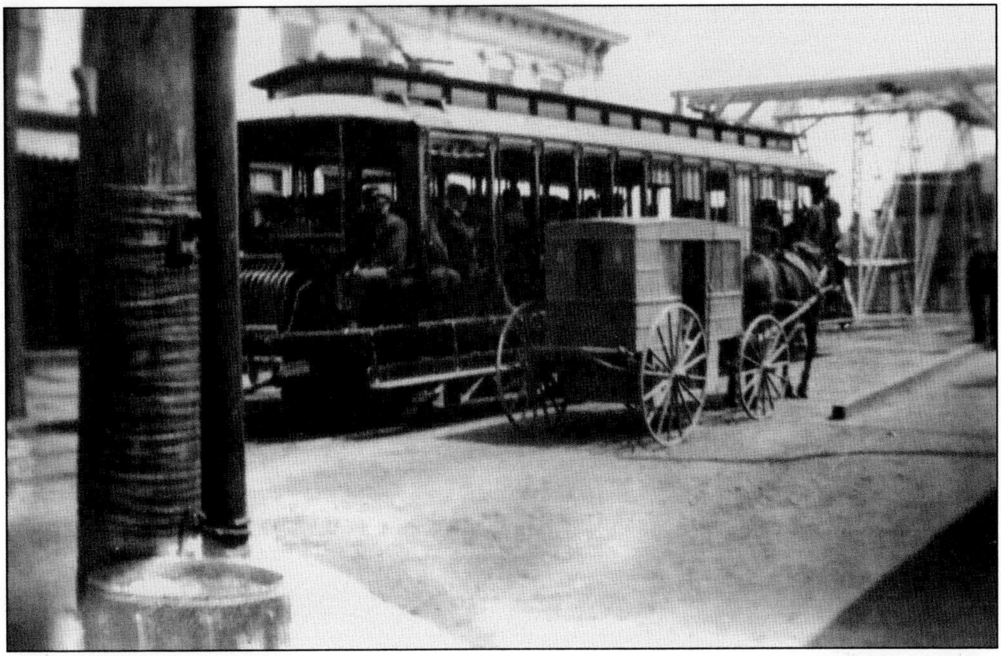

The 20th century brought new inventions, so a newer, stronger bridge over the Mystic River was needed to support trolley tracks and trolleys. In September 1904, a new steel bridge opened. This photograph shows a crowded trolley and a horse and wagon approaching the bridge. (Janet Crossman.)

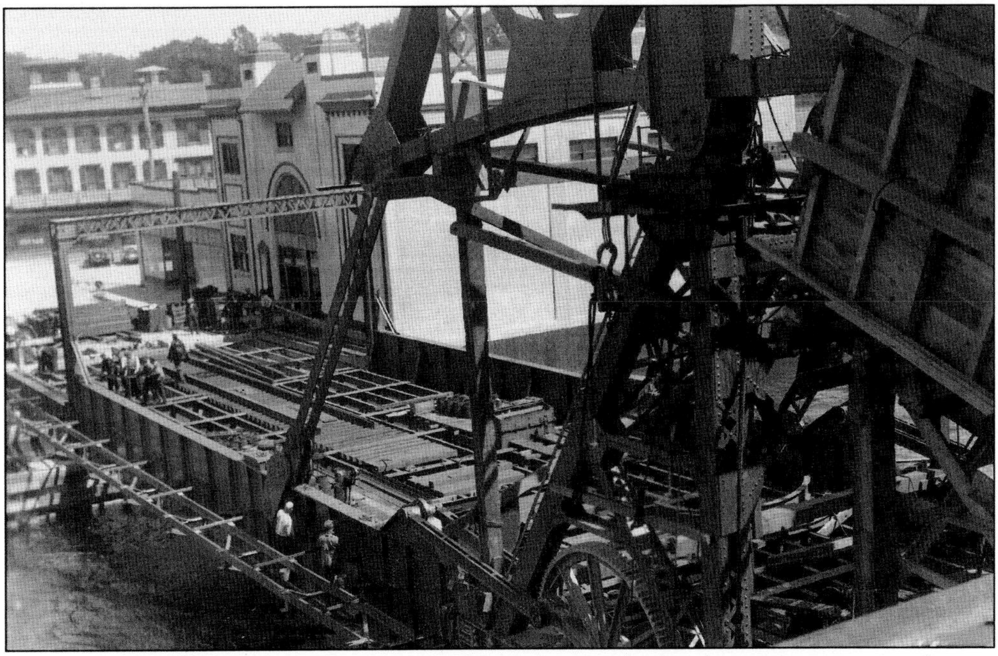

With the automobile becoming more popular and the 1904 bridge showing major signs of stress, Groton and Stonington made plans for a new bridge. Construction began in 1922. Workers cleared pilings and old piers from the river and laid a solid foundation for the bridge. (Connecticut Department of Transportation.)

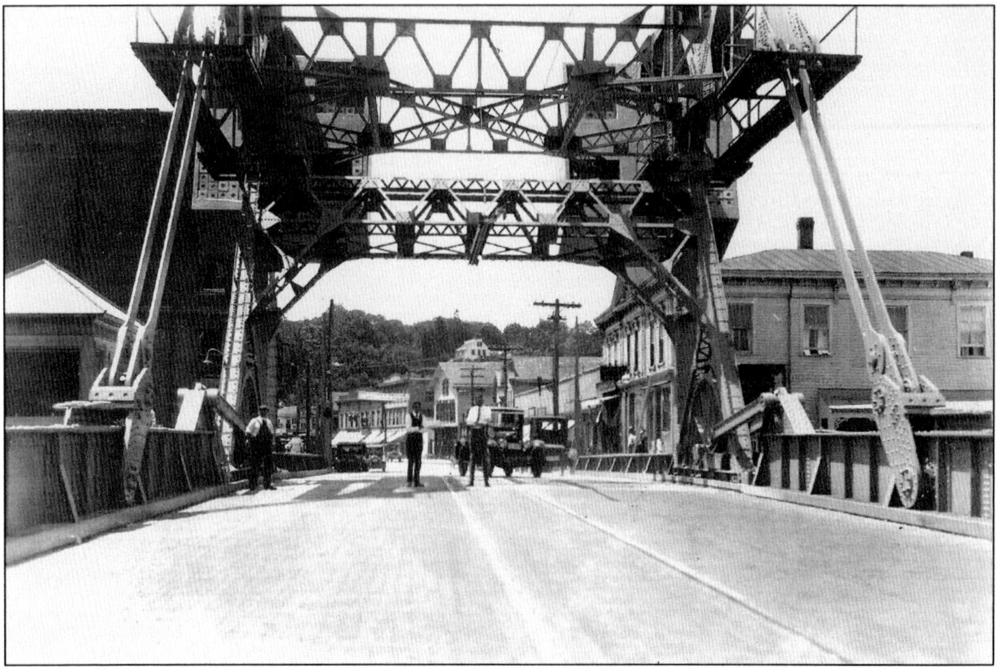

Mystic's bascule bridge was the first of its kind in the country. To open the 88-foot lift, counterweights were designed and finely balanced so two 36-horsepower motors could raise the bridge in 35 seconds. On July 10, 1922, the first automobile crossed the new bridge. The structure remains today one of Mystic's major tourist attractions. (Connecticut Department of Transportation.)

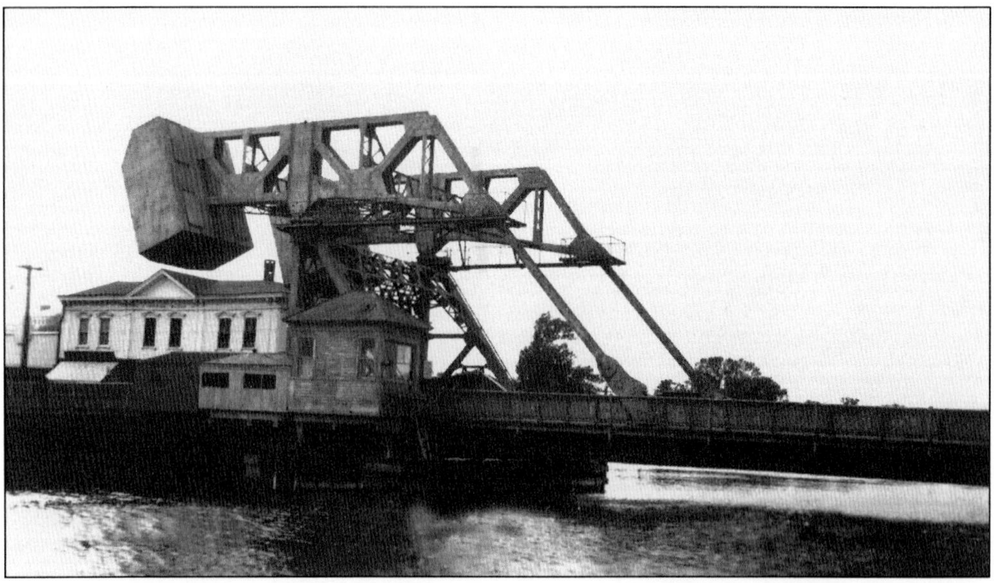

This stark photograph shows the new Mystic drawbridge looking from Cottrell Street toward the Groton side of the river. The bridge cost $254,000 to construct. Groton paid $63,000, Stonington paid $53,000 and the state paid the balance. The bridge has been part of the Mystic landscape for 85 years. The state recently announced major repairs to the structure, slated over the next two winters, so the summer tourism trade is not interrupted. (James L. Streeter.)

Five

The 1938 Hurricane

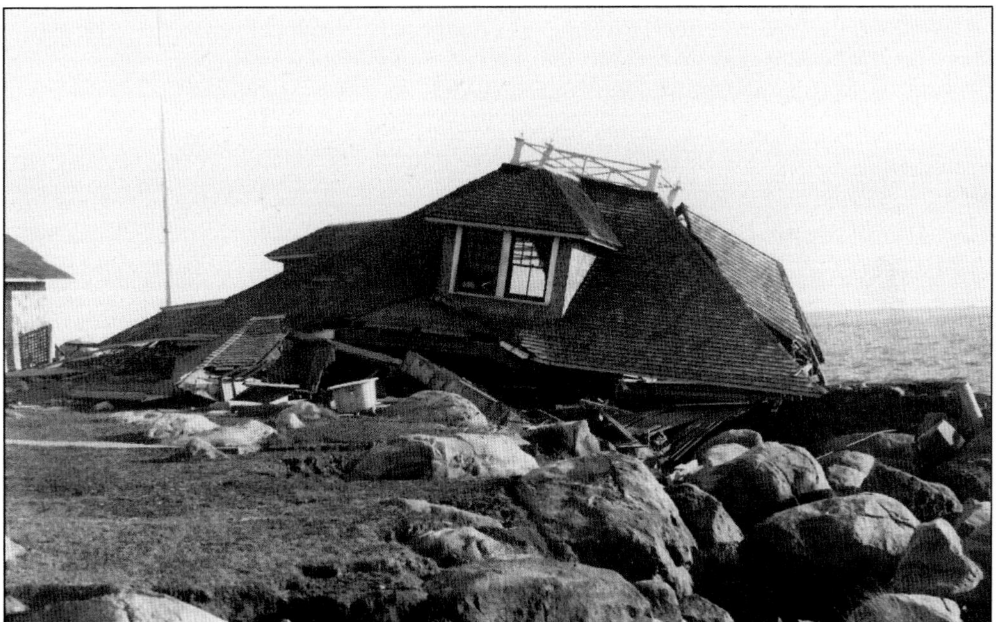

The J. J. Smith house at the end of Weston Road in Groton Long Point was flattened by the 1938 hurricane. The storm struck New England without warning on the afternoon of September 21, 1938. Hurricanes rarely hit New England, and major hurricanes are rarer still. Before 1938, records show only two other major hurricanes ever hit the region. One was in 1635 and the other in 1815, eras long before the shorelines were populated. (Sally Allyn Brousseau.)

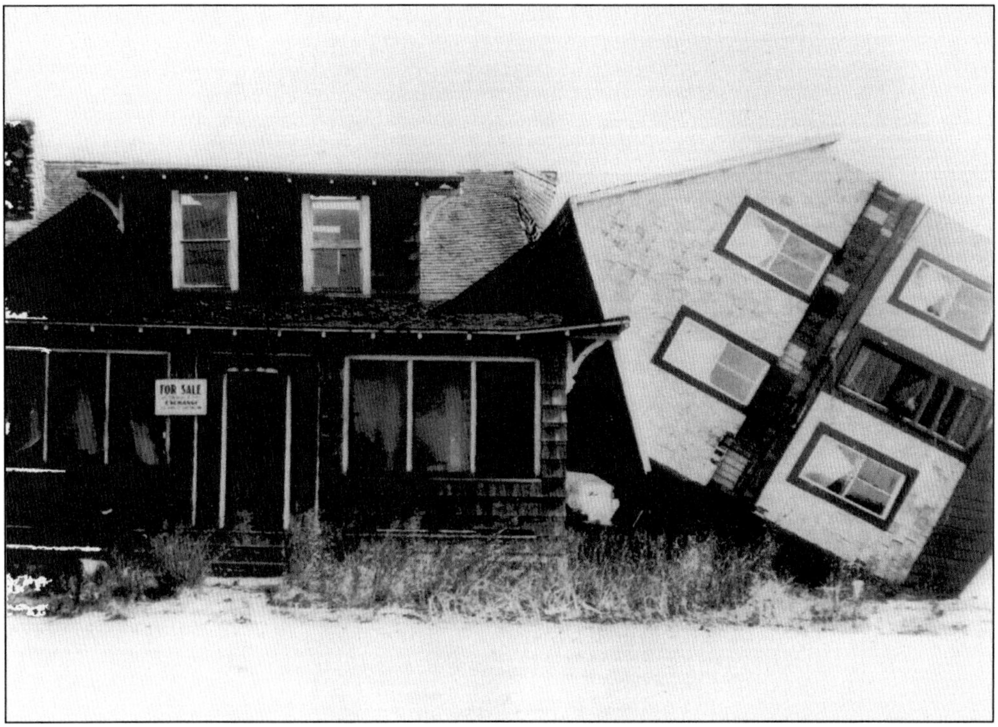

A cottage on Atlantic Avenue in Groton Long Point leans against another cottage. Both have been badly battered by the 1938 hurricane. The house on the left has a For Sale sign for anyone brave enough to rebuild along the shoreline after the storm. (James L. Streeter.)

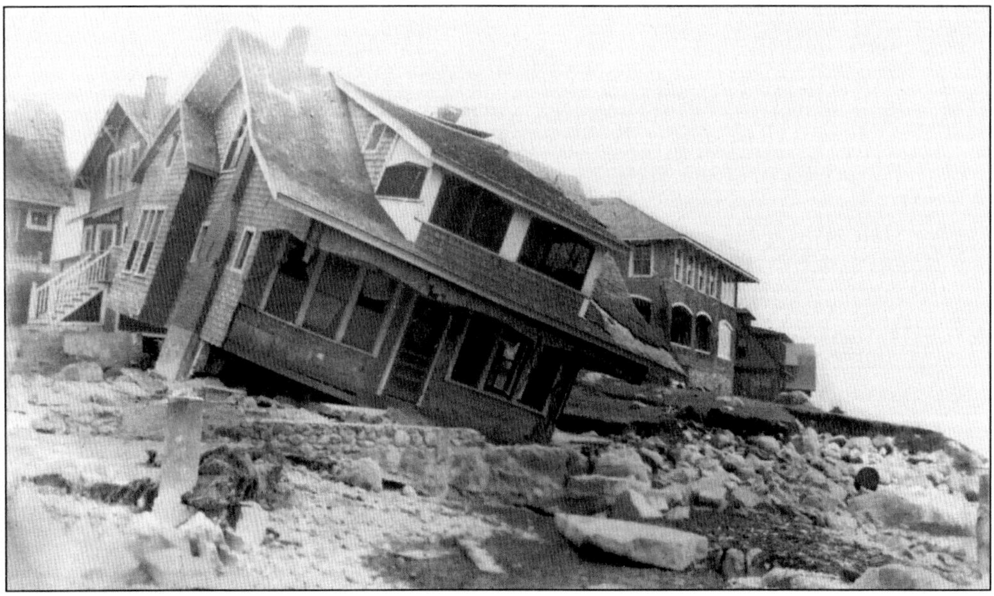

This house at South Shore Avenue and Club House Point in Groton Long Point is tilted off its foundation. (Mariellen French.)

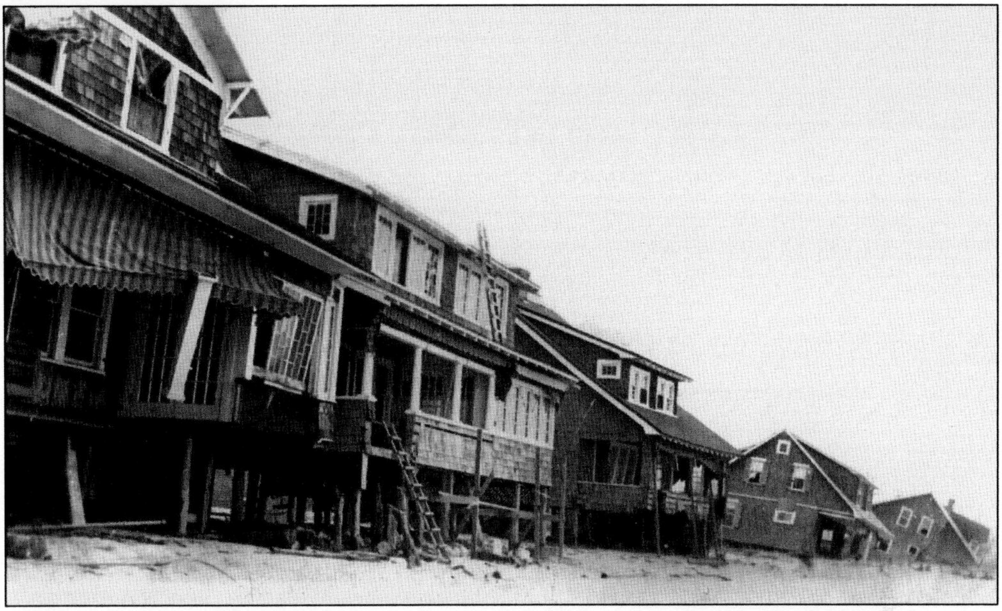

Cottages along the boardwalk at the Main Beach in Groton Long Point sustained heavy damage from the hurricane's storm surge. (Mariellen French.)

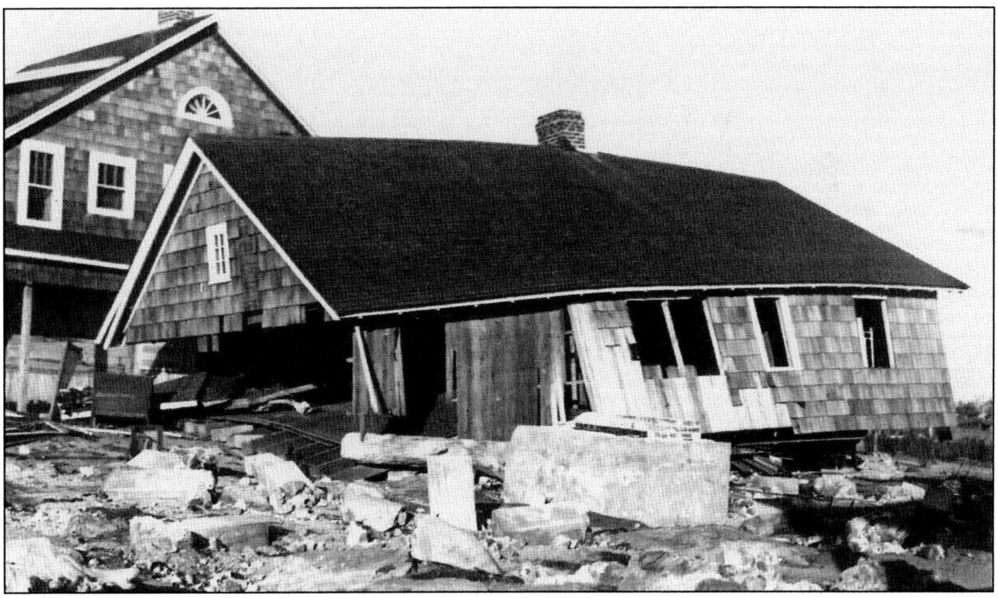

The power of the storm surge is evident in the destruction of this cottage on East Shore Avenue in Groton Long Point. Scenes like this were everywhere along the New England shoreline after the storm. (Sally Allyn Brousseau.)

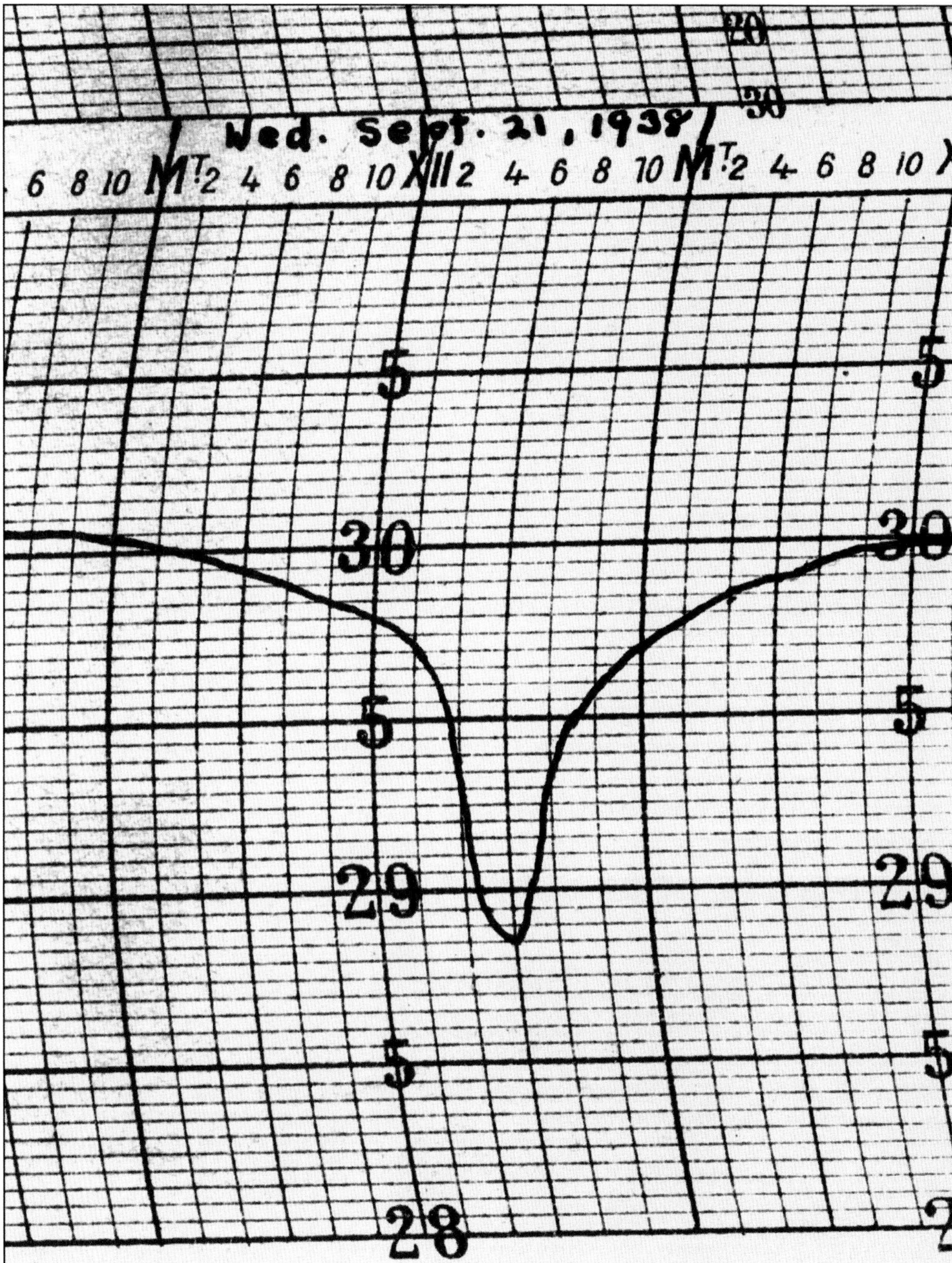

This chart shows the barometric reading for the Great Hurricane of 1938, which set a record at the time for lowest barometric pressure. The Weather Channel ranked it one of the top five storms of the 20th century. It struck without warning, killed nearly 700 people, and caused the greatest mass destruction ever suffered by the New England states. It blew salt spray as far inland as Brattleboro, Vermont, caused $400 million in damage in 1938 dollars and left 63,000 people homeless. (Mystic River Historical Society.)

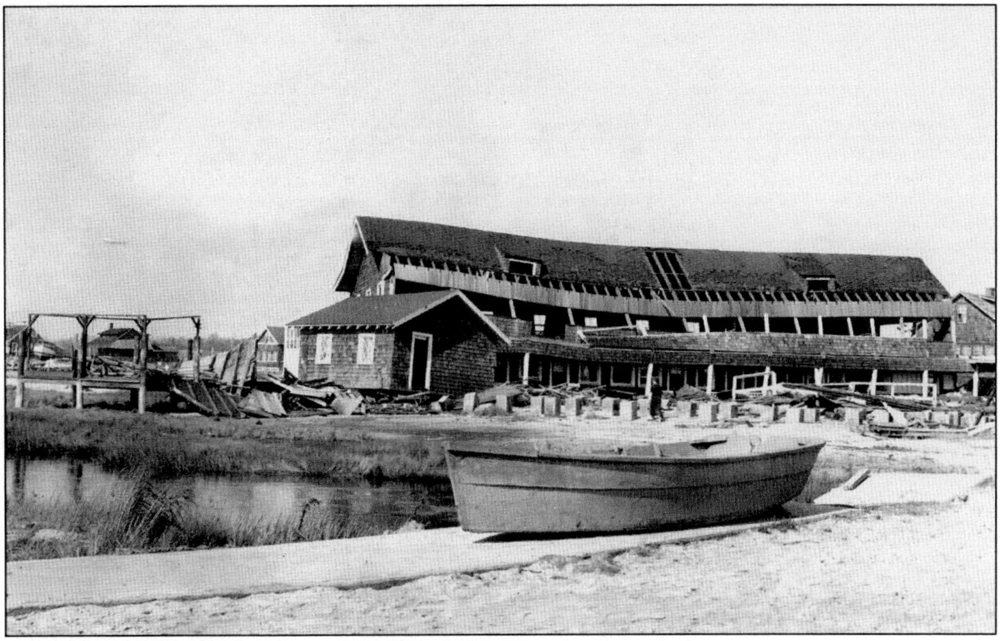

The Groton Long Point Casino, a popular venue for dances and activities in the summer resort, was damaged in the hurricane. The buildings at Groton Long Point suffered the most structural damage of any in town, probably because the summer cottages faced the open ocean and sustained a direct hit from the storm surge. In all, the hurricane destroyed 4,500 homes across Long Island and New England; 15,000 more were badly damaged. (James L. Streeter.)

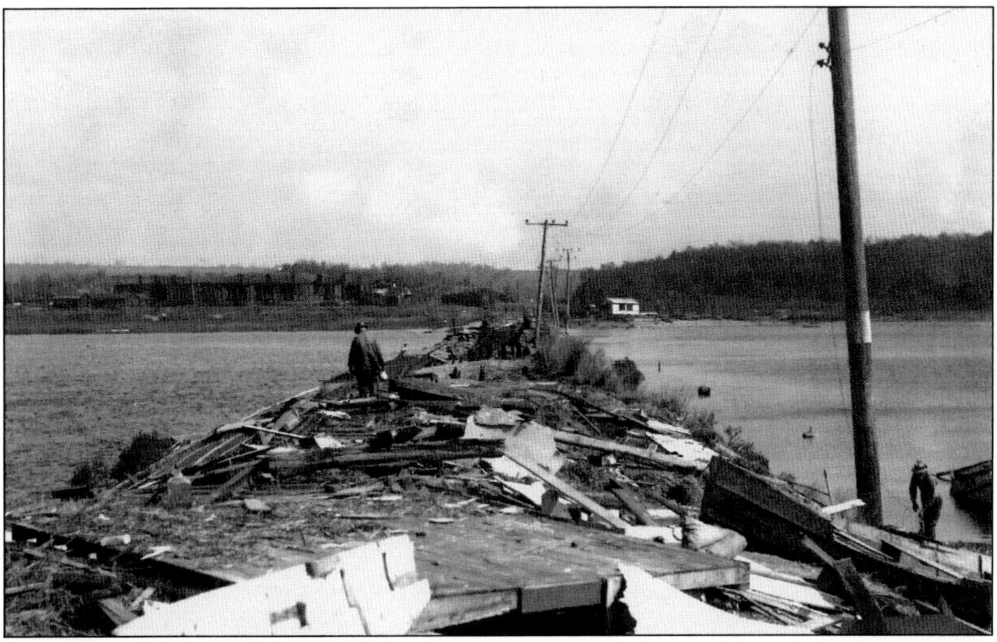

The railroad tracks to Electric Boat over the Poquonnock River are covered in debris. Train tracks along the Connecticut and Rhode Island shorelines were ripped from their beds in the storm. There was no rail service between Old Saybrook, Connecticut, and Westerly, Rhode Island, for weeks after the storm while the tracks were repaired. (Sally Allyn Brousseau.)

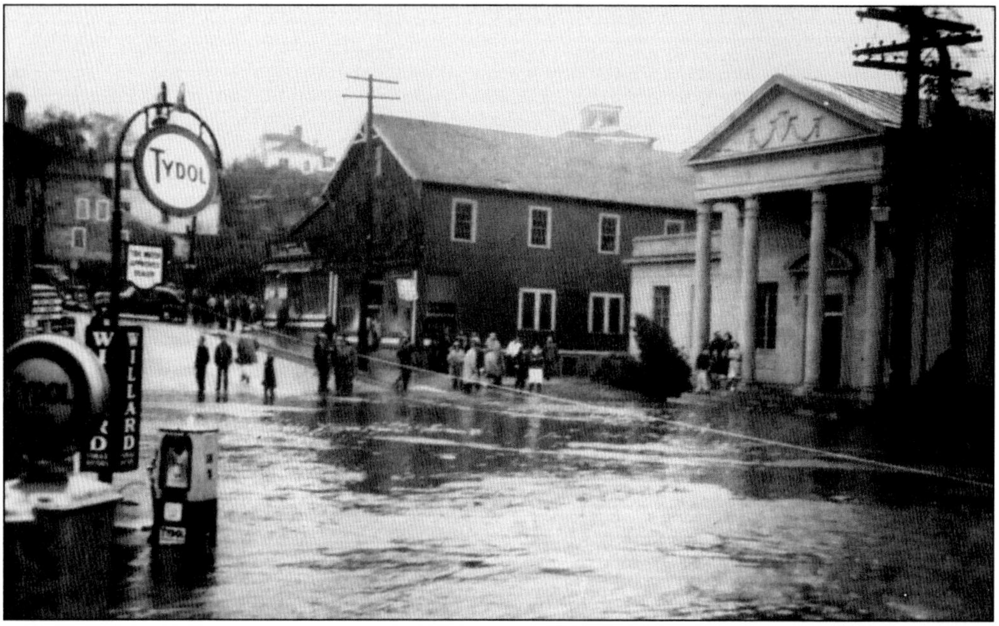

The floodwaters had started to recede in Bank Square in Mystic when these folks came out to survey the damage. The Hartford National Bank building is to the right, and the building in the middle today houses Mystic Pizza. (Mystic River Historical Society.)

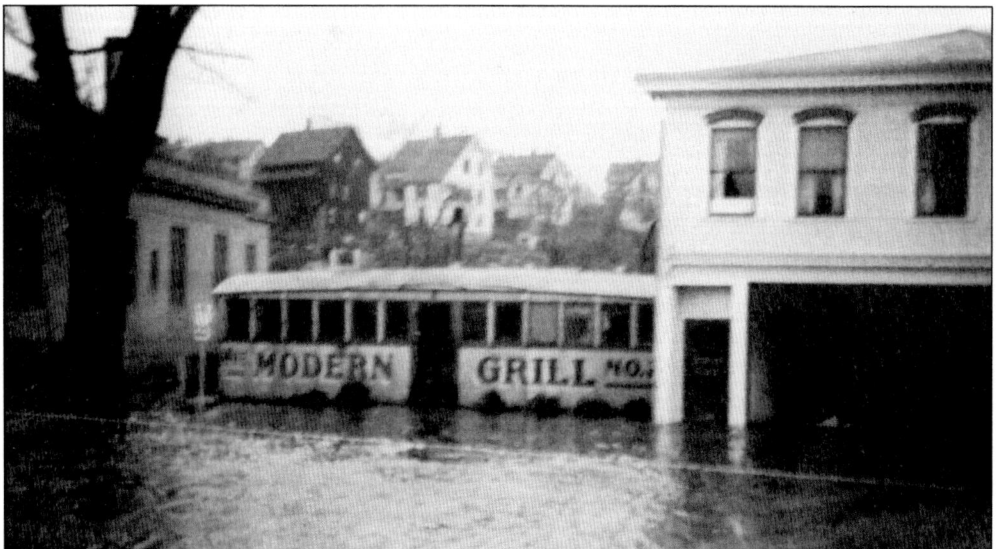

The Modern Grill diner survived the storm but is sitting in deep water in Bank Square in downtown Mystic. West Main, Pearl, Gravel, and Water Streets were all flooded by the storm surge when the hurricane struck. (Mystic River Historical Society.)

The Union Baptist Church in Mystic lost its steeple in the hurricane. The steeple had been home to the town clock, visible throughout the village of Mystic from the church's location on the top of Baptist Hill. For more than three decades after the storm, the church had no steeple. The congregation finally replaced it in May 1969. (Mystic River Historical Society.)

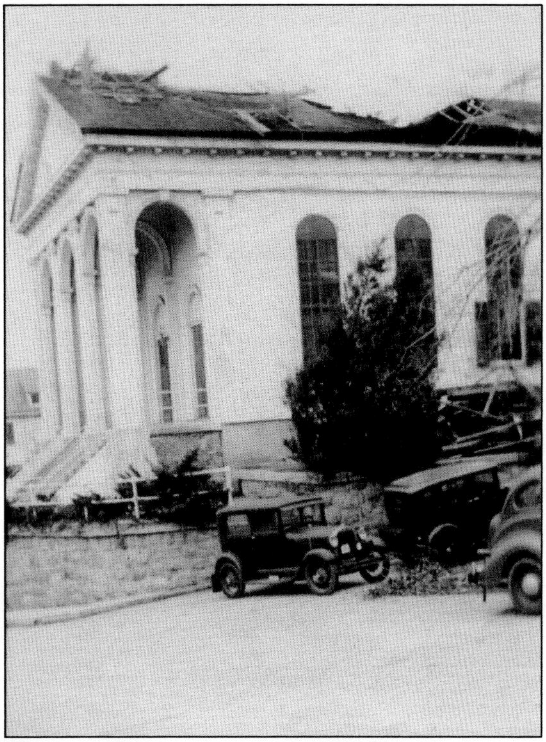

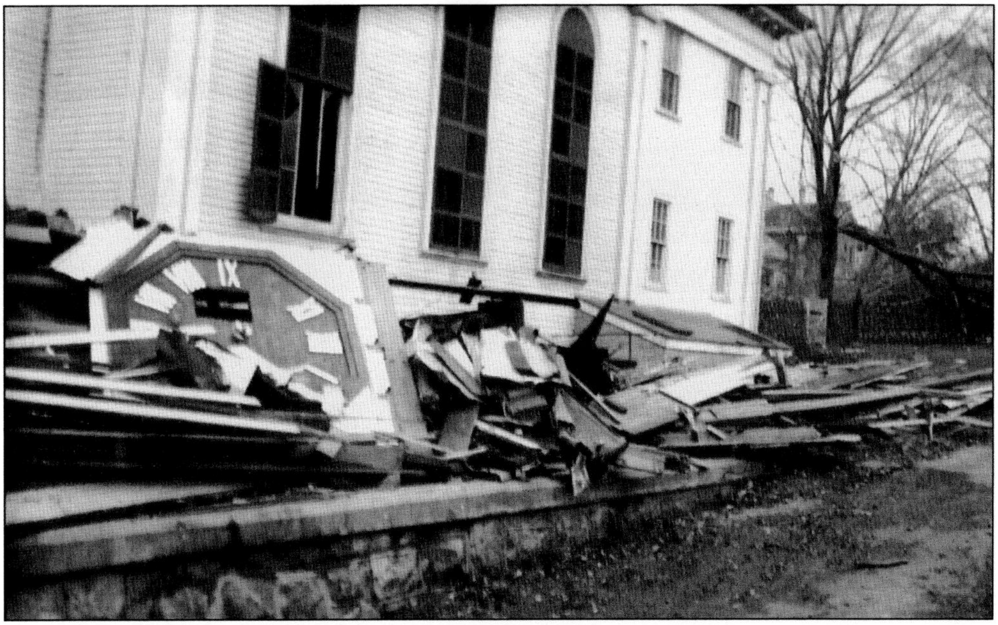

The category-three storm left the Union Baptist Church steeple a crumpled mess. The congregation replaced the steeple 31 years after the hurricane. The new one cost $90,000. In addition to a clock, it included a $25,000 Arlington carillon with a musical range of five chromatic octaves, and a 150-pound weather vane, a replica of the one atop the Old North Church in Boston. The carillon plays two concerts a day, at noon and 6:00 p.m., and its Westminster chimes strike hourly. (Mystic River Historical Society.)

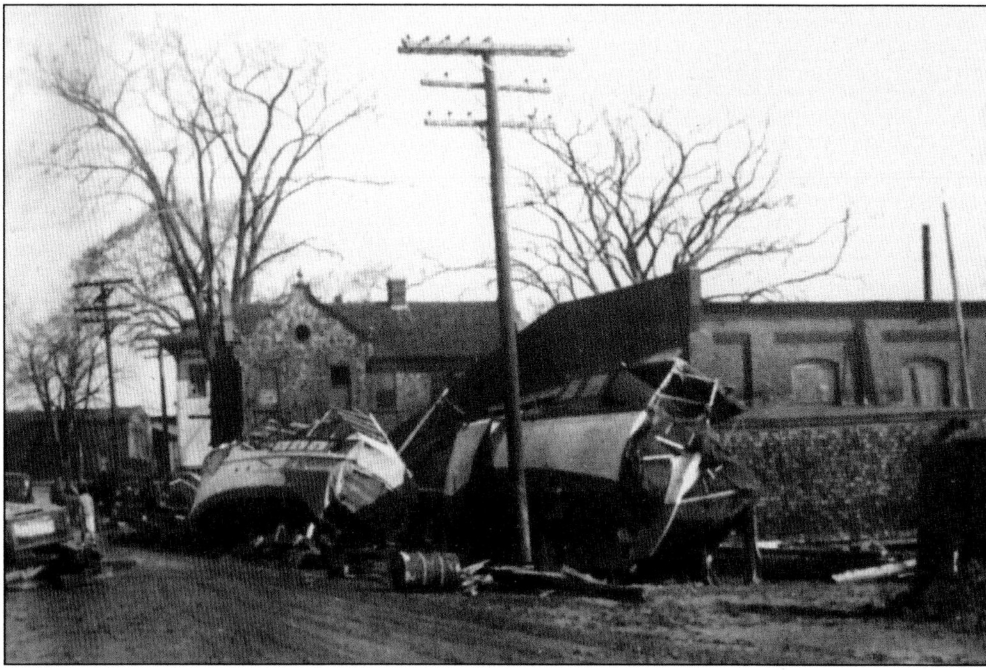

The storm surge came up the Mystic River, washing large boats from Bindloss Boatyard out on to Water Street. Here two boats lean against the old trolley barn. Water Street is slick with muck washed ashore by the rushing water. All of downtown Mystic was underwater during the storm. (Carol W. Kimball.)

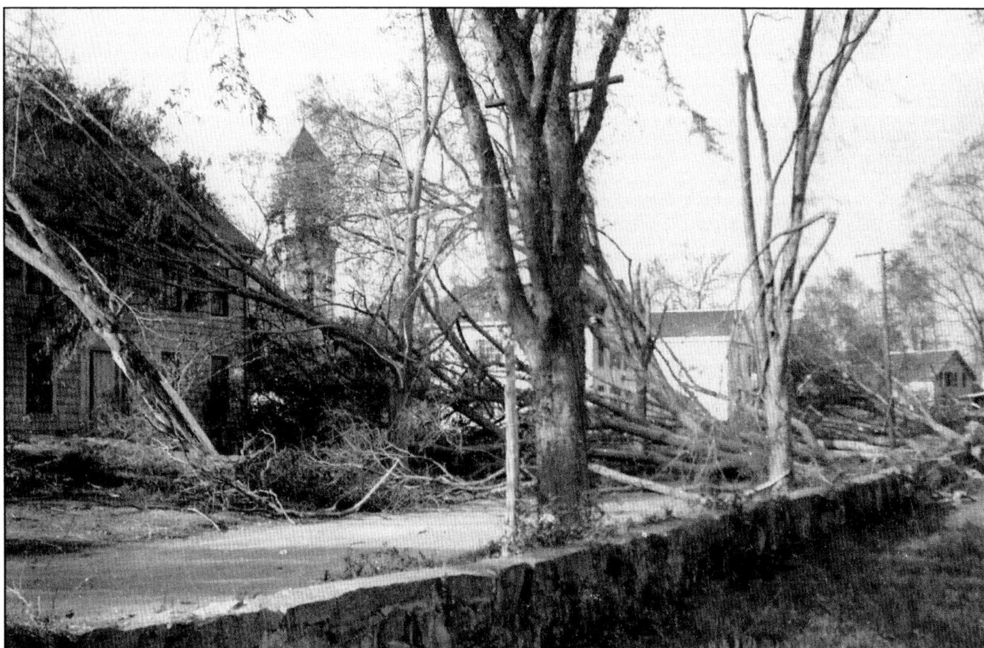

A mass of trees leans on houses, blocking River Road in Old Mystic. Cleanup after the storm took months. There were no chainsaws in 1938, so crosscut saws were used to cut up the fallen trees. (Carol W. Kimball.)

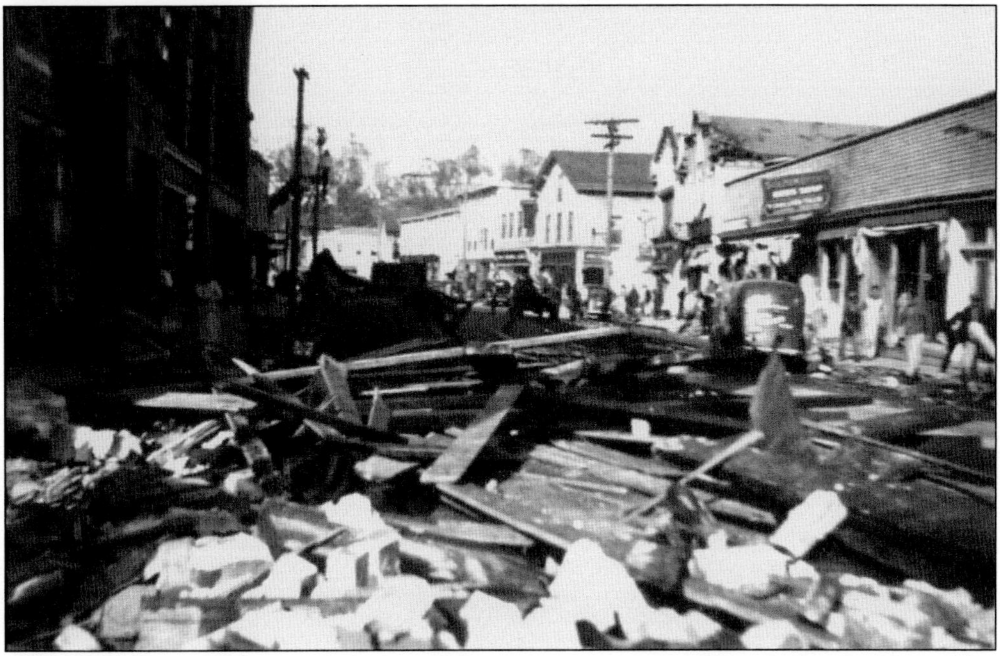

When the storm waters receded, West Main Street in Mystic was piled with debris. This photograph looks west from the Mystic drawbridge. (Mystic River Historical Society.)

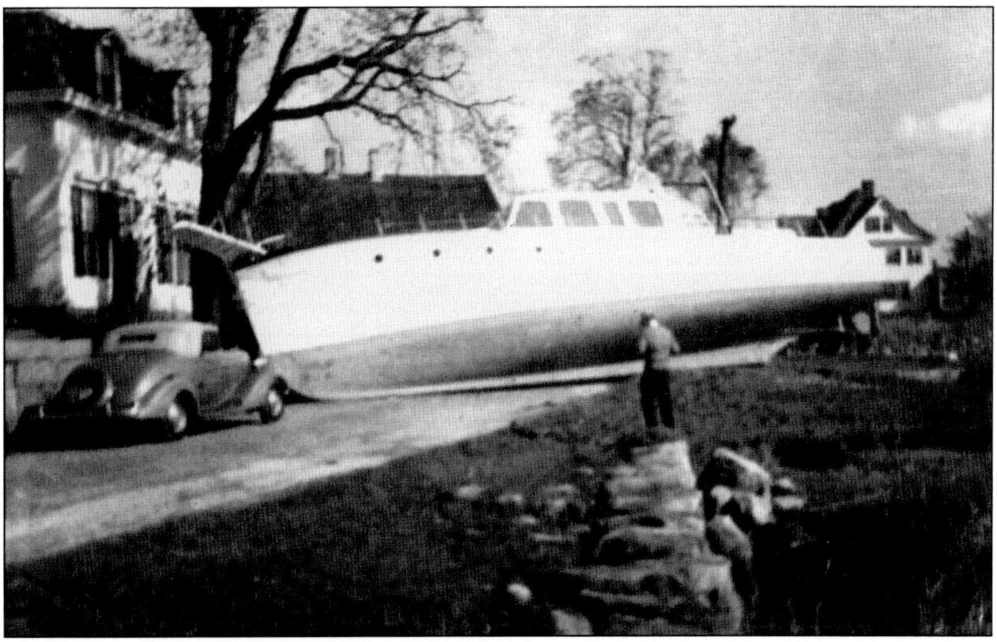

A boat from the Lathrop Engine Company floated across the Mystic River and came to rest on Gravel Street. (Mystic River Historical Society.)

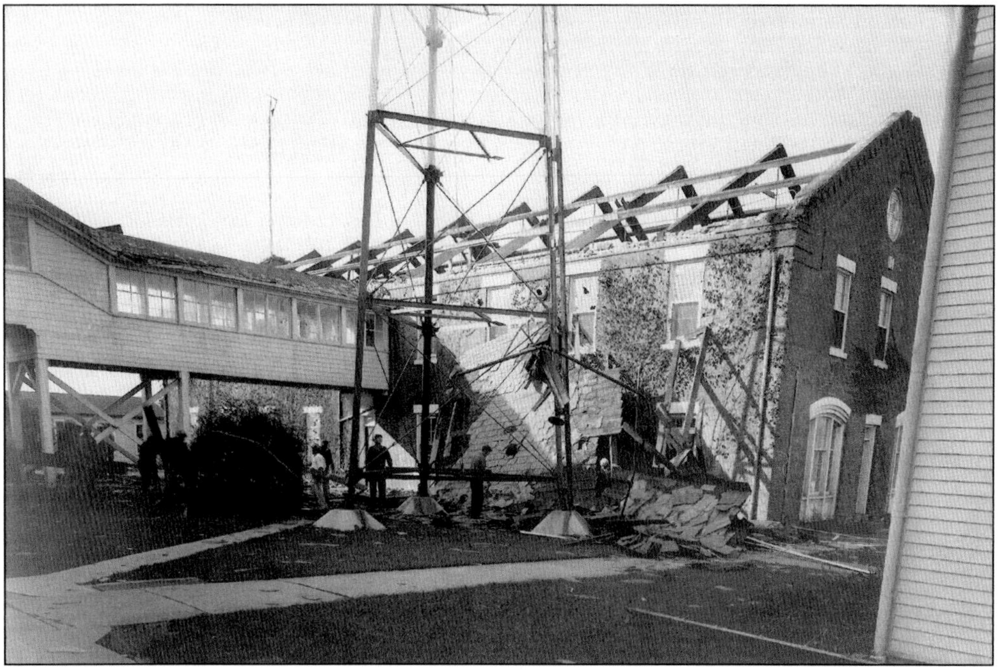

Upriver at the naval submarine base, the wind, which was clocked at 105 miles per hour in Groton before the wind gauge blew away, ripped the roof off Building One. (United States Navy.)

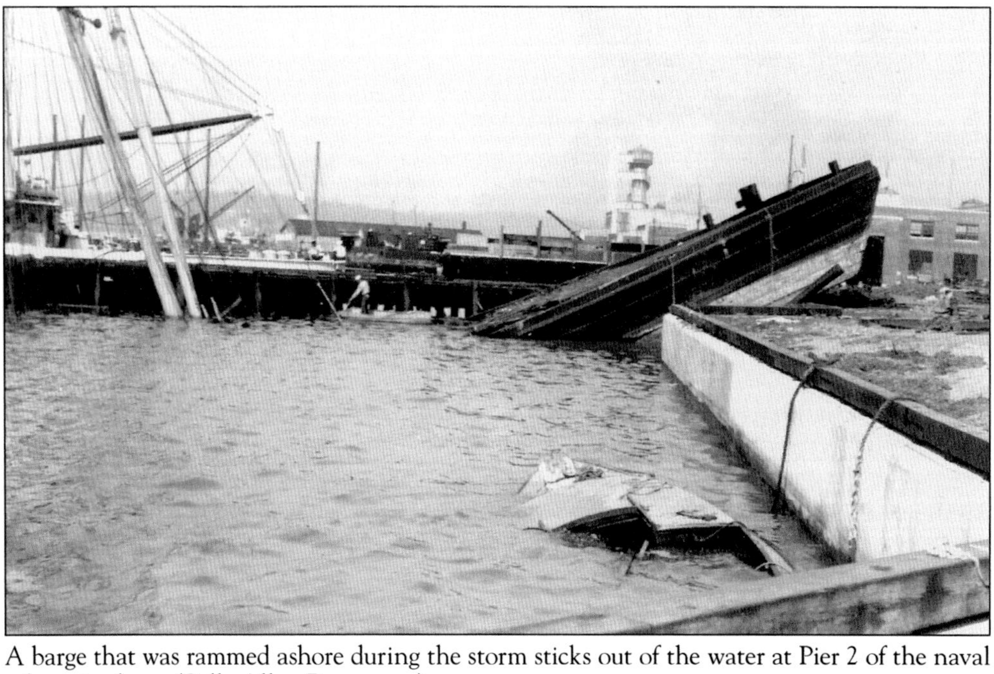

A barge that was rammed ashore during the storm sticks out of the water at Pier 2 of the naval submarine base. (Sally Allyn Brousseau.)

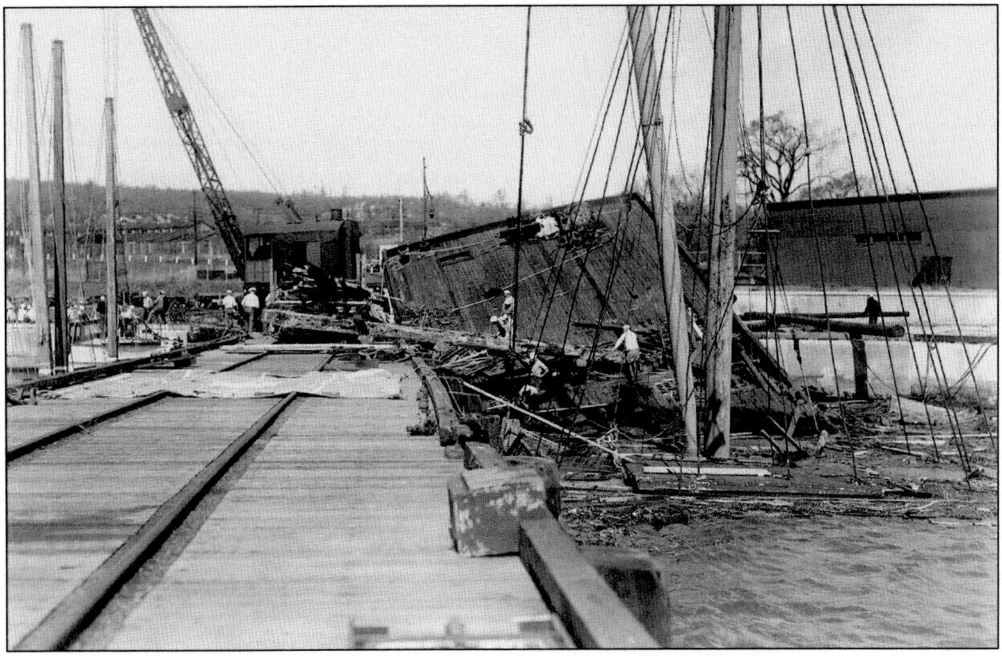

Sailors at the submarine base work to clear debris from the dock after the storm. (United States Navy.)

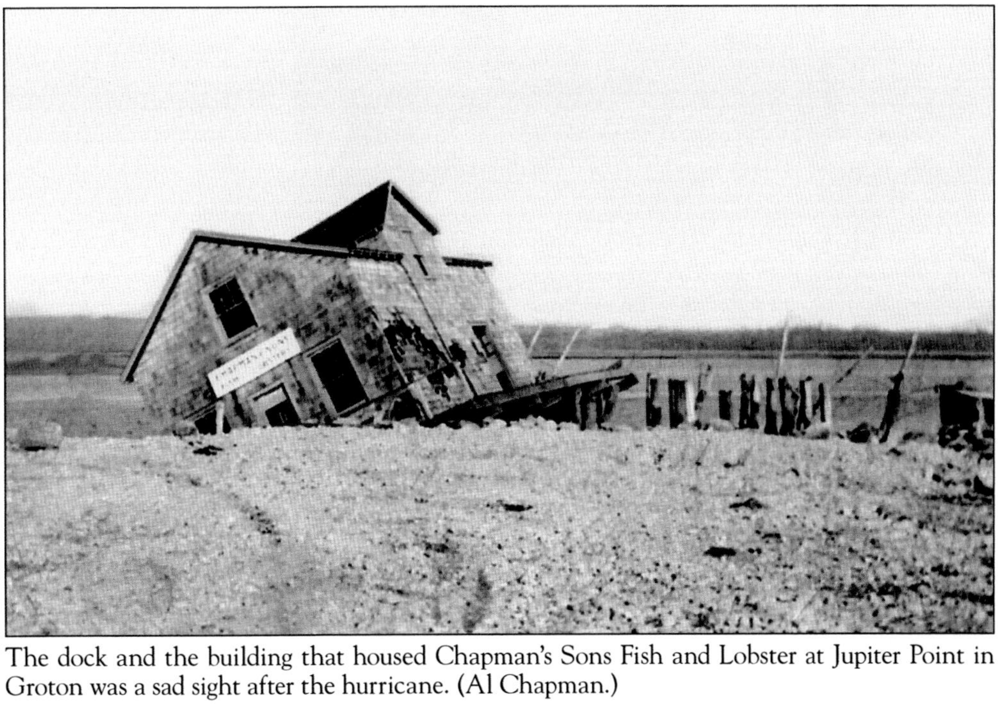

The dock and the building that housed Chapman's Sons Fish and Lobster at Jupiter Point in Groton was a sad sight after the hurricane. (Al Chapman.)

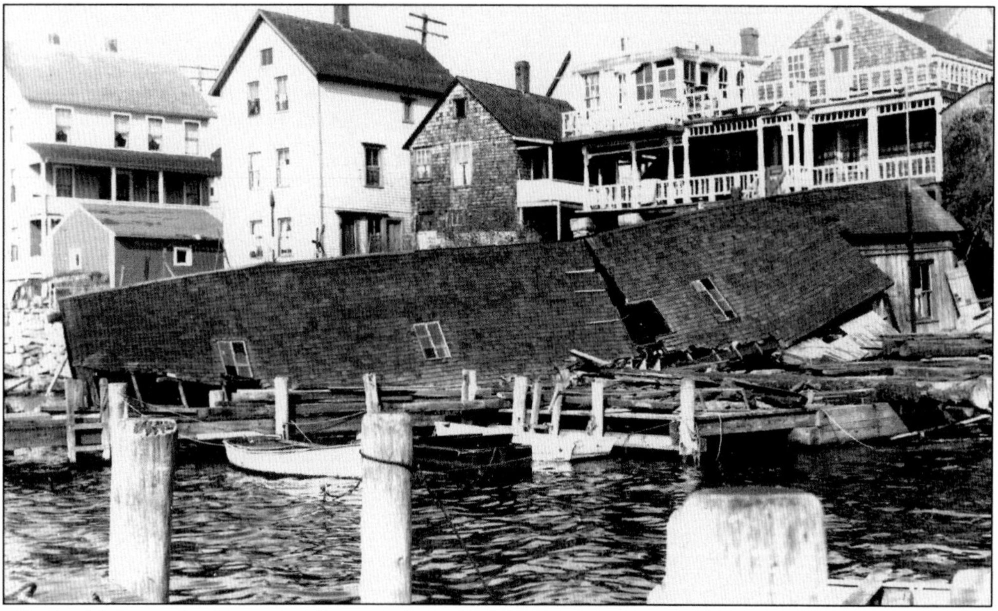

The building at the Ferguson Boatyard at 137 Thames Street was destroyed in the storm. The yard, run by Capt. Charles P. Ferguson, built many vessels. (Sally Allyn Brousseau.)

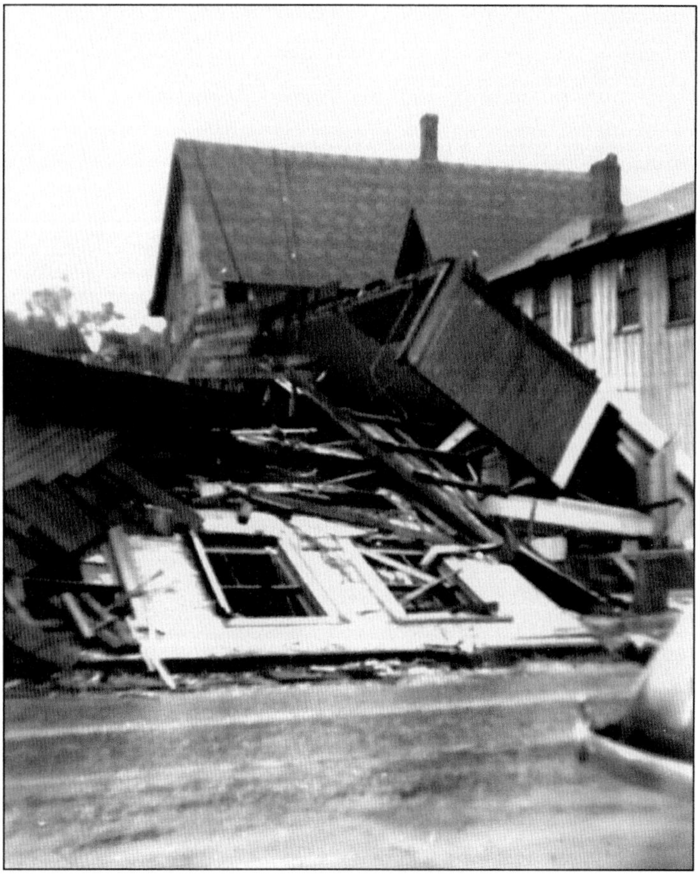

Andriola's Barber Shop on Thames Street was only rubble after the storm. (Tom Migliaccio.)

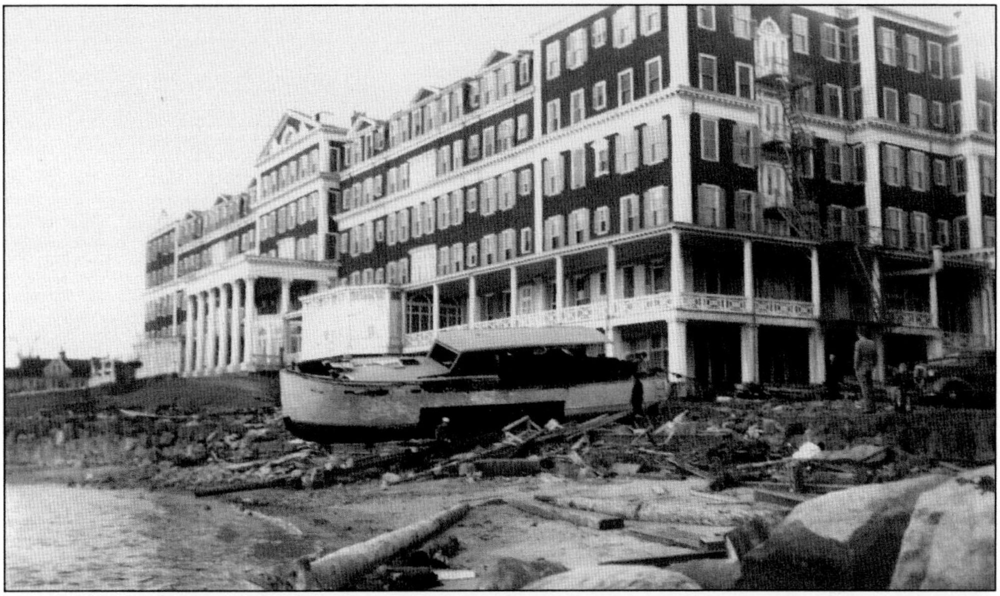

The grounds of the Griswold Hotel on the Thames River were covered in debris after the hurricane, and several boats had washed ashore. (Carol W. Kimball.)

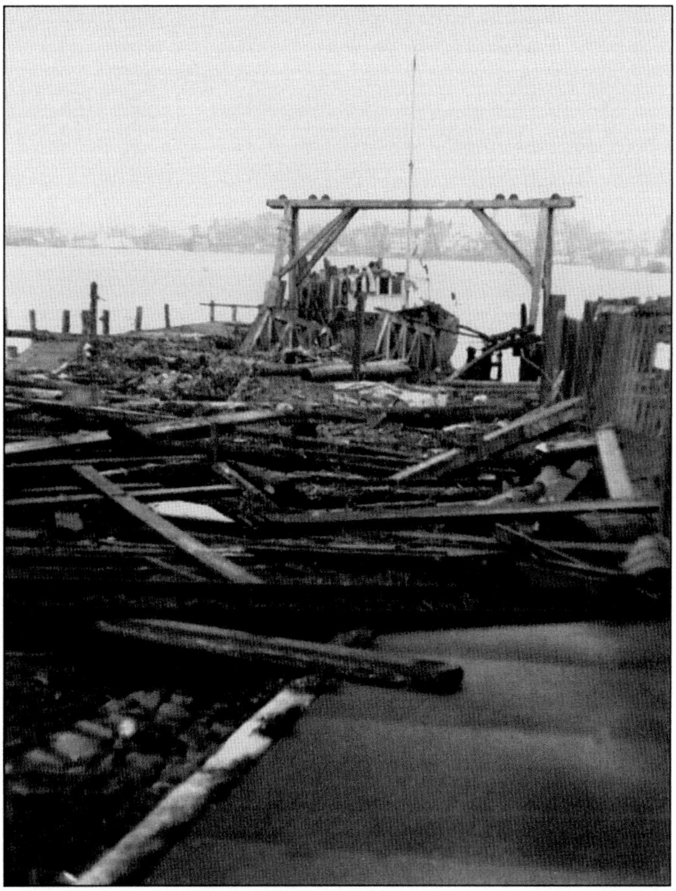

Nothing is left of the building near the ferry slip at the foot of Thames Street except a pile of debris. Passenger ferry service between Groton and New London had ceased in 1929. By then, most people traveled by car, and there was a motor vehicle bridge across the river. (Tom Migliaccio.)

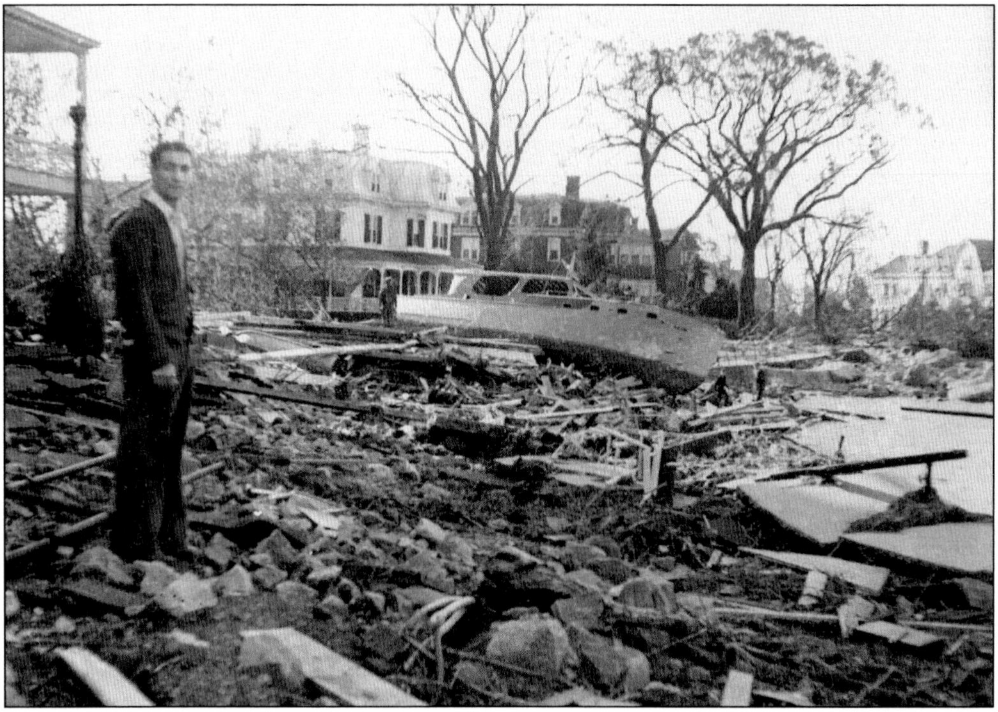

A man surveys the debris and a pleasure craft strewn along Shore Avenue after the hurricane. Fortunately the trees in the photograph are left standing, although they have been stripped of their leaves. (James L. Streeter.)

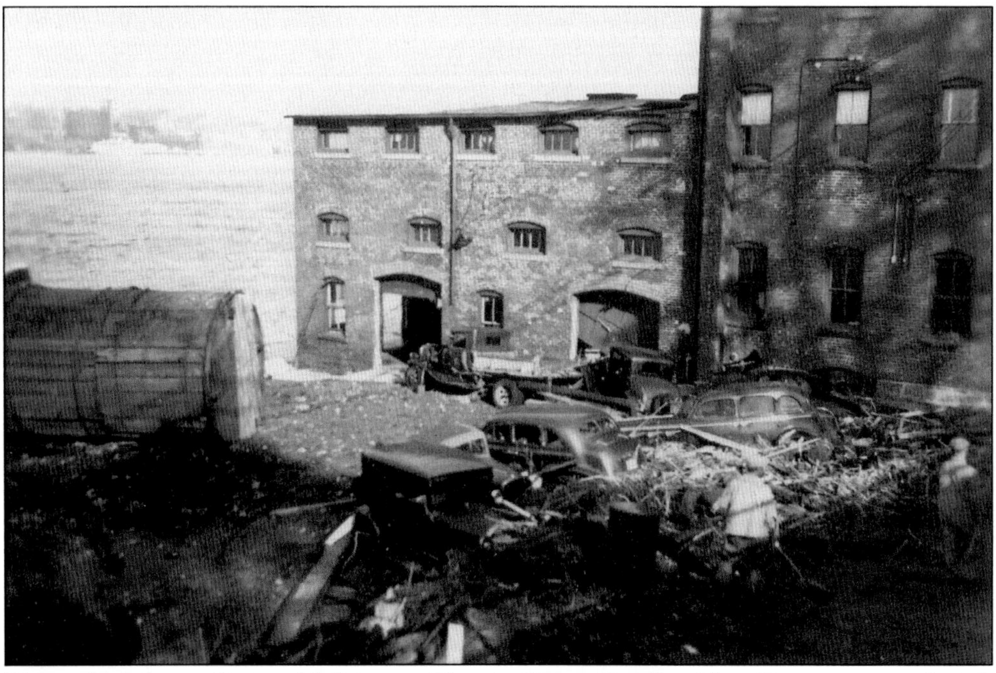

The parking lot at Groton Utilities on Thames Street is a shambles. Cars are covered with debris, and a water tower has tipped over. (James L. Streeter.)

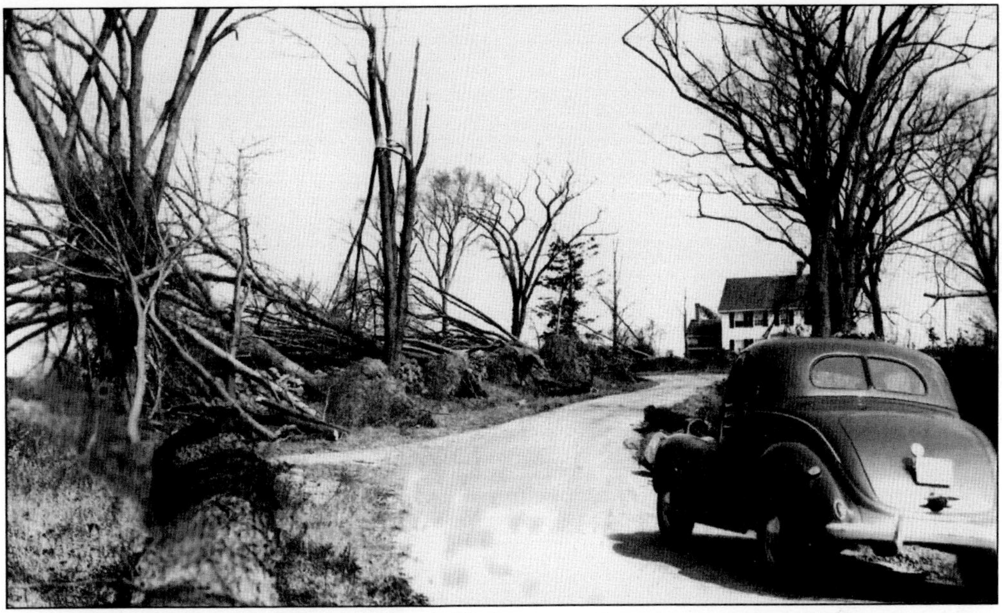

Trees near the Crouch house off King's Highway in Groton are uprooted from the storm. Connecticut lost 70 percent of its trees in the 1938 hurricane, because, when the storm hit, the ground was already saturated from four days of heavy rain. The strong winds easily blew even giant trees down. Throughout New England, 275 million trees were uprooted or broken off. Many were never replaced. (Sally Allyn Brousseau.)

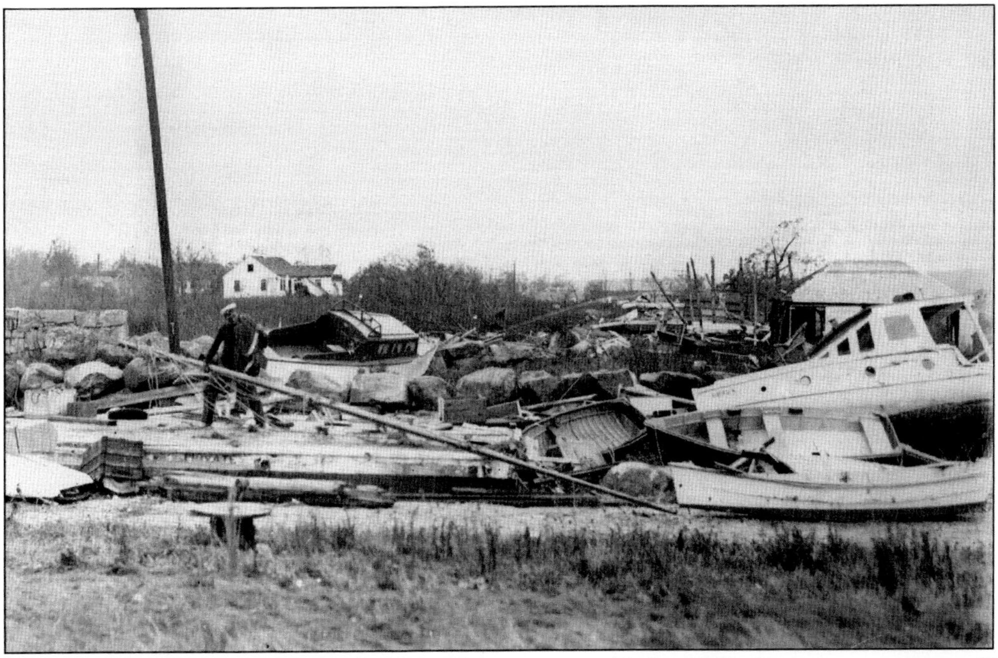

A man pulls the mast from a boat at Shennecossett Yacht Club. Boats were strewn all along the shoreline. More than 2,600 boats across New England were lost in the hurricane. (James L. Streeter.)

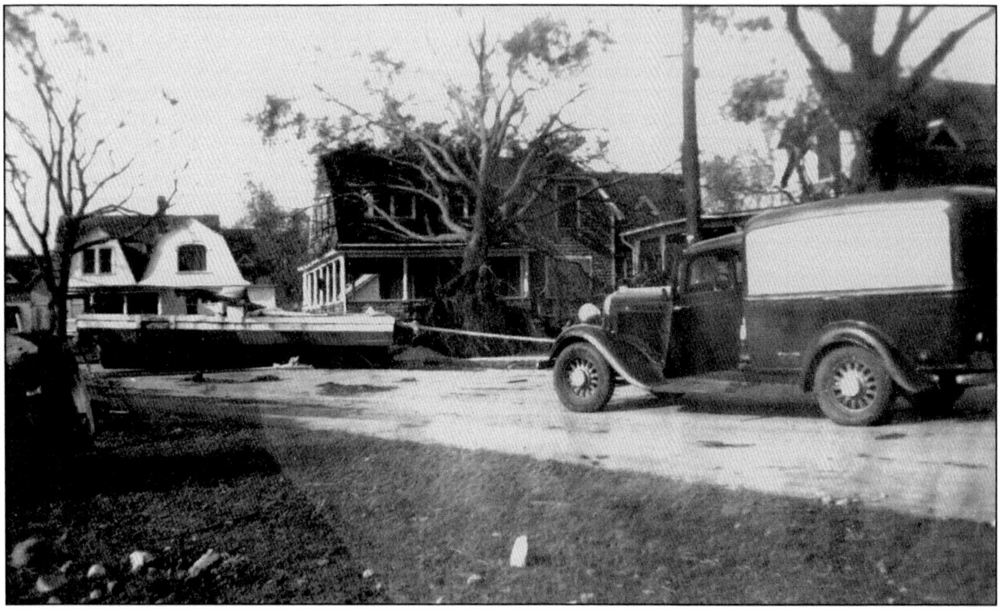

Debris fills the road on Shore Avenue in Groton, not allowing this van to pass. (Tom Migliaccio.)

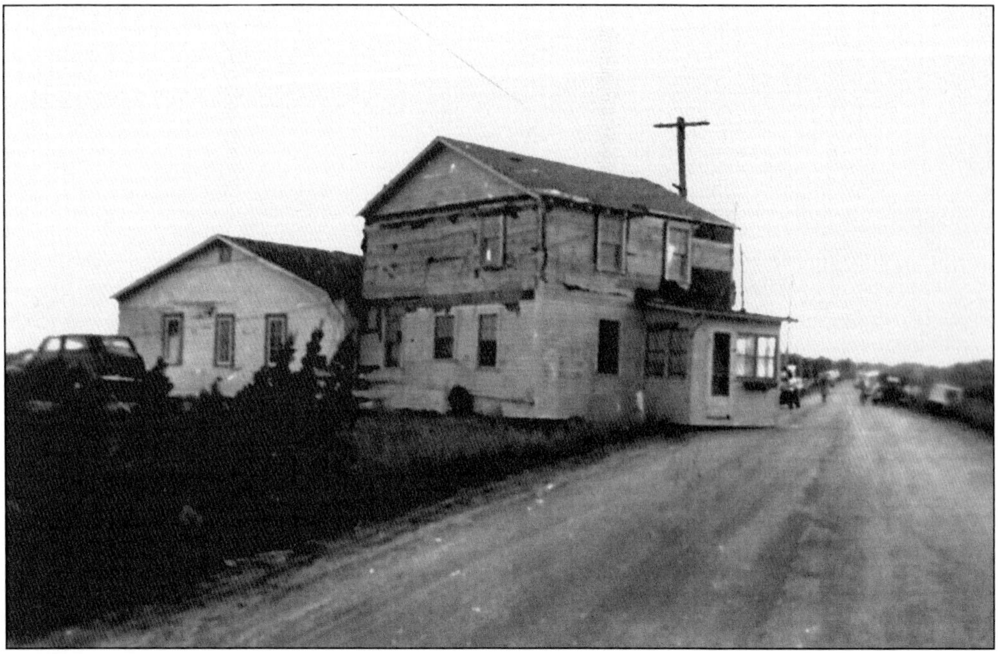

The fierce wind from the hurricane pushed this house on Groton Long Point Road off its foundation and into the road. (Tom Migliaccio.)

Six

VILLAGES

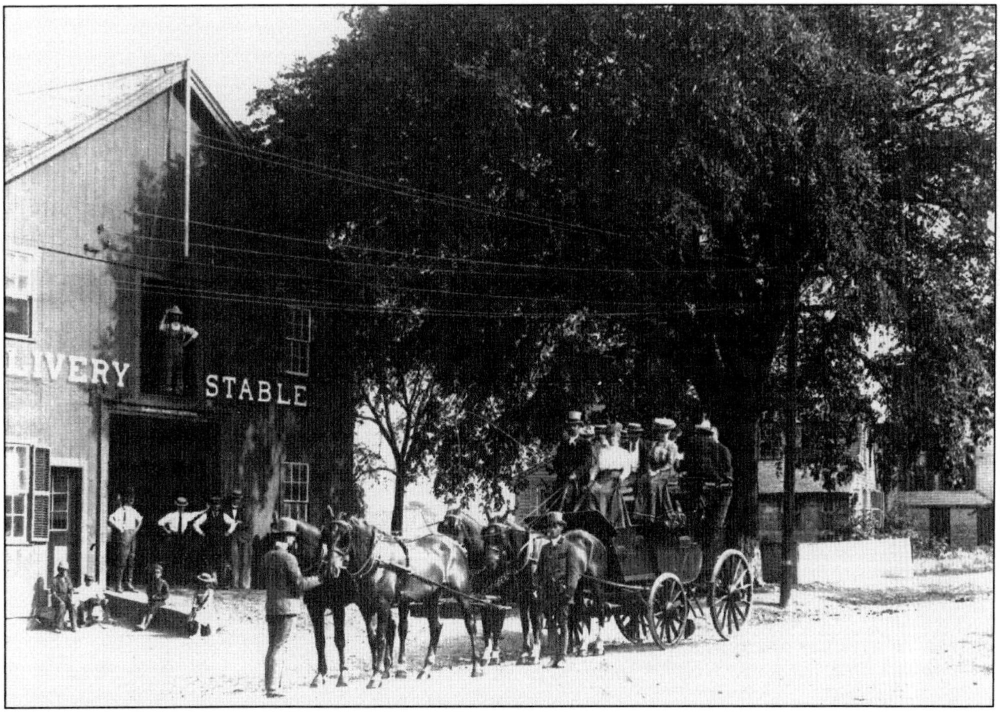

Roswell Brown's livery stable was at Bank Square in Mystic for more than 70 years. Brown founded the business on Water Street around 1850. His son James E. F. Brown joined him in 1883. The livery and boarding stable, shown here, with Charles P. Williams's coach waiting outside, had 24 stalls. It provided carriages to and from the railroad station. The property later was the site of Albertus B. Brown's automobile storage and Wally's Service Station. (James L. Streeter.)

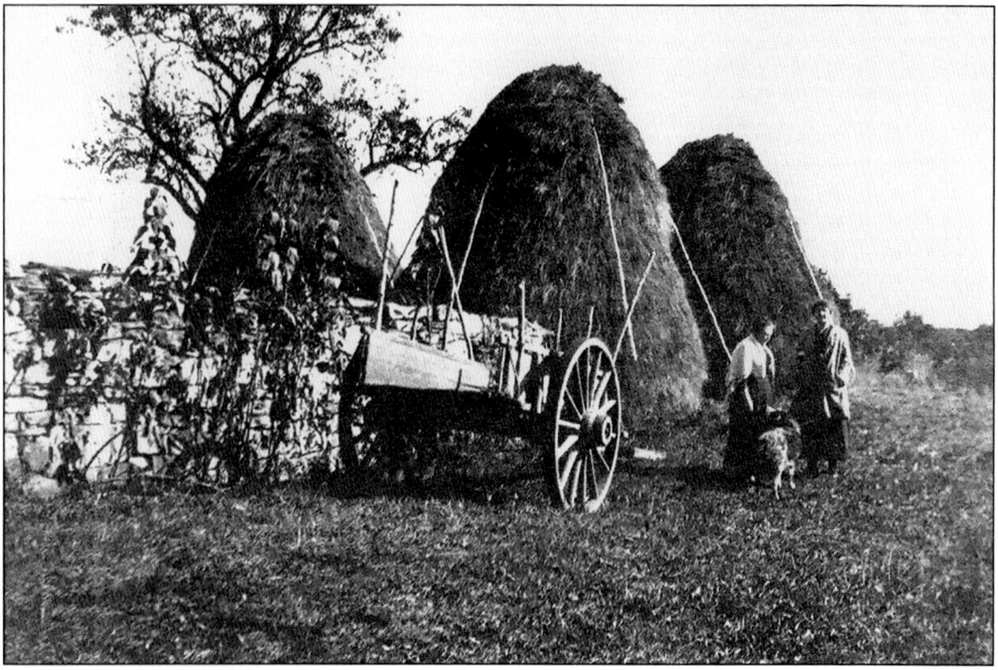

Haying was a part of the farming scene in Groton during the years when farms dominated the landscape. Here farmers create haystacks on the Daniel Brown farm in the Fishtown section of Mystic around 1900. The Bel-Aire housing development was built on the property in the 1960s. (Robert Bankel.)

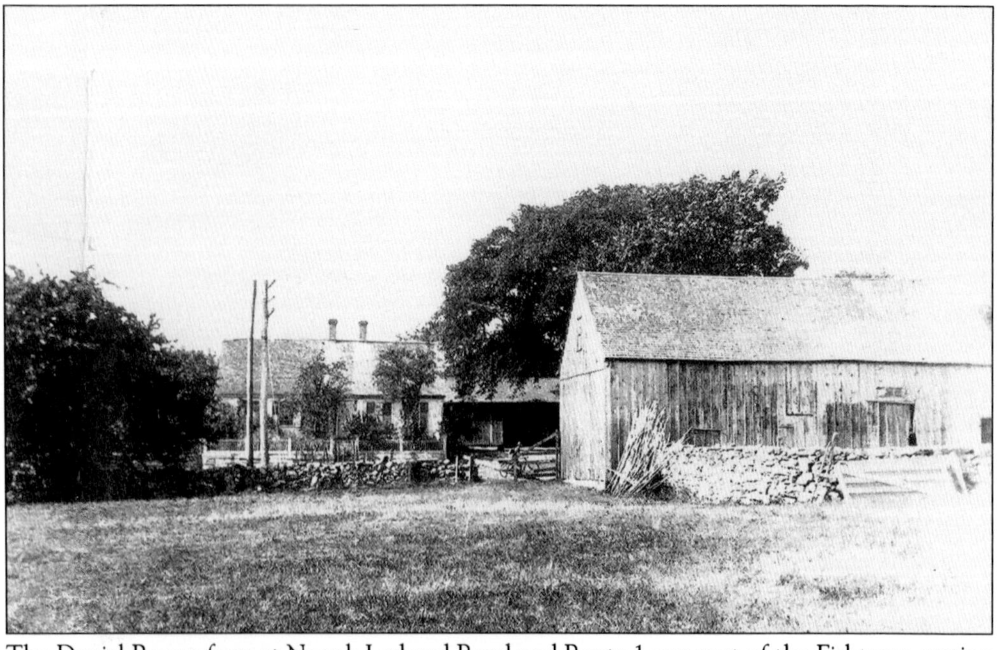

The Daniel Brown farm at Noank Ledyard Road and Route 1 was part of the Fishtown section of Mystic for years. The house was taken down in the early 1960s when the Bel-Aire housing development was built. Daniel Brown Drive in the Bel-Aire housing development is named for the farm that once stood there. (Robert Bankel.)

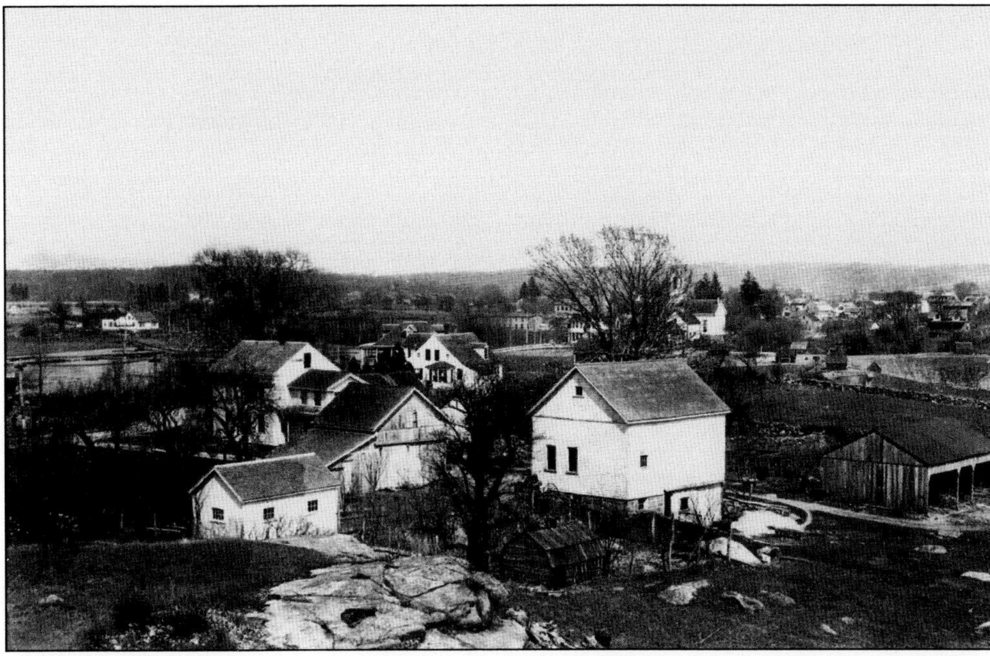

This view of Poquonnock Bridge is of the Chapman farm, which stood where the Groton Regency is today. Lyman Chapman owned the farm and raised trotting horses that raced at Poquonnock Driving Park. His son Glenn carried on the farm. Glenn also worked as superintendent of grounds and buildings at Connecticut College in New London. (LaRoue family.)

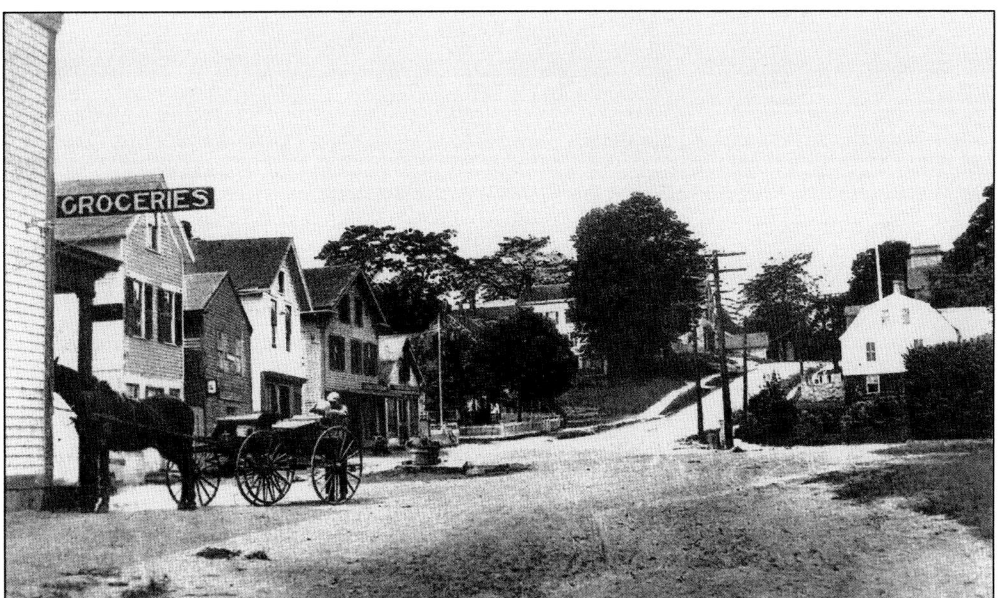

This early-20th-century photograph, taken from the foot of the hill near the Chester Latham Store, shows Main Street in Noank. (Janet Crossman.)

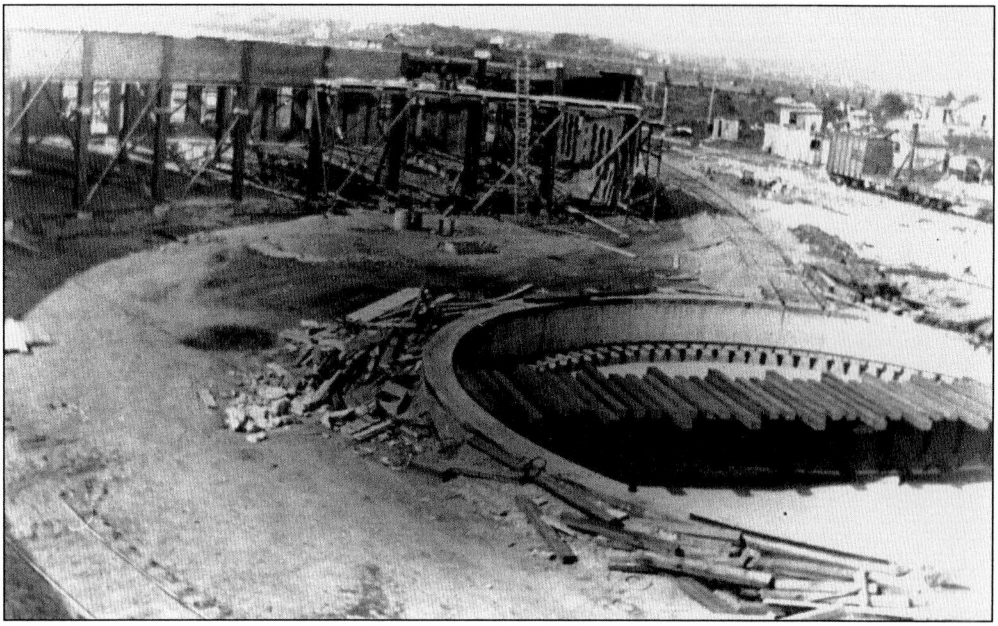

For the first three decades of the 20th century, the New York, New Haven and Hartford Railroad ran the Midway Yard off Depot Road in Poquonnock Bridge for its coal-burning trains traveling between Boston and New York to take on fuel. In this photograph, the roundhouse at the Midway Yard in Poquonnock Bridge is under construction. When it was completed, it could accommodate 20 locomotives. At its peak, Midway Yard employed nearly every man in Poquonnock Bridge. The yard closed in the late 1920s, when changes in transportation and economic condition rendered it obsolete. (Robert Bankel.)

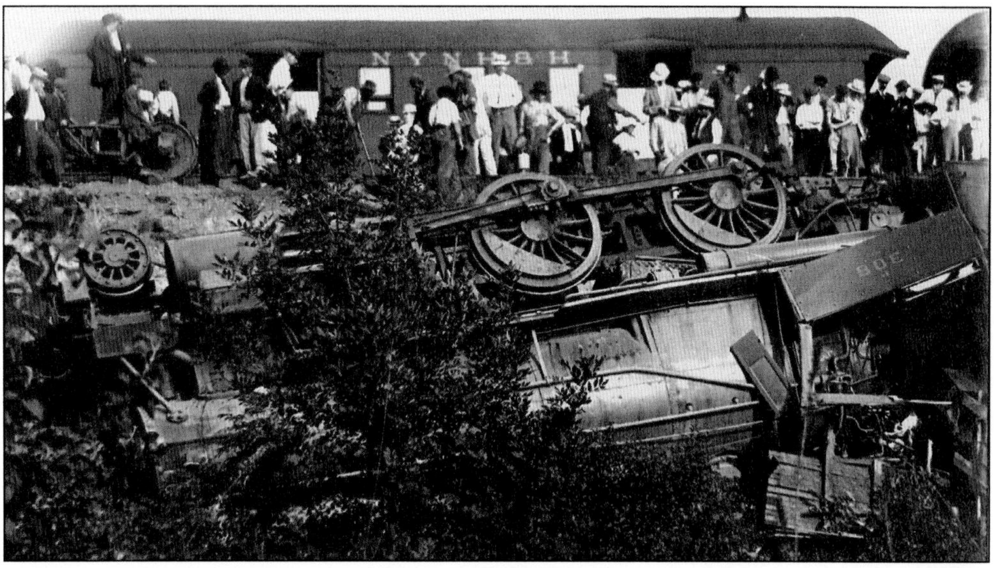

The most spectacular train wreck in Poquonnock Bridge history occurred at 8:00 a.m. on Sunday, December 21, 1924. The Boston-bound Pittsburgh Express crashed into a 72-car, westbound freight train. The locomotive derailed, eight boxcars were destroyed, and 200 passengers were thrown from their seats or bunks. Only eight people were slightly injured. Debris was strewn all over the tracks, including gravestones and many Pullman blankets. (Johnson family.)

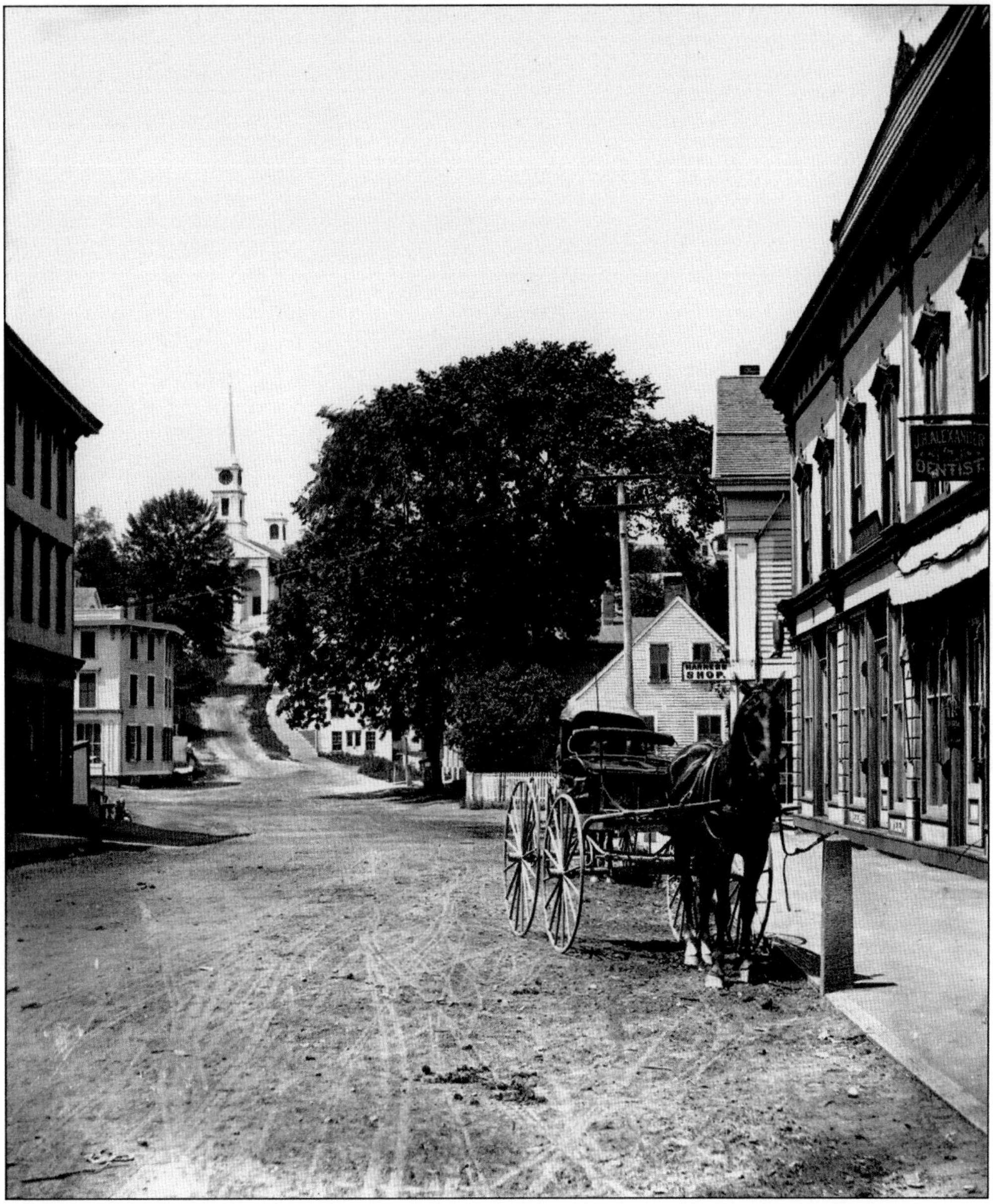

West Main Street in Mystic is tranquil in this early-20th-century photograph. Today Route 1 runs up Baptist Hill past the Union Baptist Church, and summer days often find traffic backed up the hill past the church, waiting as Mystic's famous bascule bridge opens to let boat traffic pass up and down the Mystic River. (Carol W. Kimball.)

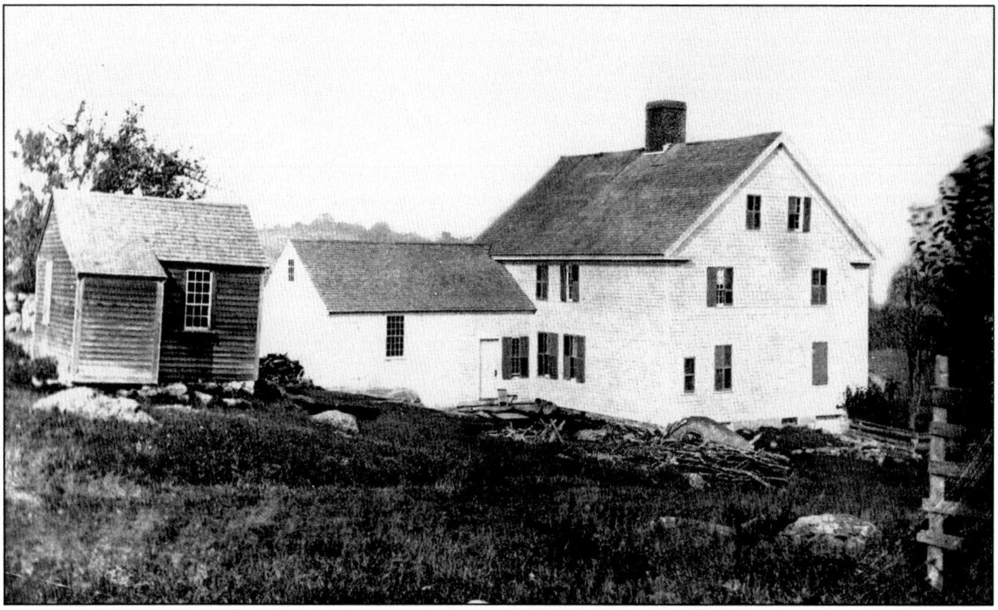

The Fish farm on High Street has been in the Fish family since John Fish came to Mystic in 1655. The Fishes were among the region's founding families, and a descendant still lives in the house today. This photograph was taken around 1900, before Martha Edgecomb Fish had the front porch built on the house. (Fish family.)

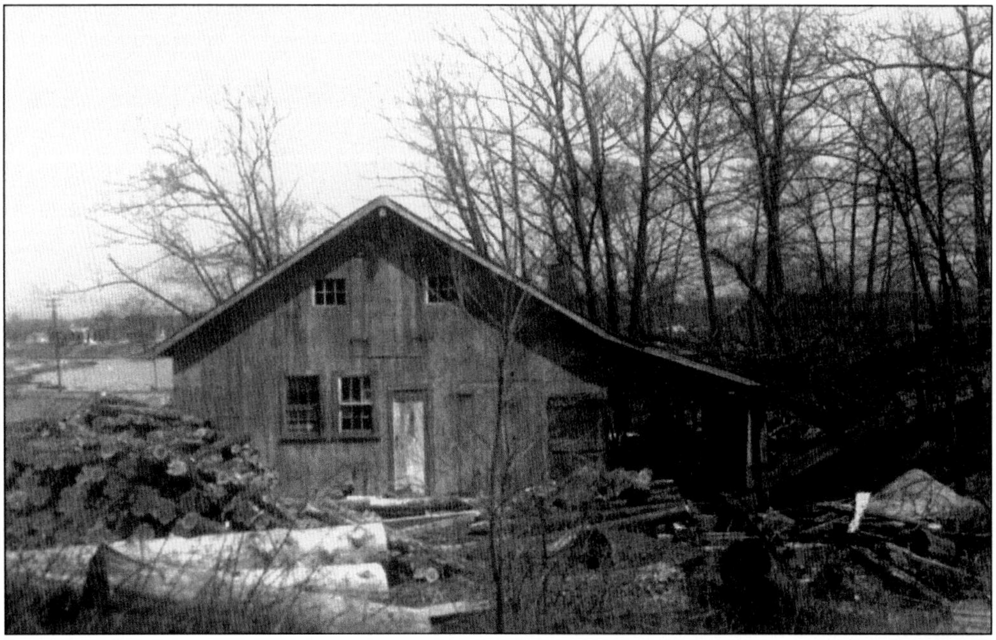

From 1750 to the mid-1930s, there was a mill on Bindloss Brook in Mystic. The first owner, Joseph Parks, ran a gristmill at the site on Bindloss Road. Later William Bindloss bought the property and was known for the cornmeal he produced for making Rhode Island johnnie cakes. About 1914, the mill was converted to a sawmill, but by 1935, it was no longer operational. The building was destroyed in the 1938 hurricane, but its foundation is still visible just below the dam that forms Bindloss Pond. (Paul Ingle.)

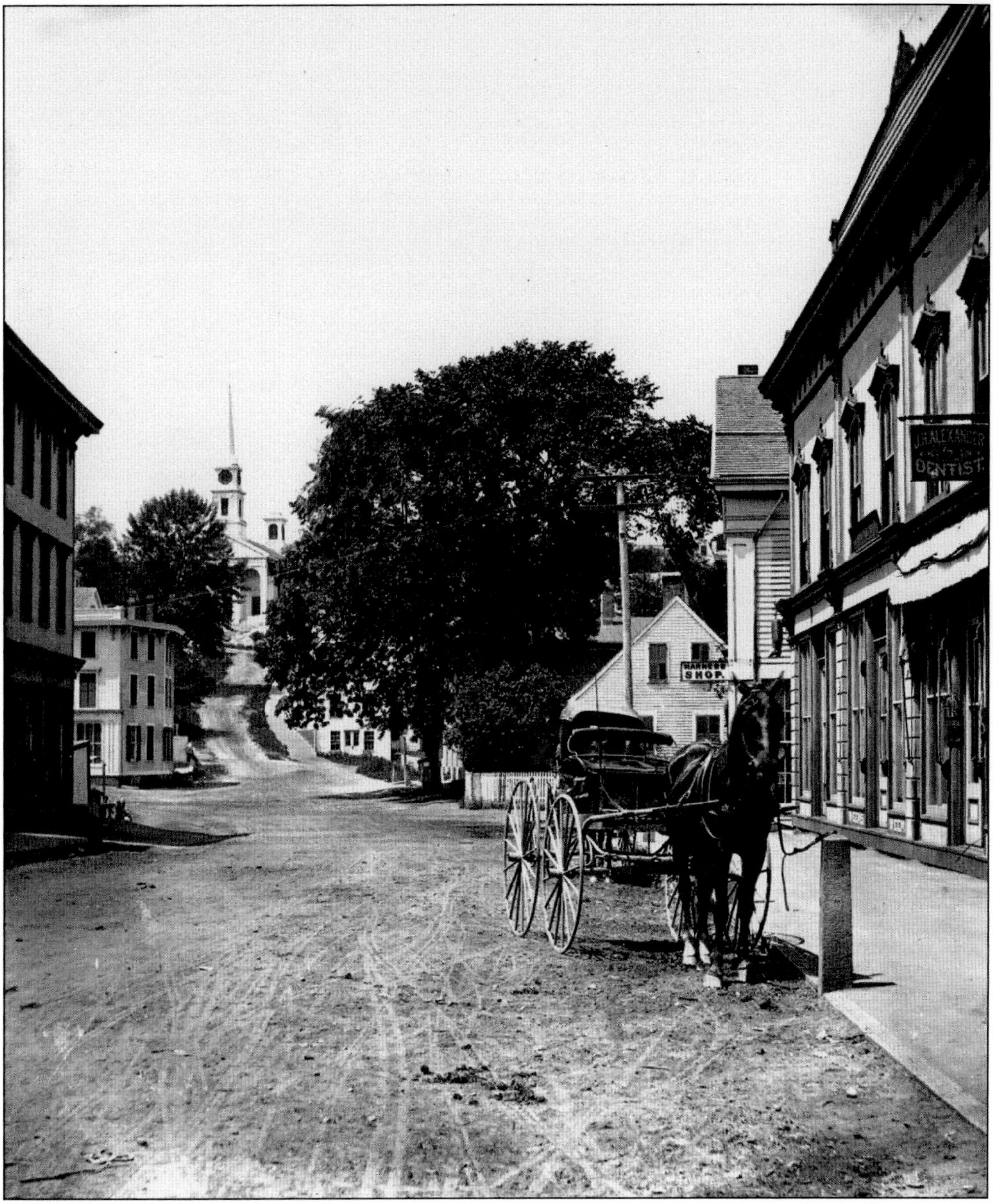

West Main Street in Mystic is tranquil in this early-20th-century photograph. Today Route 1 runs up Baptist Hill past the Union Baptist Church, and summer days often find traffic backed up the hill past the church, waiting as Mystic's famous bascule bridge opens to let boat traffic pass up and down the Mystic River. (Carol W. Kimball.)

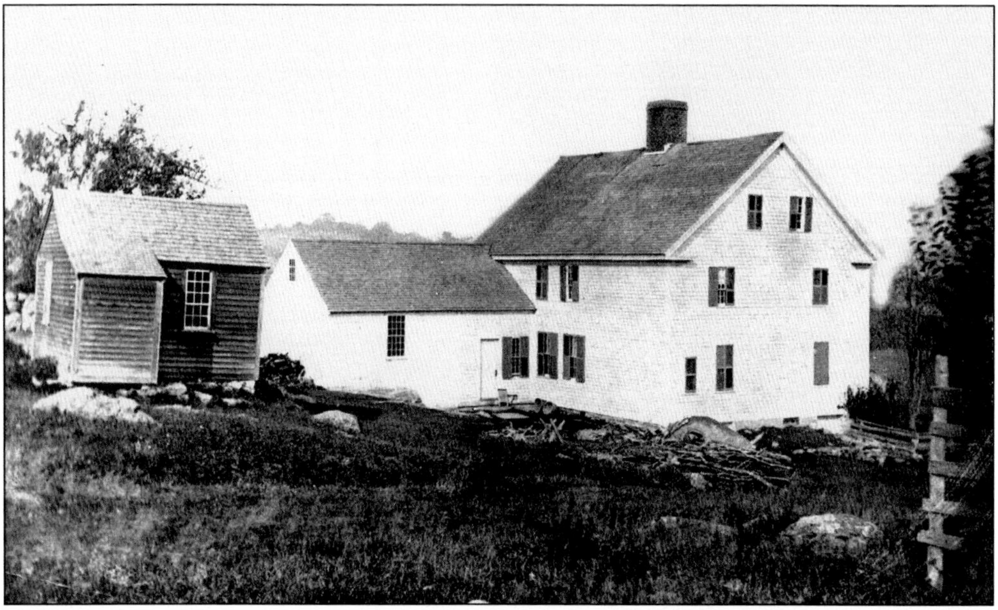

The Fish farm on High Street has been in the Fish family since John Fish came to Mystic in 1655. The Fishes were among the region's founding families, and a descendant still lives in the house today. This photograph was taken around 1900, before Martha Edgecomb Fish had the front porch built on the house. (Fish family.)

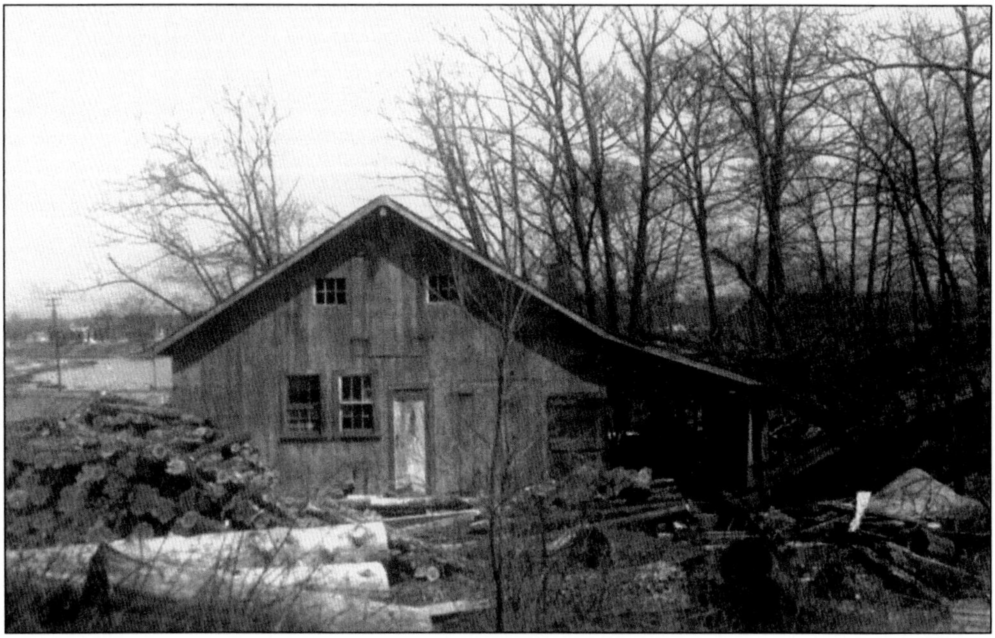

From 1750 to the mid-1930s, there was a mill on Bindloss Brook in Mystic. The first owner, Joseph Parks, ran a gristmill at the site on Bindloss Road. Later William Bindloss bought the property and was known for the cornmeal he produced for making Rhode Island johnnie cakes. About 1914, the mill was converted to a sawmill, but by 1935, it was no longer operational. The building was destroyed in the 1938 hurricane, but its foundation is still visible just below the dam that forms Bindloss Pond. (Paul Ingle.)

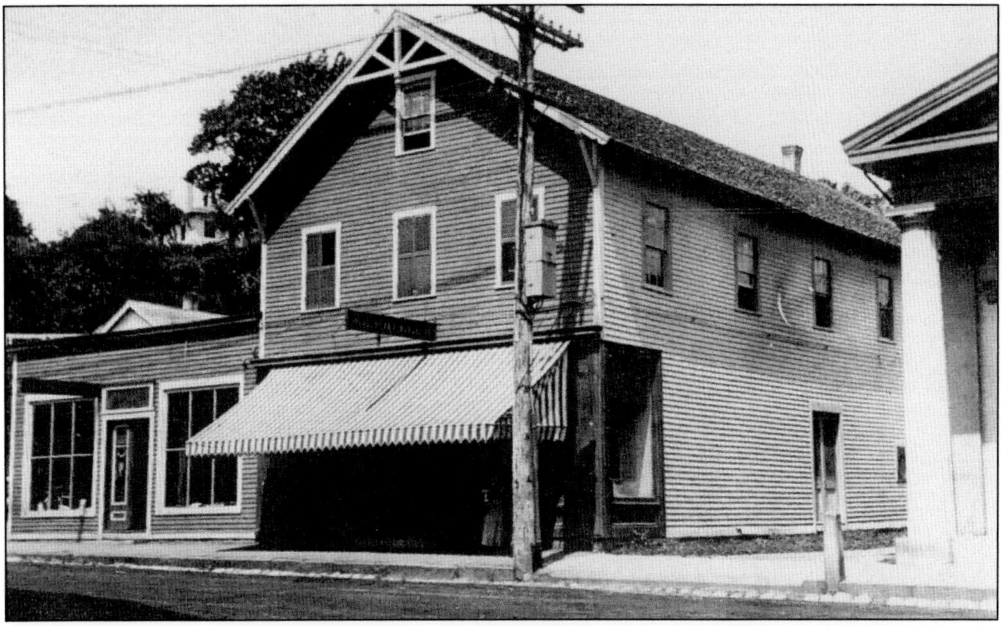

The building that today houses Mystic Pizza, made famous in the 1988 Julia Roberts movie, has been a part of downtown Mystic for years. In 1868, William E. Wheeler ran a grocery store, William E. Wheeler and Son, with his son William Jr. The senior Wheeler retired in 1876, and in 1885, the son built his own store, at West Main and Bank Streets, selling groceries, hardware, and dry goods. Over the years, the building has been home to a variety of businesses, including a Laundromat. (Robert Bankel.)

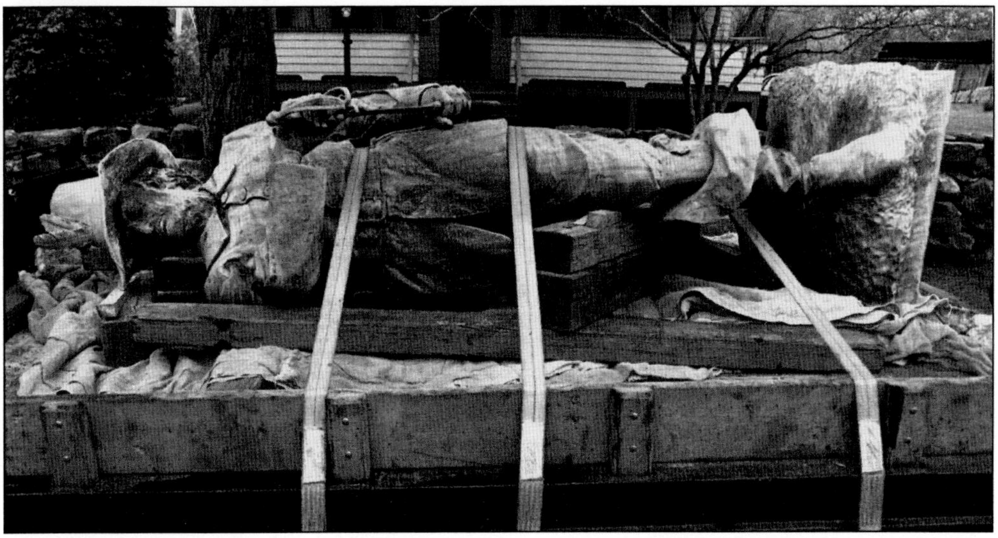

For 106 years, a statue of Capt. John Mason stood at the top of Pequot Hill in Mystic. The state erected the Cromwellian figure in 1889, near the site where Mason led the 1637 Pequot massacre, a dawn raid that killed hundreds of Pequot. The Mashantucket Pequot tribe objected to the statue being on sacred ground, and the state removed it in May 1995. In this photograph, the statue sits on a flatbed truck on Pequot Avenue waiting to be hauled away. It was refurbished and, in June 1996, was erected on the Palisado Green in Windsor, where Mason was a founding father. (Westerly Sun.)

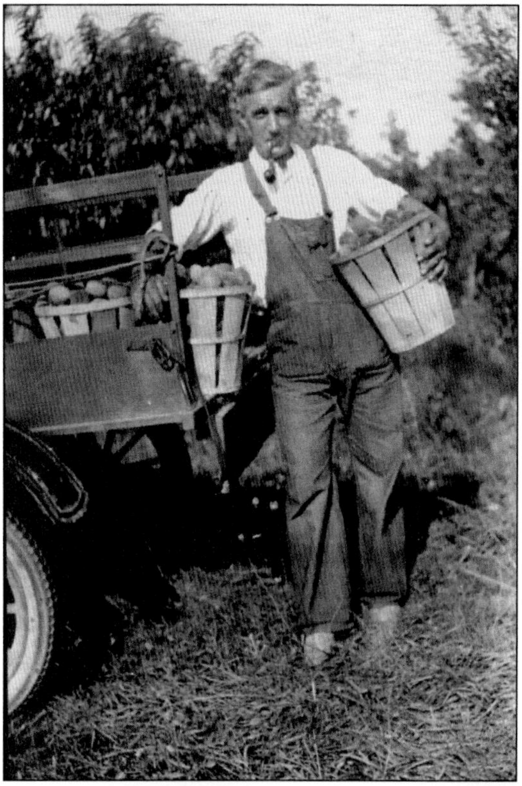

Center Groton, once the geographical center of Groton when Ledyard was part of the town, developed into a choice area for farming. John Ross Haley, who lived in the former Smith-Haley Tavern at Routes 184 and 117, was well known in the 1920s and 1930s for his extensive apple orchards. He is shown here with part of his harvest. (Henry Haley.)

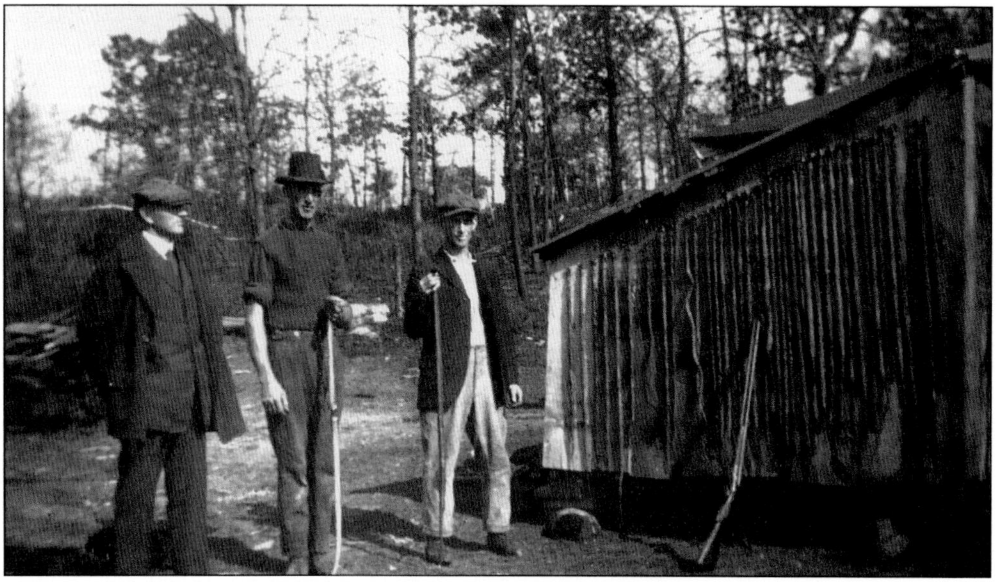

Center Groton was once famous for its snakes. Copperheads and rattlesnakes lived in the rocky ledges of Candlewood Hill and were so plentiful that the town once offered bounties for killing them. One section was known as Rattlesnake Ledge, where in 1896, a rattler, measuring four feet six inches long with 10 rattles, was shot. In this photograph, John Ross Haley, center, and two of his neighbors show off their catch while other trophies are nailed to the side of the outbuilding. (Henry Haley.)

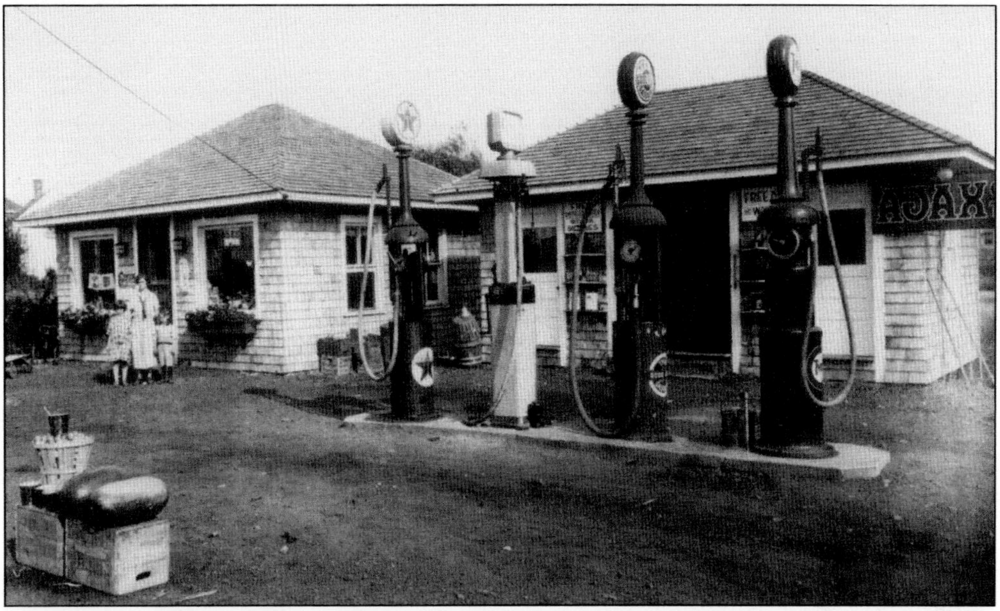

Lu Johnson and her children, William A. Johnson and Gert Johnson, stand in front of the Kum-See-Me filling station and lunch shop, at the corner of Fort Hill and North Roads in the 1920s. The business expanded to include groceries and ice cream. When son William bought the store in the 1950s, he added a meat department and hardware section. Today Johnson's Hardware and Home Center survives as one of Groton's last family owned and operated businesses. (Johnson family.)

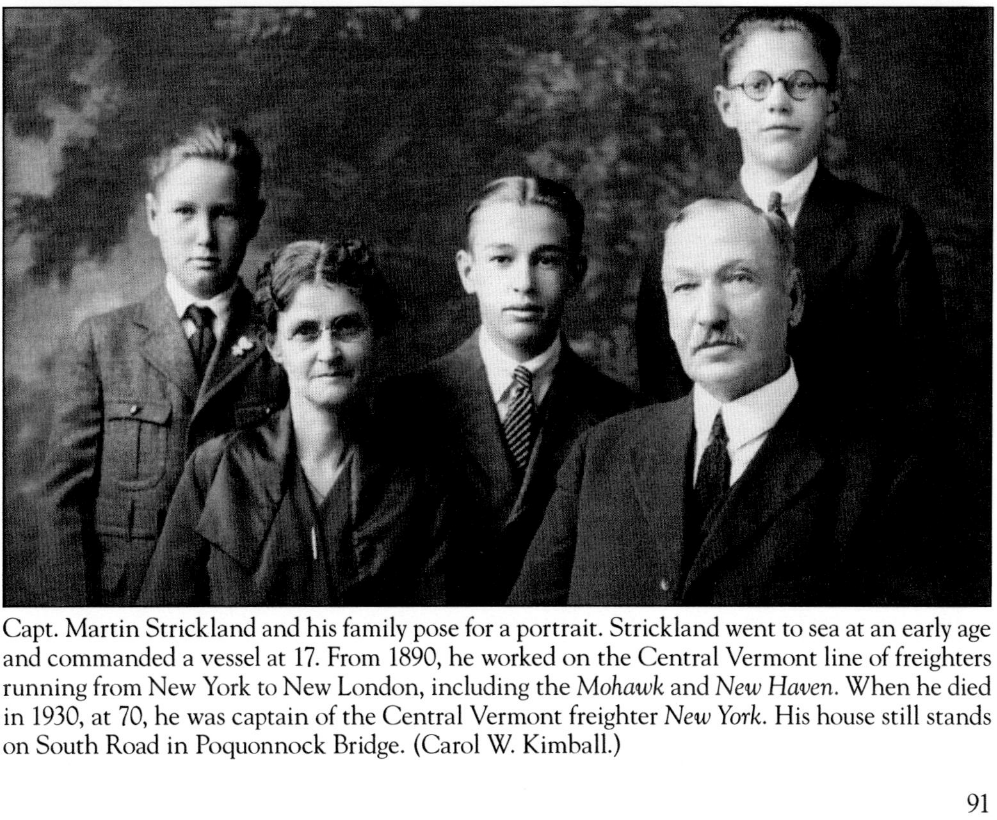

Capt. Martin Strickland and his family pose for a portrait. Strickland went to sea at an early age and commanded a vessel at 17. From 1890, he worked on the Central Vermont line of freighters running from New York to New London, including the *Mohawk* and *New Haven*. When he died in 1930, at 70, he was captain of the Central Vermont freighter *New York*. His house still stands on South Road in Poquonnock Bridge. (Carol W. Kimball.)

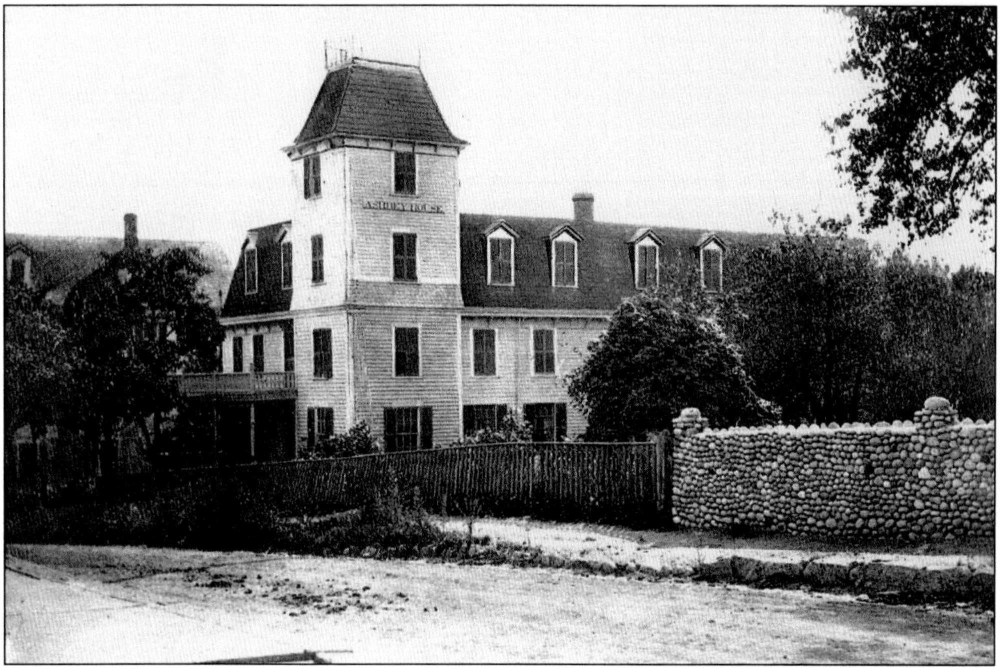

The Ashbey House in Noank was one of the popular summer hotels in the village. It could accommodate 40 to 50 guests. In an 1890 advertisement, proprietor L. D. Ashbey listed the rates for the hotel at $1.25 per day, $8 per week. He touted the facility as a place "where city guests could enjoy sea breezes and fresh seafood as well as famous clam chowder." (James L. Streeter.)

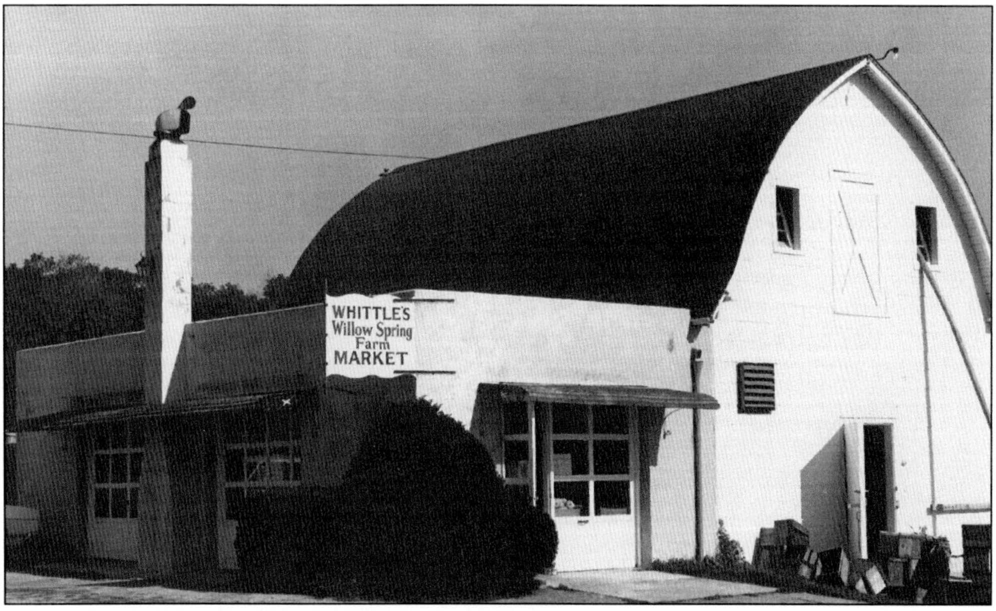

Willow Spring Farm Market on Noank Ledyard Road in Mystic is a popular place to buy fresh vegetables. Robert Whittle bought the farm in 1907 after seeing it advertised in the *New York Times*. Whittle had just finished work digging on the Panama Canal and wanted to invest his money in a farm. His descendants still own and run the business, one of the few working farms still in town. (Whittle family.)

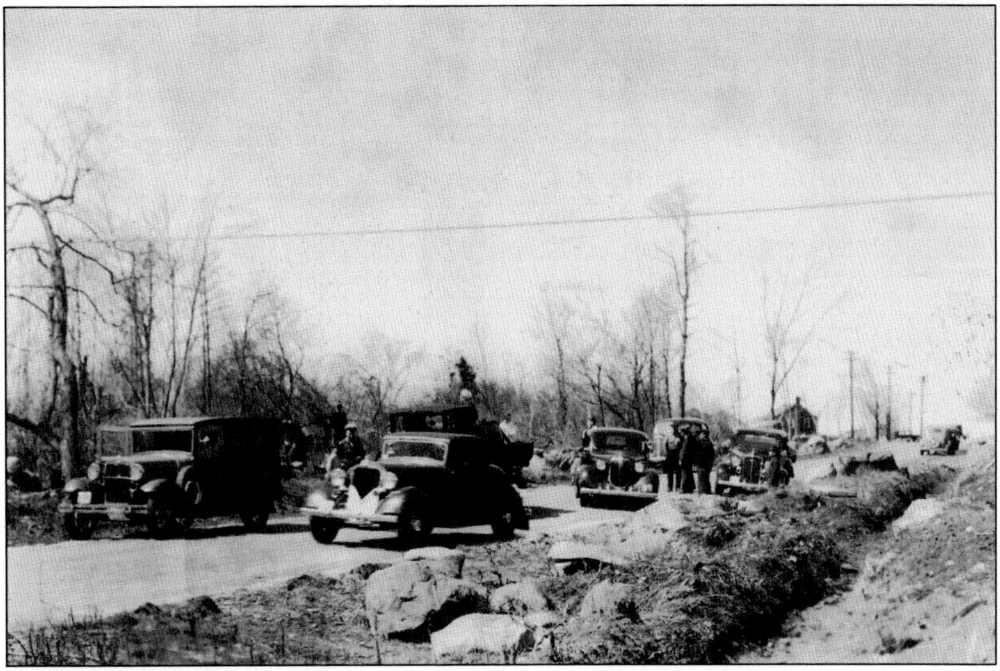

Several vehicles respond to a forest fire in the Pleasant Valley section of town. Forests are fewer in Pleasant Valley today, which is home to the naval submarine base and several areas of navy housing. (Sally Allyn Brousseau.)

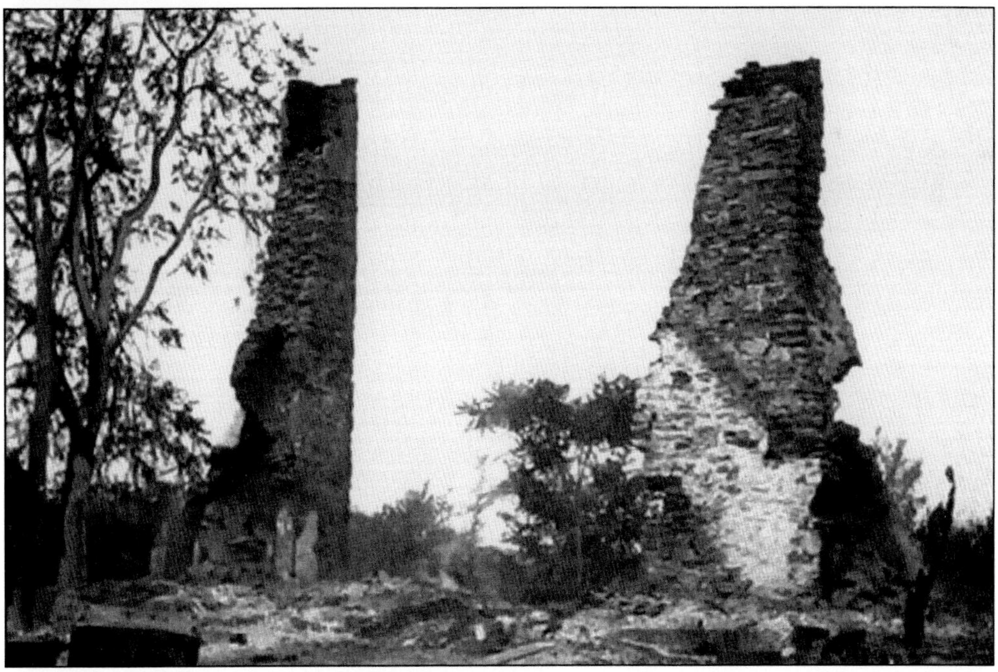

All that remained of the Avery homestead were its two chimneys after a spark from a passing locomotive set fire to the 200-year-old Groton landmark on Poquonnock Road in 1894. Generations of Averys had lived in the house, known as the Hive of the Averys. The Avery Memorial Association erected a memorial on the site in 1900. (James L. Streeter.)

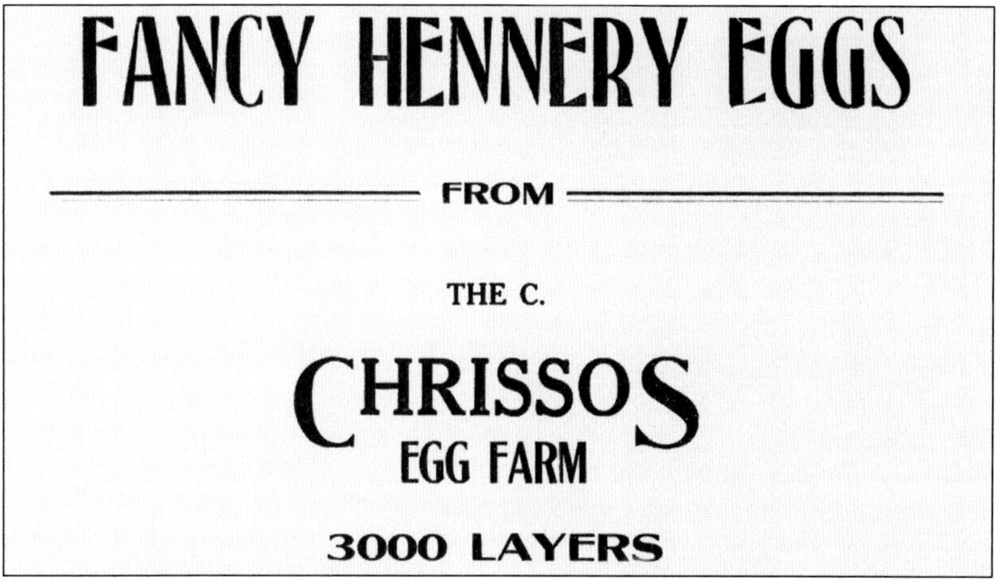

The Chrissos Poultry Farm spread across 50 acres on Grove Avenue in Pleasant Valley. Founded in 1919 by Christopher Chrissos, a former assistant manager on Morton F. Plant's farm at Avery Point, the farm was in business from the 1920s to the 1950s and, at one point, was one of the largest egg farms in New England. (Dorothy Chrissos.)

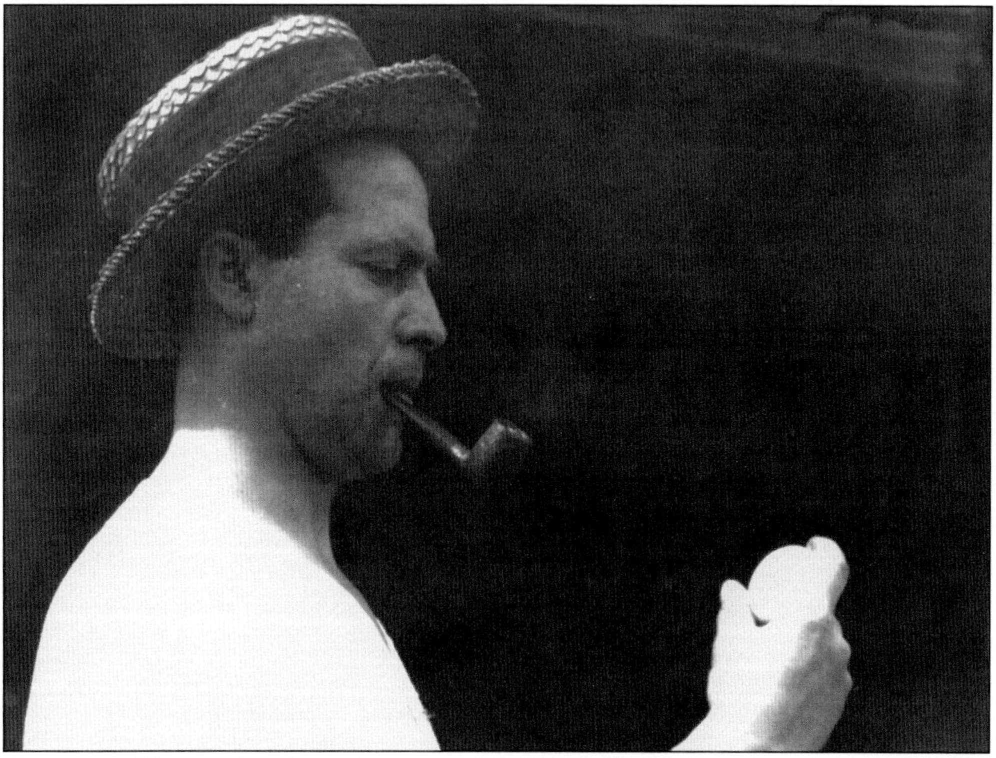

Christopher Chrissos, founder and owner of the Chrissos Poultry Farm, inspects an egg. At its peak, the farm had five full-time workers and was considered one of the most modern poultry facilities in the country. (Dorothy Chrissos.)

Seven

Borough of Groton

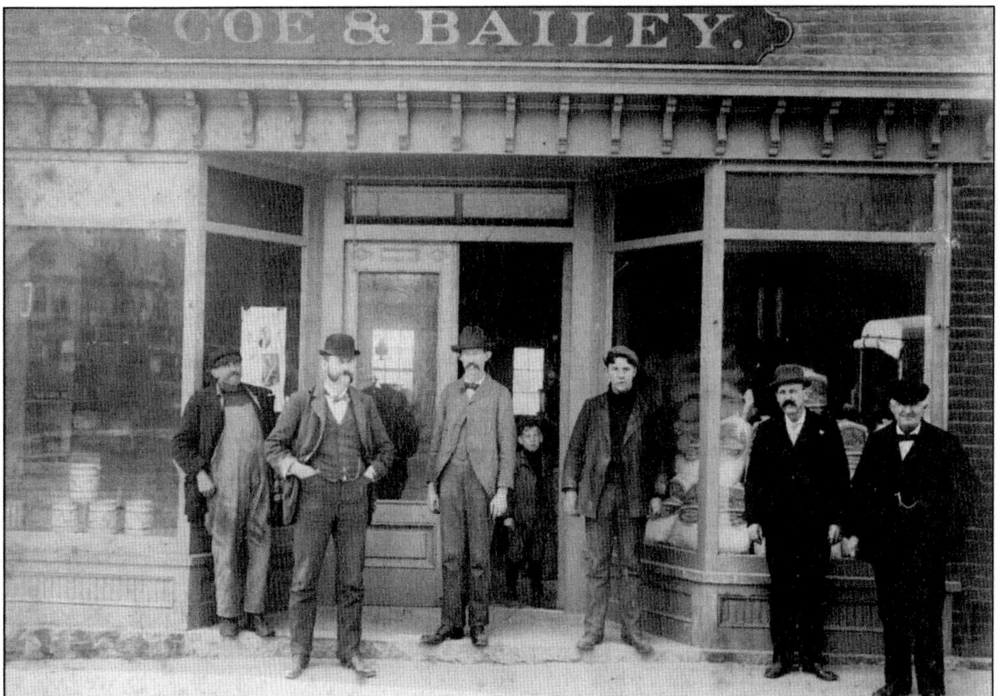

Coe and Bailey General Store was at 241 Thames Street. Henry L. Bailey, who also served as Groton town clerk from 1907 to 1941, is pictured second from the left, and Ernest Coe is second from the right. (Ed Stebbins.)

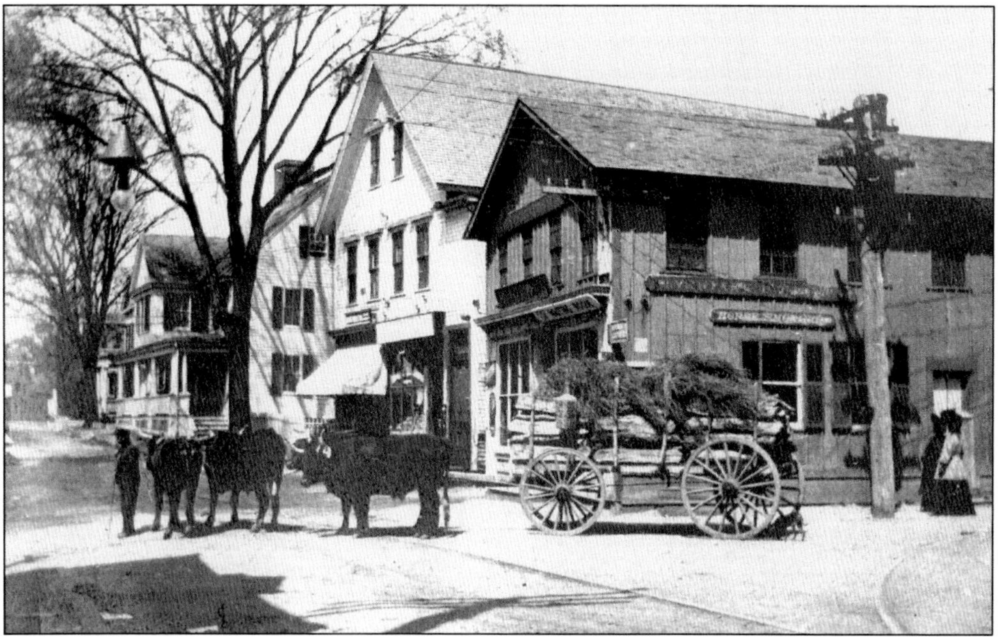

A wagon and oxen stand at Thames and School Streets in front of the streetcar waiting room. (Winifred Newbury.)

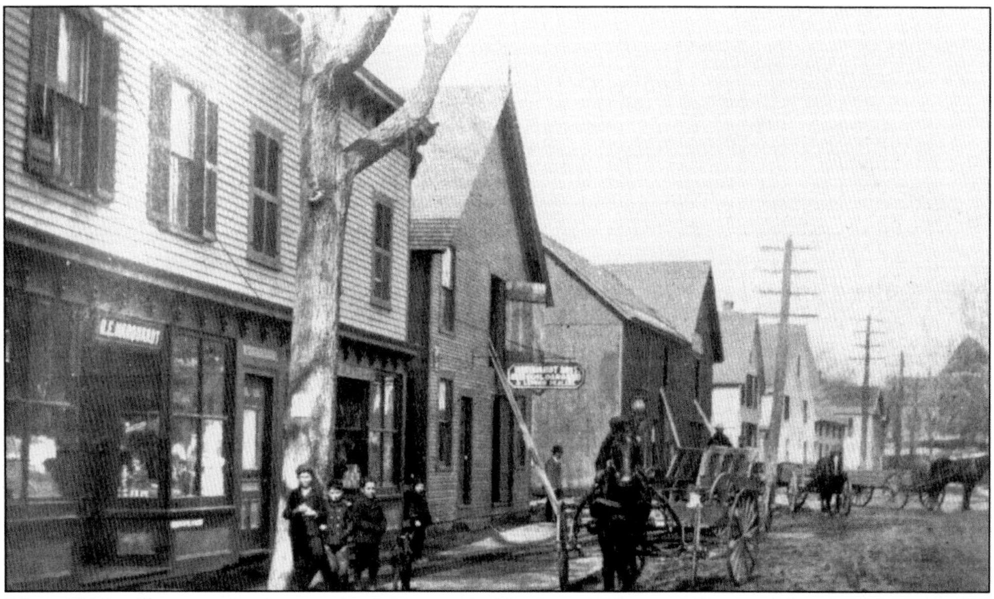

This 1890s photograph shows the Marquardt block on Thames Street. The building in the center by the telephone pole became Groton Hardware. The first three buildings on the left exist today. (James L. Streeter.)

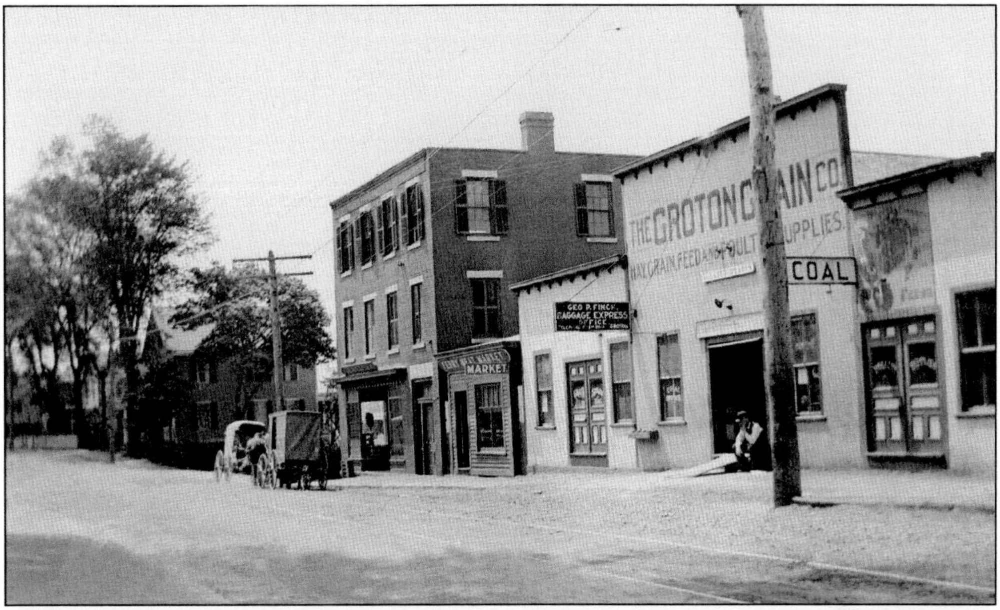

The Groton Grain Company on Thames Street, across from Pleasant Street, was the largest hay, grain, and feed supply store in Groton. The upper floors of the three-story brick building on the left were home to Groton's first YMCA. (James L. Streeter.)

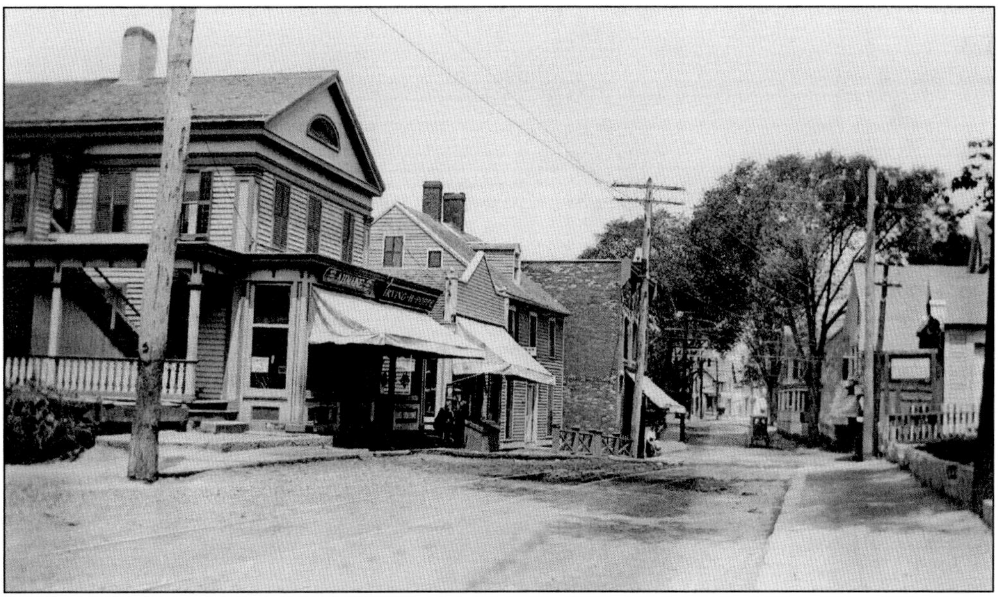

This late-1920s photograph shows the block of stores on Thames Street near the ferry slip. Businesses in these buildings included Edgcomb and Poppe tailors and C. W. Allyn Groceries and Provisions. (James L. Streeter.)

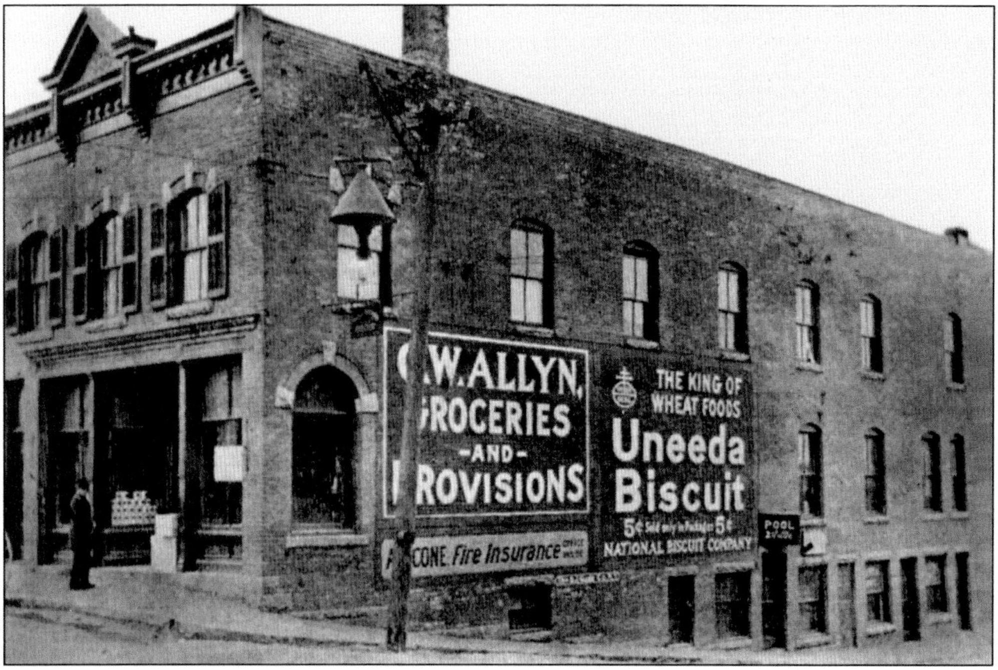

This early-20th-century photograph shows C. W. Allyn Groceries and Provisions at 213 Thames Street. Several small businesses operated from the basement of the building, and the second floor was used as offices. (James L. Streeter.)

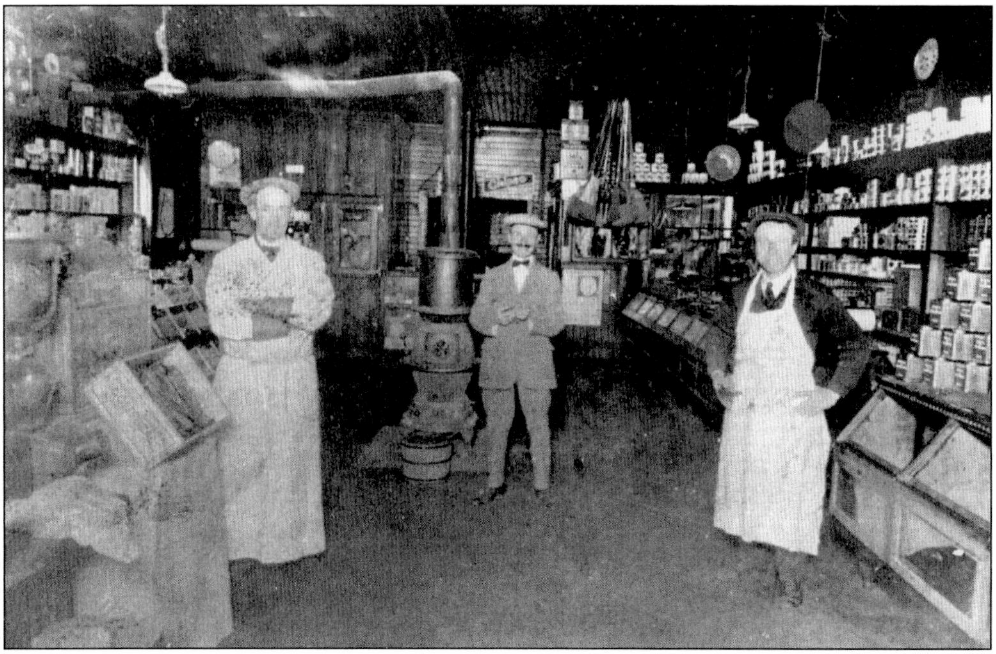

Carlos W. Allyn, center, stands inside his store, C. W. Allyn Groceries and Provisions, which was at 213 Thames Street. It was the largest grocery store in Groton and made home deliveries. (Betsey Allyn VanDressie.)

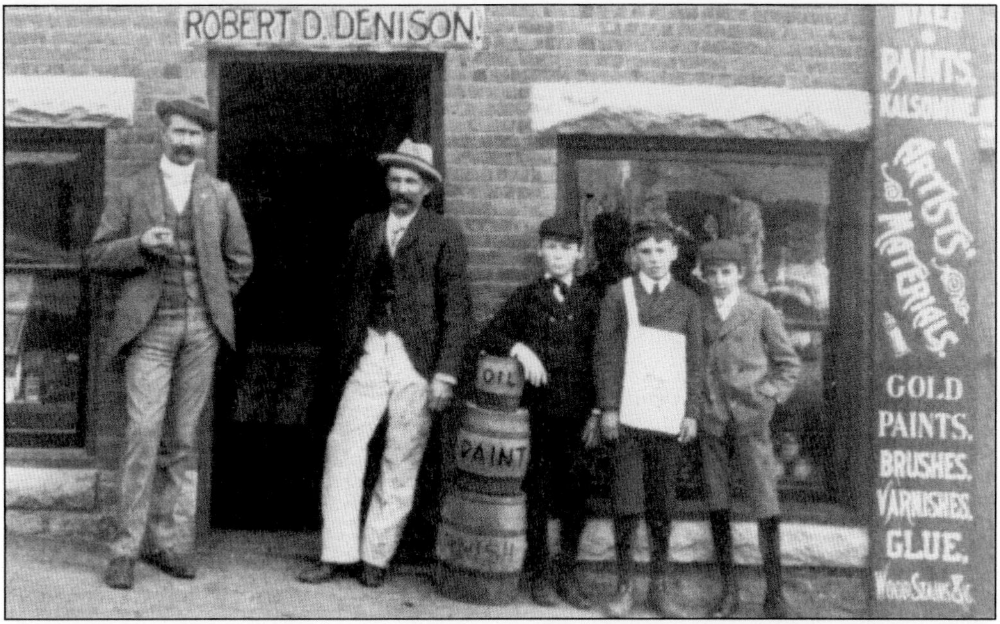

The Robert D. Denison paint store was housed in the basement of the C. W. Allyn Groceries and Provisions building at 213 Thames Street. It sold painting supplies and materials for artists as well as housepainters. (James L. Streeter.)

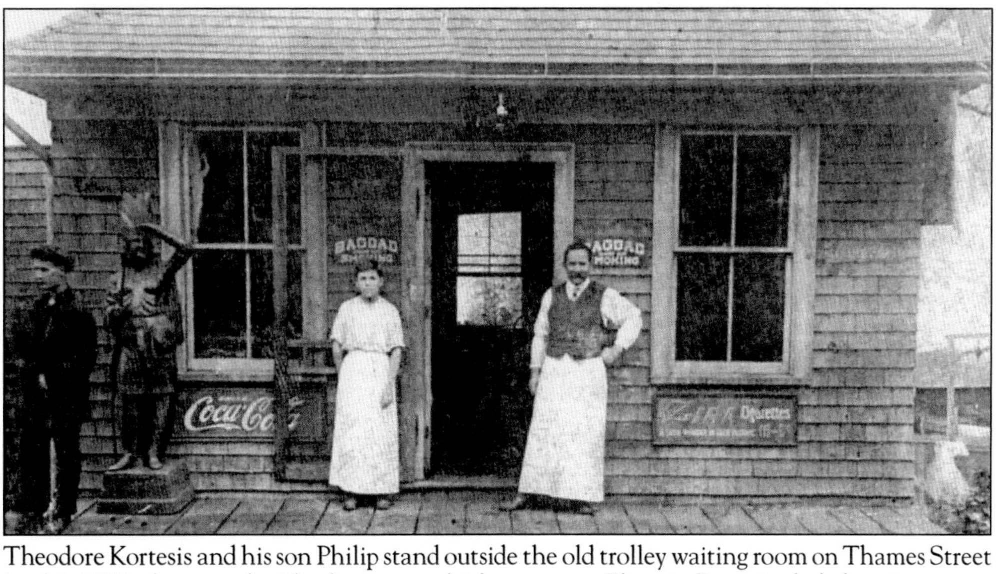

Theodore Kortesis and his son Philip stand outside the old trolley waiting room on Thames Street in this 1913 photograph. The business, which was near Electric Boat, included an ice-cream parlor and candy shop. (Helen Kortesis.)

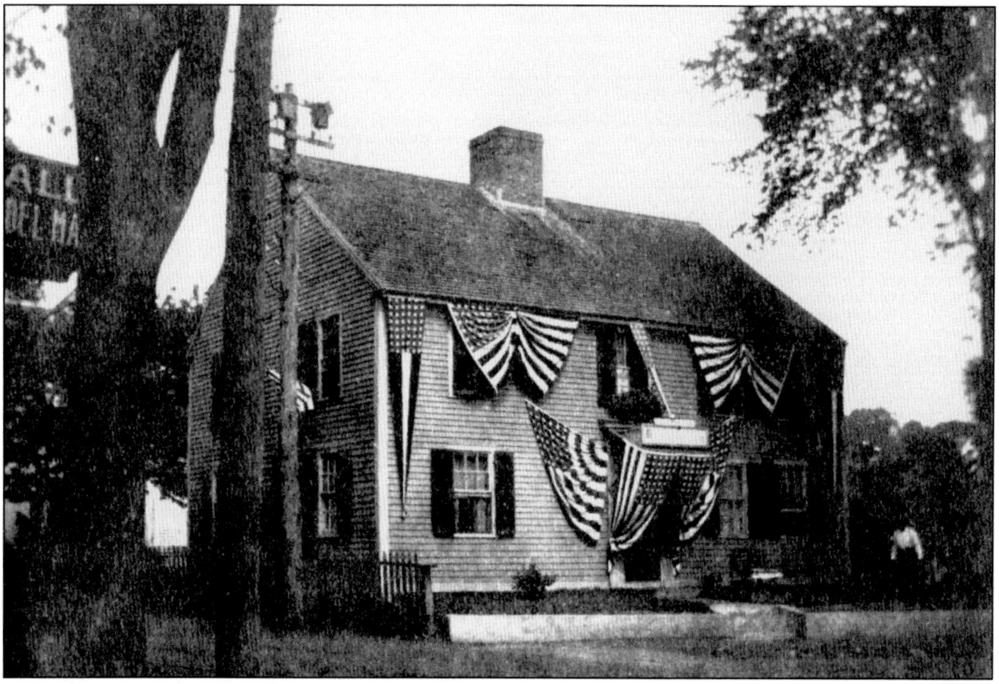

The Ebenezer Avery house was where badly wounded defenders from the September 6, 1781, Battle of Groton Heights were taken after the battle. The house was moved from Thames Street to Fort Griswold Battlefield State Park in 1971. (Winifred Newbury.)

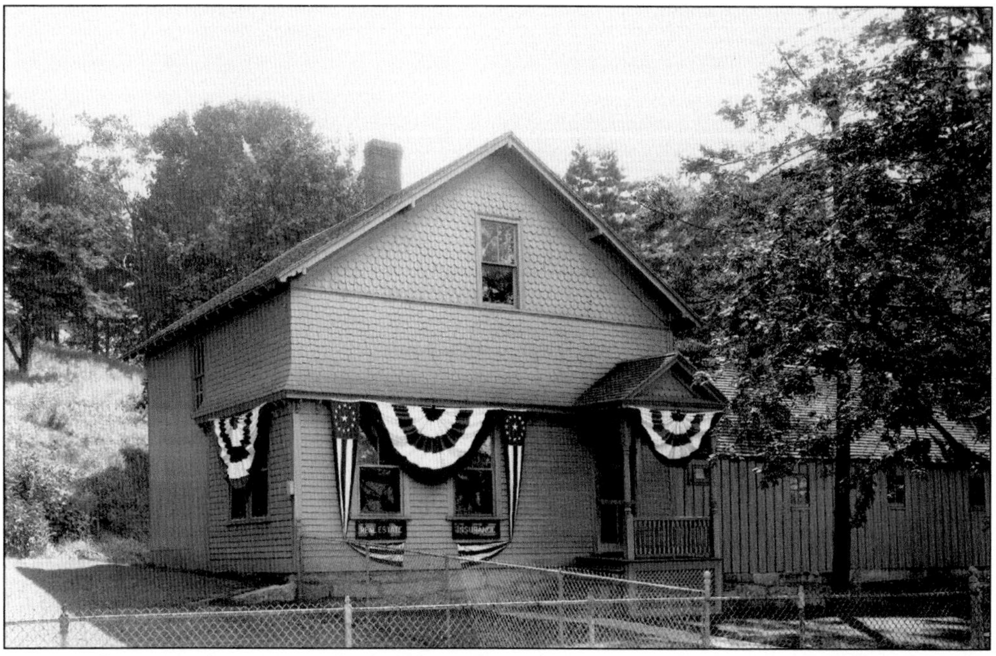

Bunting decorates the carriage shed of the Avery-Copp House. The building initially was used as a horse carriage barn. In the 1940s, it served as the business offices for Bailey Insurance. Recently the Avery-Copp Museum restored the structure as a repository for Groton historic documents. (John Scott.)

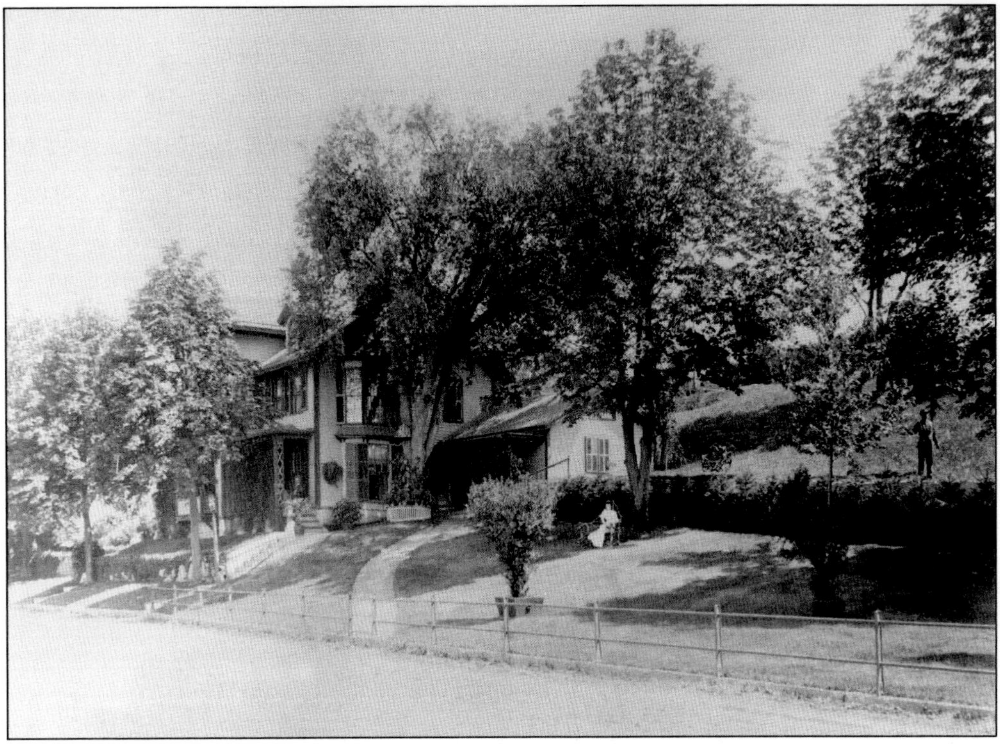

The Avery-Copp House at 154 Thames Street is a museum today, depicting the life of Belton Copp and Bessie Avery Copp, who lived in the Victorian home more than a century ago, about the time this photograph was taken. (Avery-Copp Museum.)

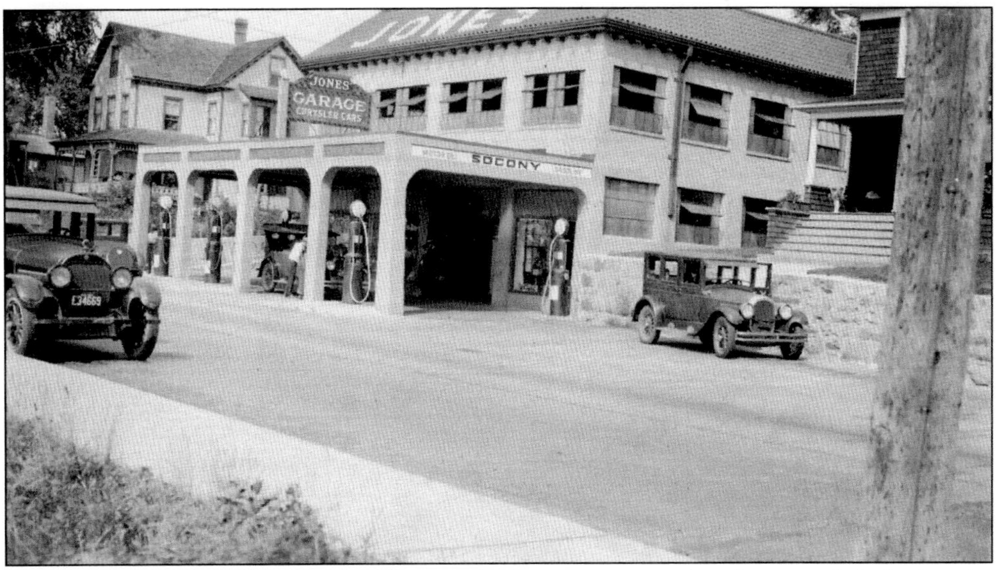

In the 1930s, Jones Garage at 28 Thames Street was a main distributor and dealership for Chrysler. The garage was built on property that once was the site of the Groton Congregational Church. (Harold C. Cornet.)

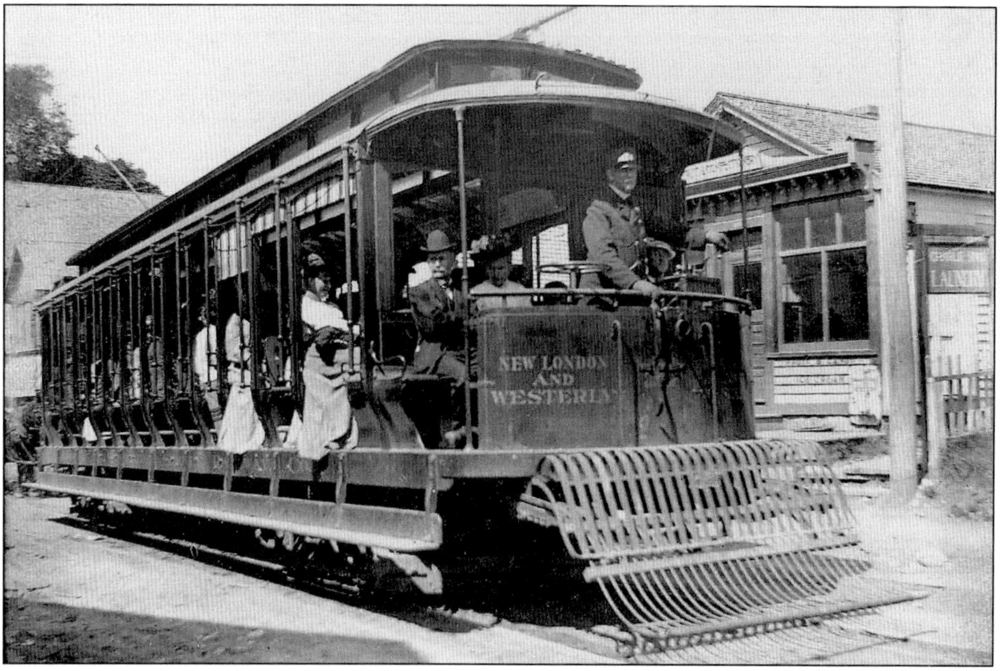

A New London and Westerly trolley travels down Thames Street near School Street, where there was a trolley turnaround. Trolleys were a popular mode of transportation at the beginning of the 20th century, before automobiles became prevalent. (Bob Irons.)

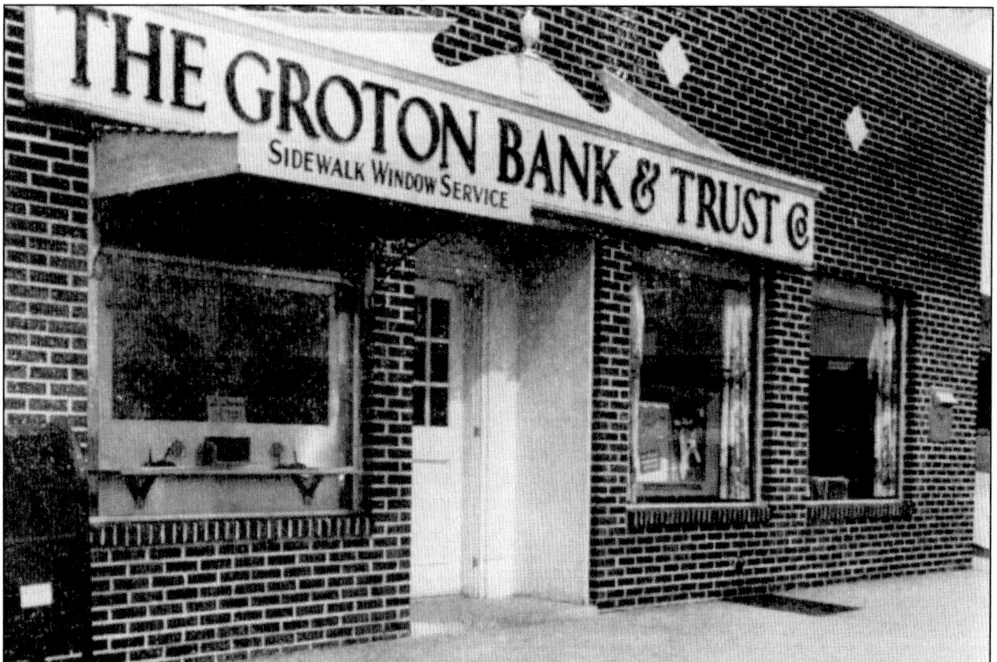

The Groton Bank and Trust Company, the borough's first bank, opened in April 1953 at 486 Thames Street and offered window service. The bank moved to the Groton Shopping Plaza in 1957. Today the Riverfront Children's Day Care Center uses the building. (James L. Streeter.)

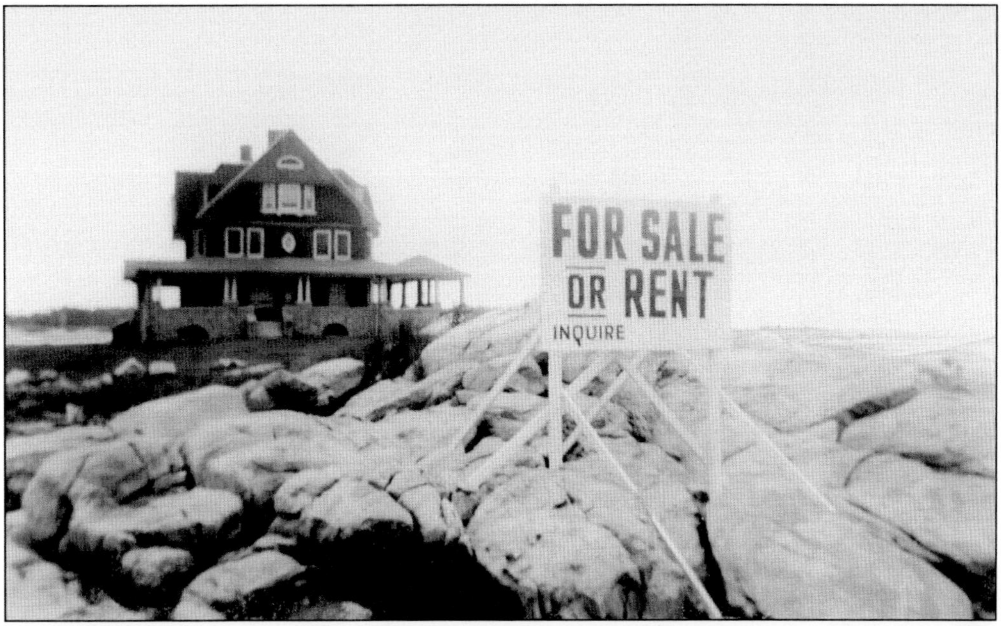

The Borough of Groton was the buyer for the Tyler estate shown here. The 1945 purchasing price was $40,000 and included the 23-room house, a barn, a detached apartment, and 2,000 feet of waterfront. The waterfront became the city of Groton's public beach. (Bill Sanford.)

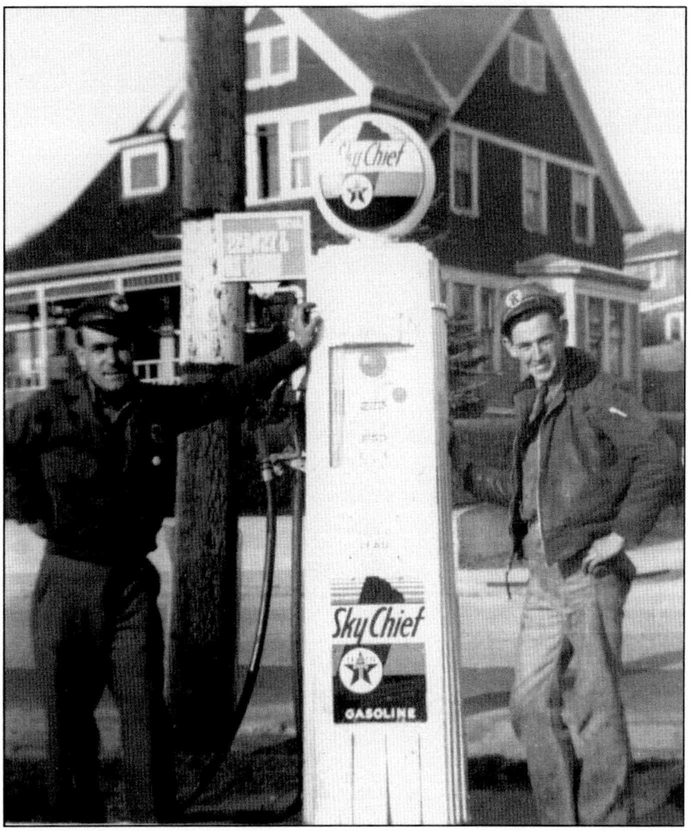

Rudy Santacroce, left, and Joe Hollis stand by a gas pump at Rudy's Texaco Station at 435 Thames Street across from Allen Street. Gasoline was only 22.9¢ per gallon. (John Santacroce.)

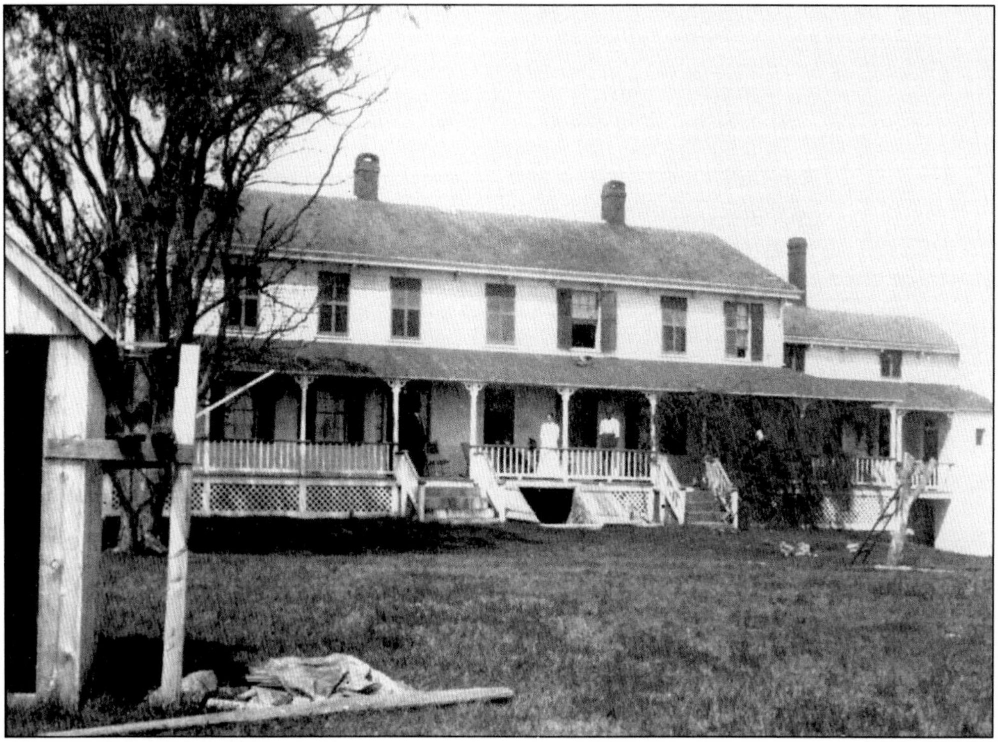

This farmhouse, the original John Grant Spicer home and hotel, became part of the J. Everett Spicer property at Avery Point. Morton F. Plant later bought the property and built his summer home, Branford House, there. Today it is the Avery Point campus of the University of Connecticut. (Mike Boucher.)

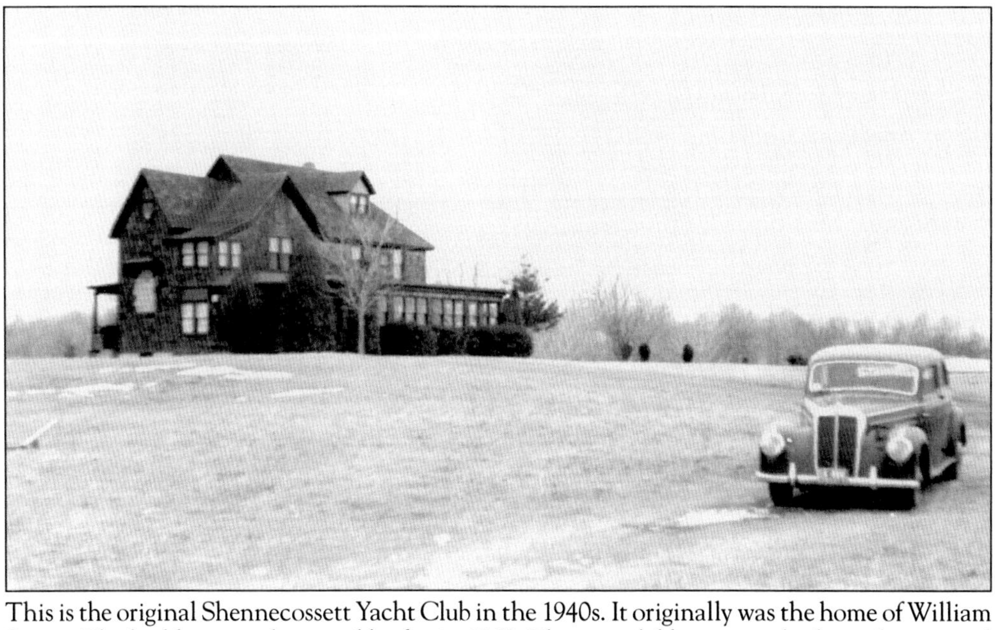

This is the original Shennecossett Yacht Club in the 1940s. It originally was the home of William Spicer. The building was destroyed by fire in 1969. The new clubhouse was built on the original foundation. (Shennecossett Yacht Club.)

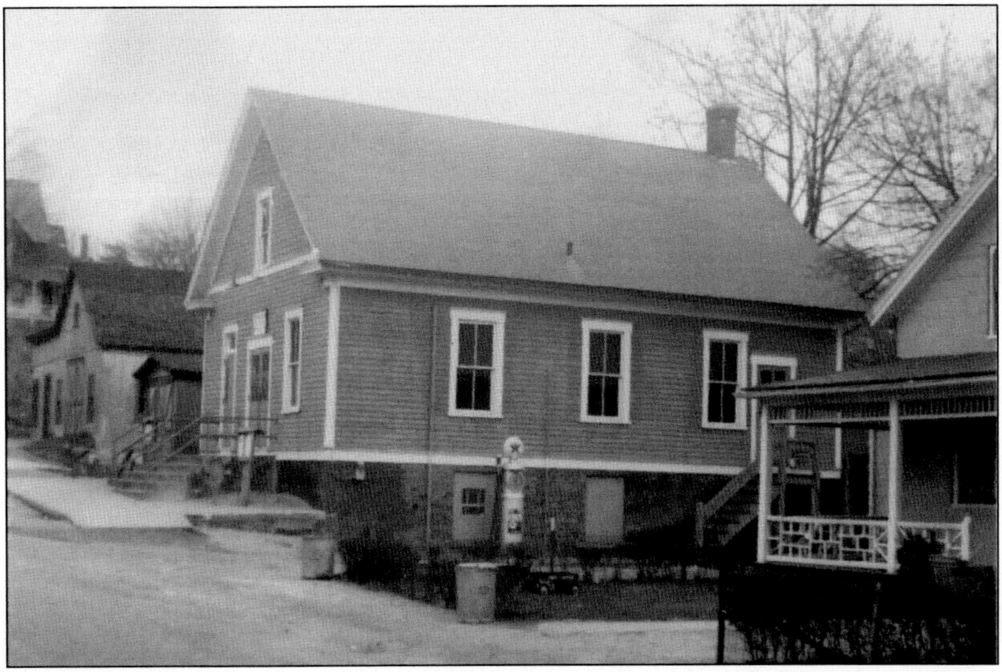

The Borough of Groton used the district meeting hall on School Street for borough government meetings through the 1950s. Today the building is an apartment house. (Town of Groton Department of Public Works.)

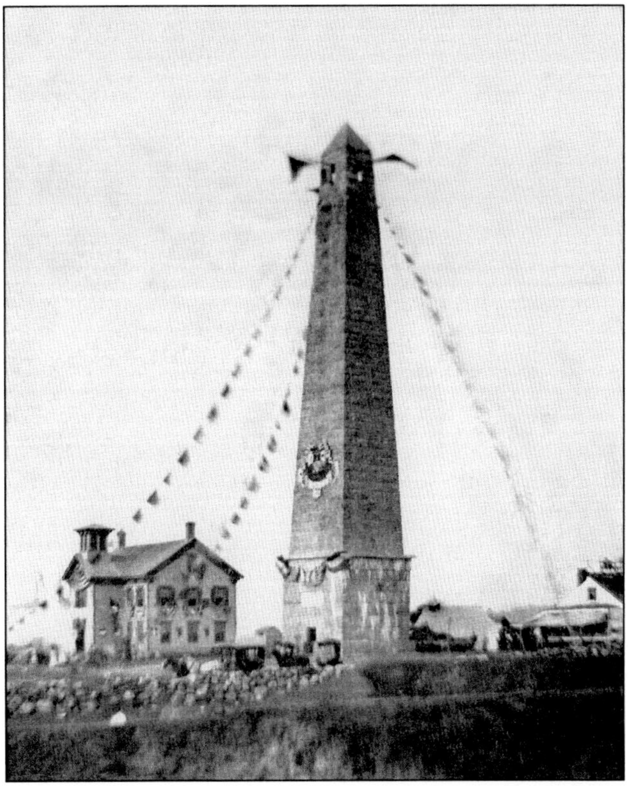

The Groton Monument is decked out with flags and bunting in preparation for the monument's 100th anniversary in 1930. The monument was erected to commemorate the September 6, 1781, British attack on Groton and New London, commanded by the traitor Benedict Arnold. The 185 defenders of the fort were overwhelmed by the superior British force. The original Groton Heights School is to the left of the monument. (James L. Streeter.)

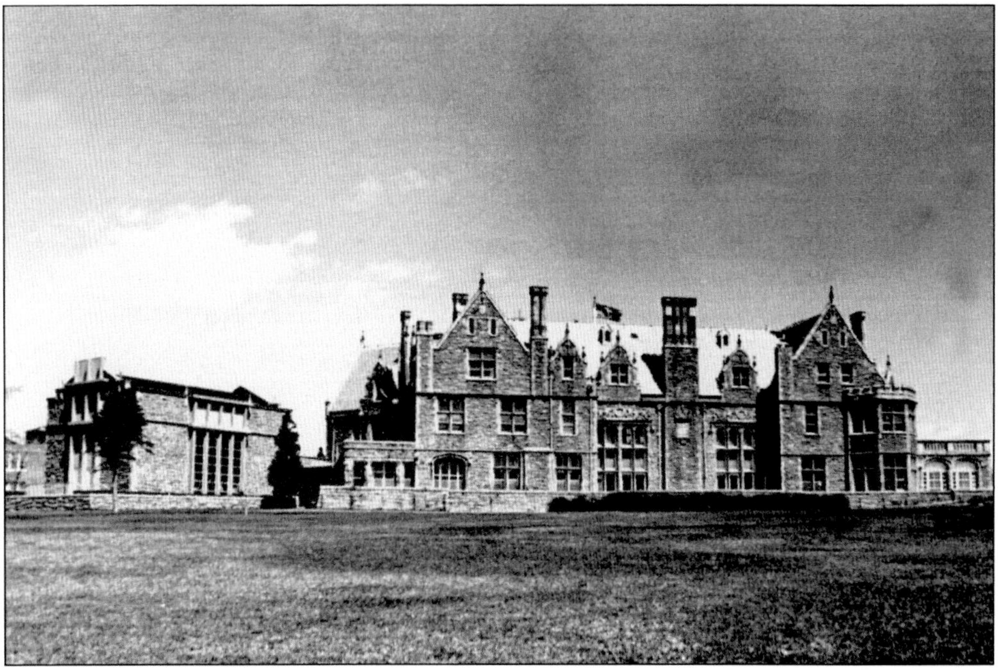

From 1938 to 1967, Branford House housed the administrative offices and residence of the commanders of the U.S. Coast Guard training station at Avery Point. This 1950s photograph shows the chapel the U.S. Coast Guard built at the left of the mansion. It was torn down after its interior suffered extensive termite damage. (James L. Streeter.)

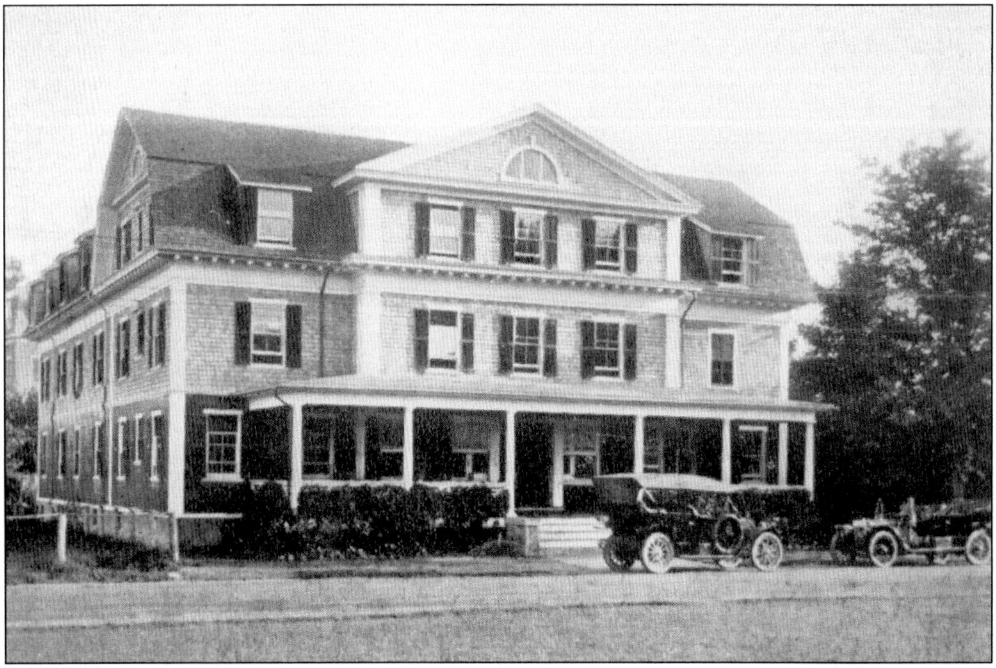

The Griswold Hotel Annex, shown around 1930, was across the street from the famed Griswold Hotel, built by hotel magnate Morton F. Plant. It was used as a rooming house for the hotel workers. (James L. Streeter.)

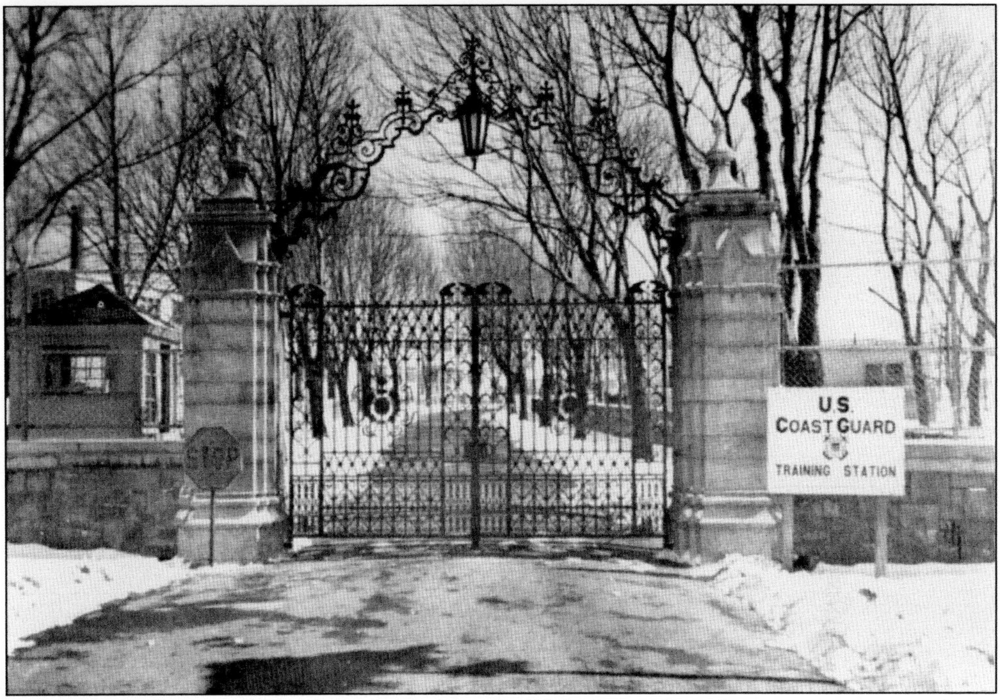

Snow covers the ground at the main gate to the U.S. Coast Guard training station at Avery Point in the late 1940s. The station was on property that once was the summer home of Morton F. Plant. The ornate iron gates and archway in the photograph were built for Plant. (James L. Streeter.)

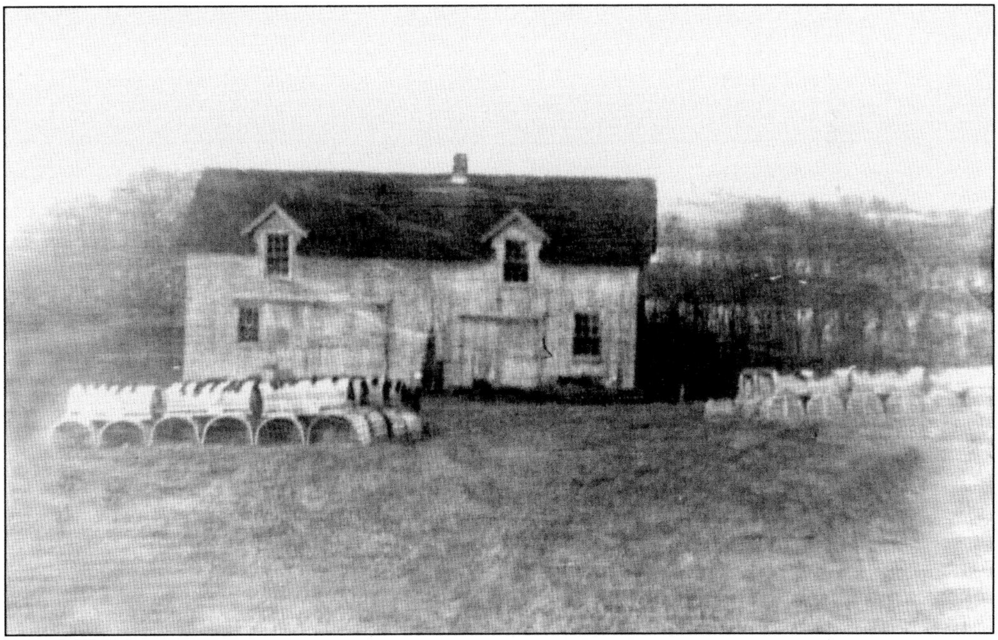

This barn originally was part of the Mather Farm off Thomas Road, where the Sound Breeze Condominiums are today. Before the condominiums were built, the Chapman family owned the barn and used it to store its fishing and lobstering equipment. (Al Chapman.)

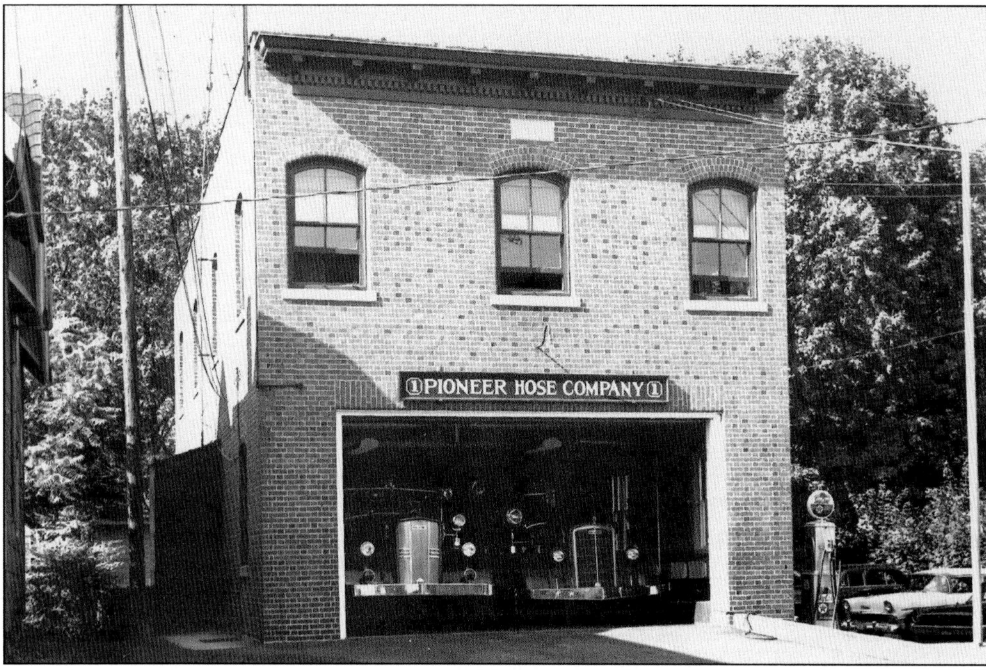

The Pioneer Hose Company firehouse on Pleasant Street, built in 1917, was the first building used exclusively for the fire department in the borough of Groton. Today the building is occupied by the Machinists' Union. (James L. Streeter.)

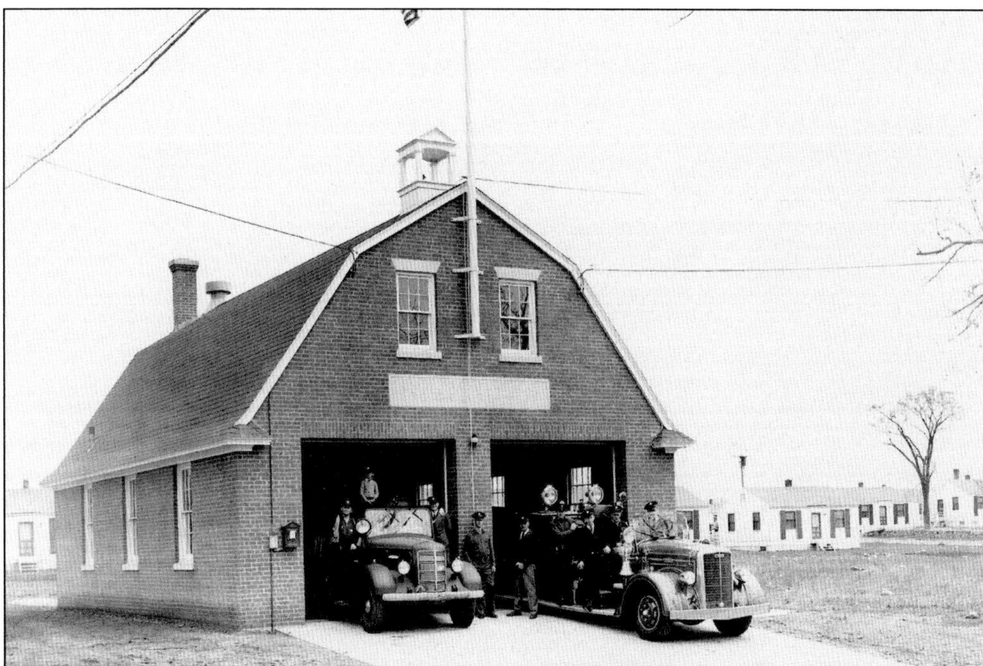

In the 1950s, the Borough of Groton established the Eastern Point Volunteer Fire Department to support all the housing projects that had been built in that part of town to house military and government contract workers. (James L. Streeter.)

Eight

HERE AND THERE

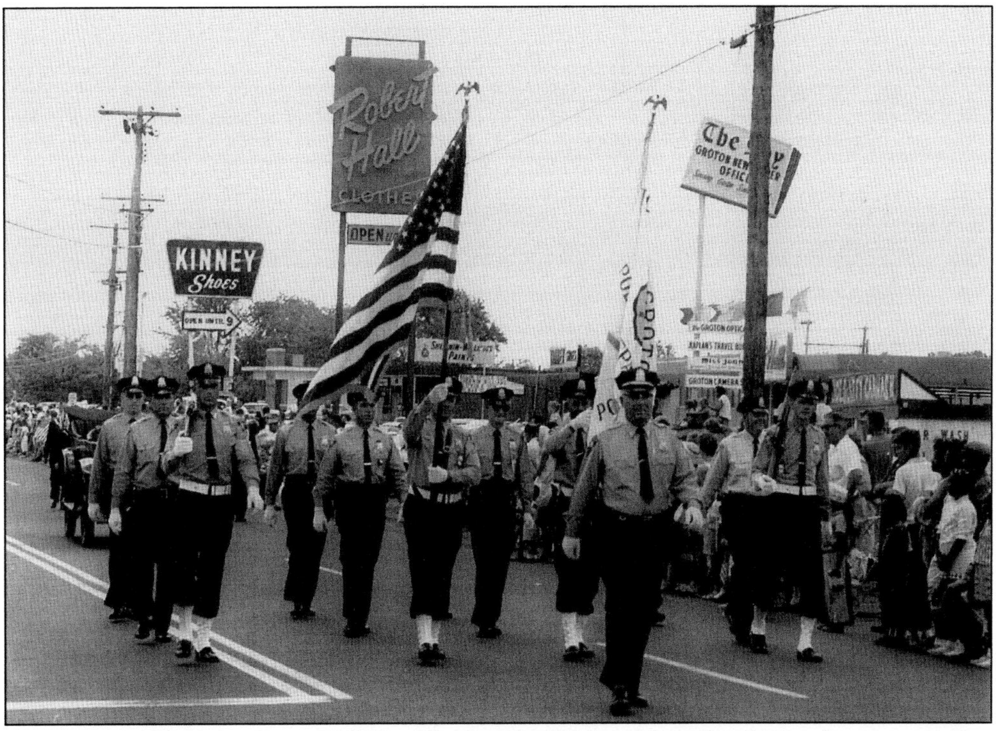

The commercial strip on Long Hill Road for decades has been the official route for town parades, including Fourth of July and the annual holiday parade each December. This 1950s photograph shows Groton police officers leading a parade past Kinney Shoes and Robert Hall Clothes, two popular stores of the era. (Groton Town Police.)

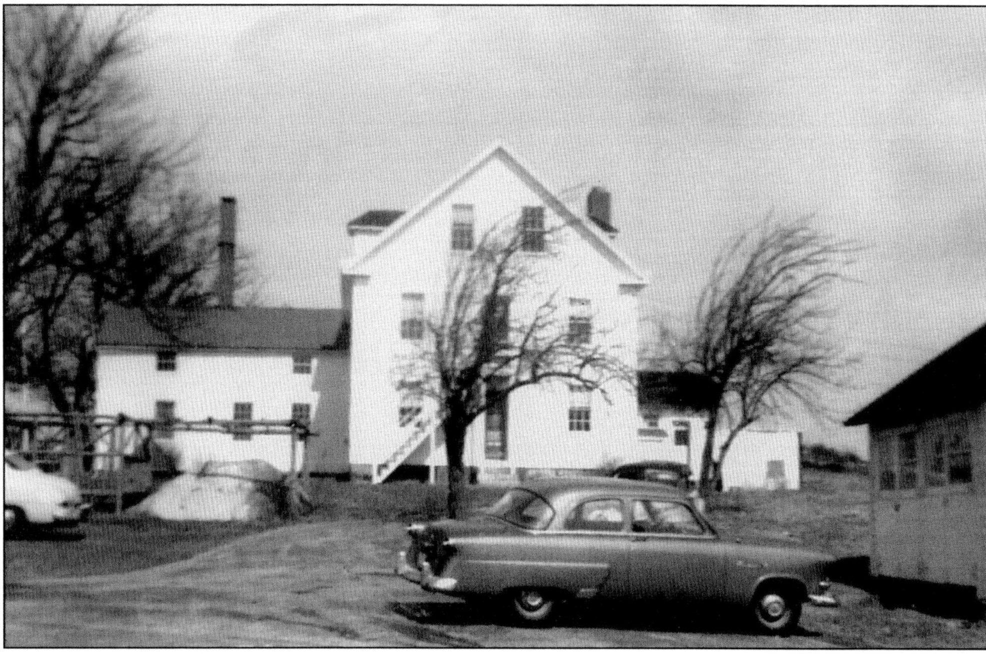

In 1886, Capt. Elihu Spicer of Mystic, who also built the Mystic and Noank Library as a gift to the people of those two villages, gave the town the former Comfort Brown farm with its 554 acres and two buildings, as well as $1,000 in cash, to establish the Spicer Home for the Poor. At the time, towns often had poor farms, a place for indigent people to live. Today the Robert E. Fitch High School, the public works department, and the town police department are built on the property. The only remnant of the poor farm is a walled cemetery, in front of the high school, where the poor were buried. (James L. Streeter.)

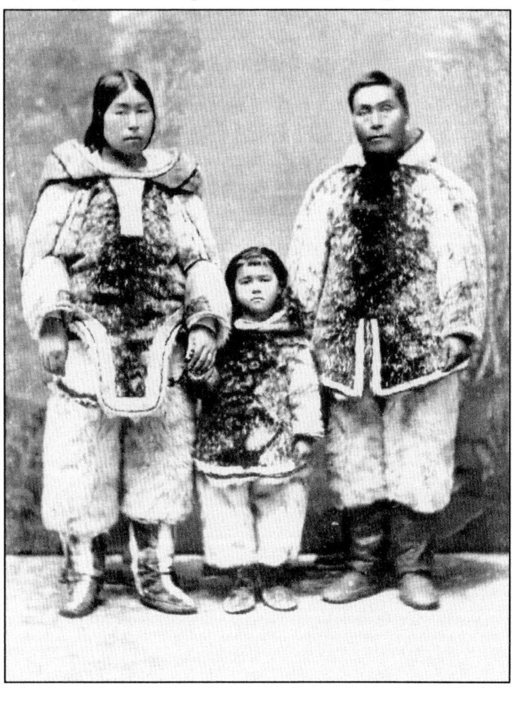

John Bull and his family, Eskimos from Cumberland Gulf in Hudson Bay, were brought to Groton by whaling captain John O. Spicer. John Bull's testimony, needed in a lawsuit, won the case for Spicer against a New Bedford whaling firm whose men had stolen Spicer's oil stored at Cumberland. Spicer wanted Bull to stay in Groton, but Bull said he could not stand the climate. (Carol W. Kimball.)

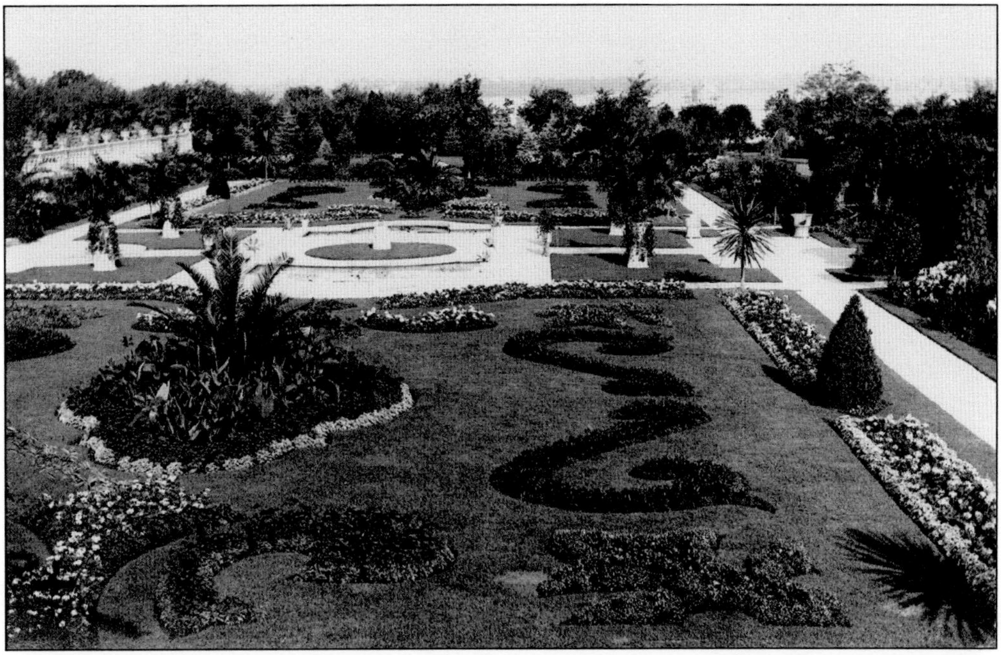

The gardens at Branford House, Morton F. Plant's summer home at Avery Point, were opulent and expansive. (James L. Streeter.)

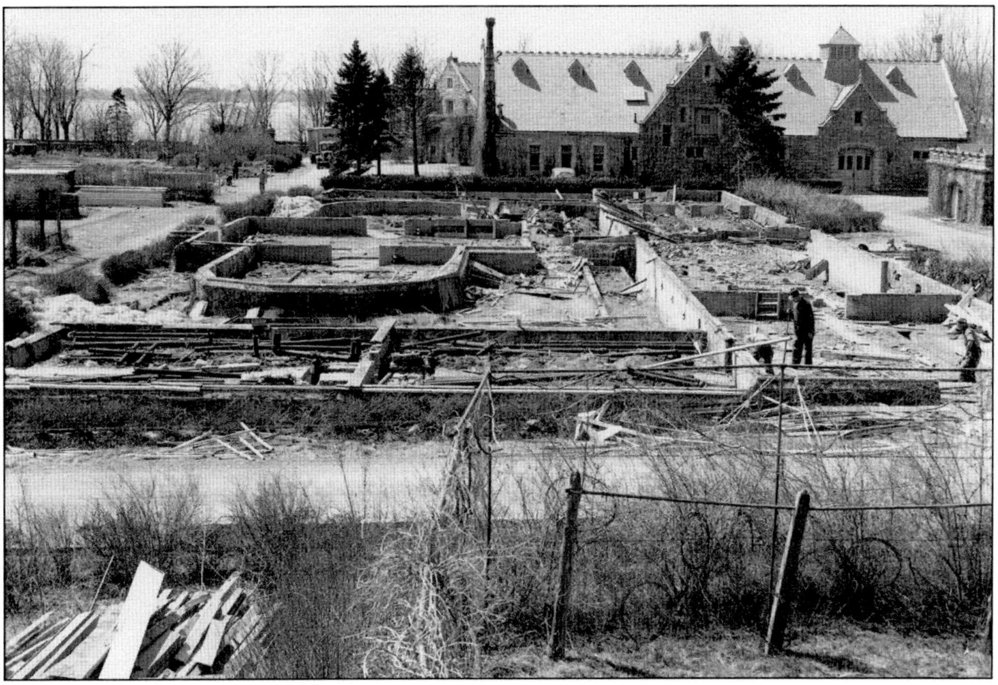

Plant had expansive greenhouses at Branford House, his summer home at Avery Point. The greenhouses supplied flowers for Branford House and for the nearby Griswold Hotel, which Plant owned, as well as exotic plantings for the many formal gardens on the grounds. The greenhouses fell into disuse after Plant's death from influenza in 1918, and workmen are shown here dismantling them. (Spicer family.)

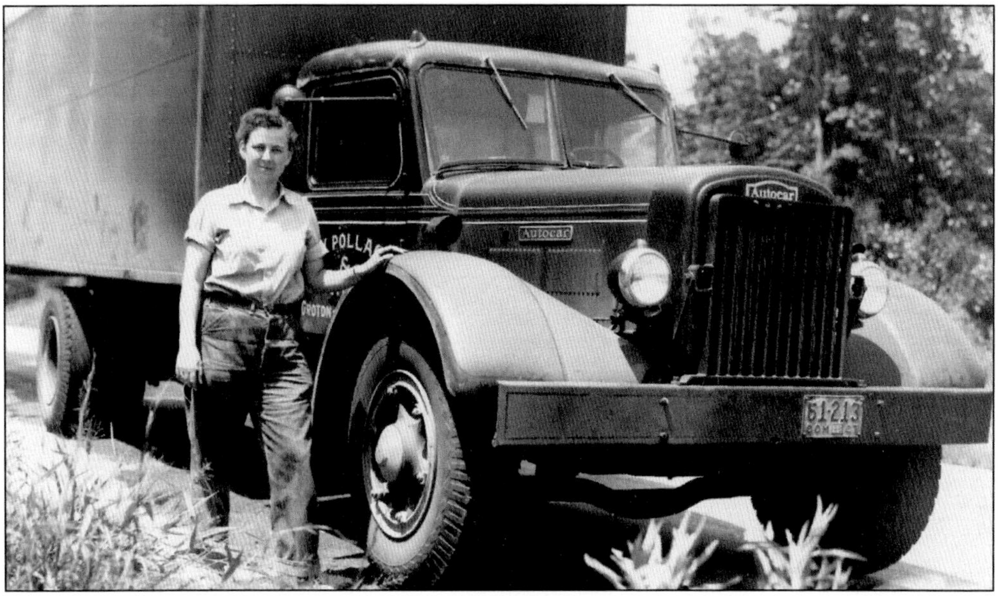

Anne Thompson was the primary truck driver for the Max Pollack Mills on Poquonnock Road. Thompson was a 1939 graduate of Robert E. Fitch High School and was one of the first women drivers for the mill, which produced sewing and other types of threads. It was in business from 1920 to 1958. Today the building is an annex for Electric Boat. (Sally Allyn Brousseau.)

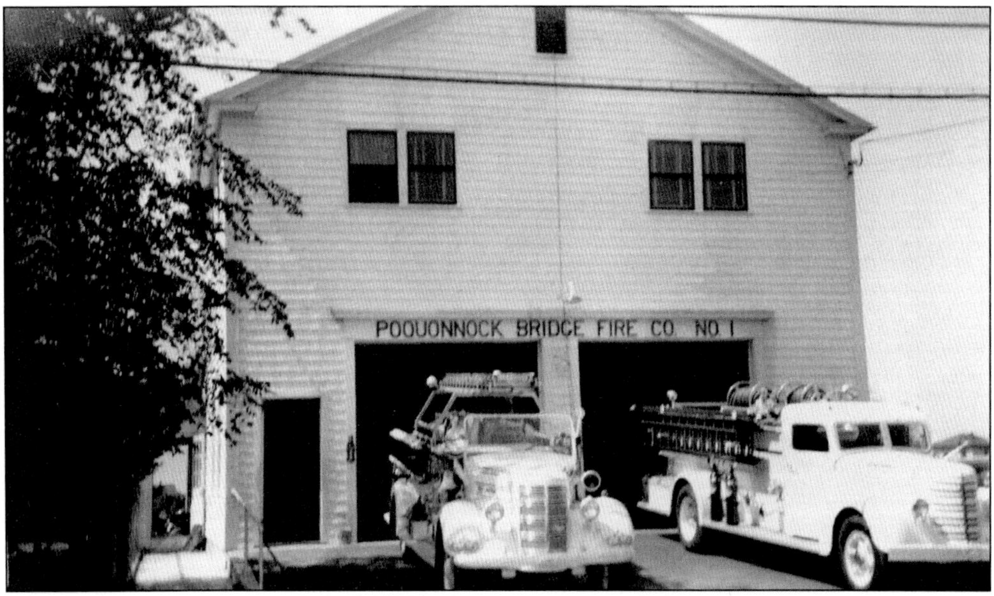

The first Poquonnock Bridge firehouse, on Route 1, opened in January 1946. The firehouse and its equipment answered a need for fire protection as Poquonnock Bridge's population grew during World War II when 1,100 prefabricated homes were built there to house workers in war industries. Today Poquonnock Bridge has a second firehouse, built in 1990 on Long Hill Road, about a mile from the firehouse pictured here in 1949. (Janet Crossman.)

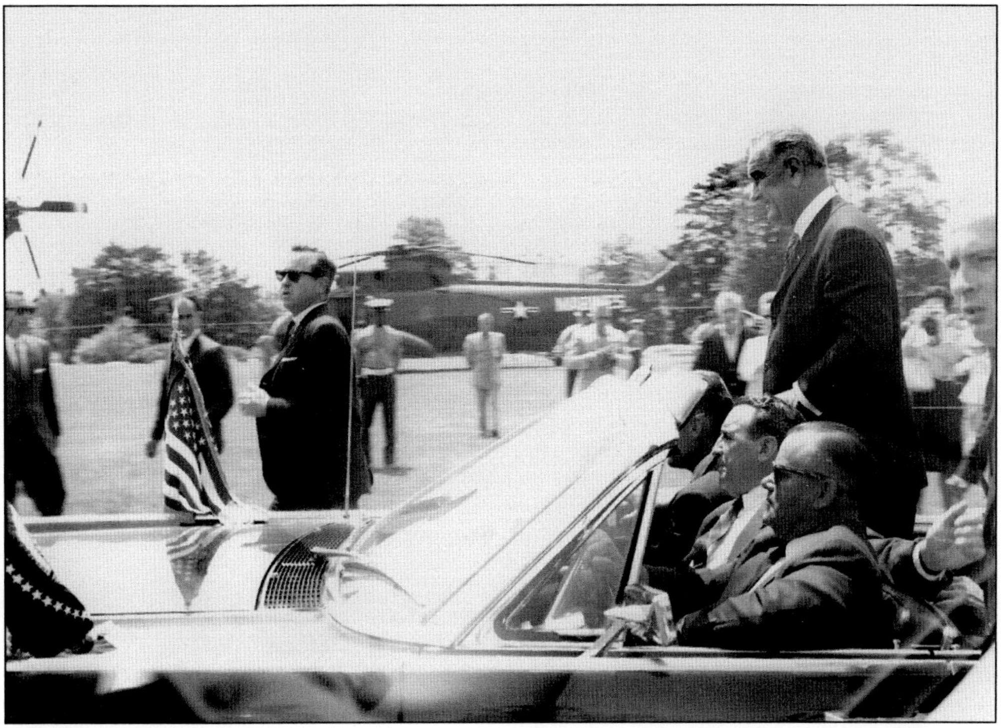

Pres. Lyndon B. Johnson stands in his car to greet crowds in Groton on June 3, 1964. The president spoke at General Dynamics Electric Boat that afternoon for the keel laying of the submarine USS *Pargo*. Seated in the center of the front seat is Connecticut governor John Dempsey. (City of Groton.)

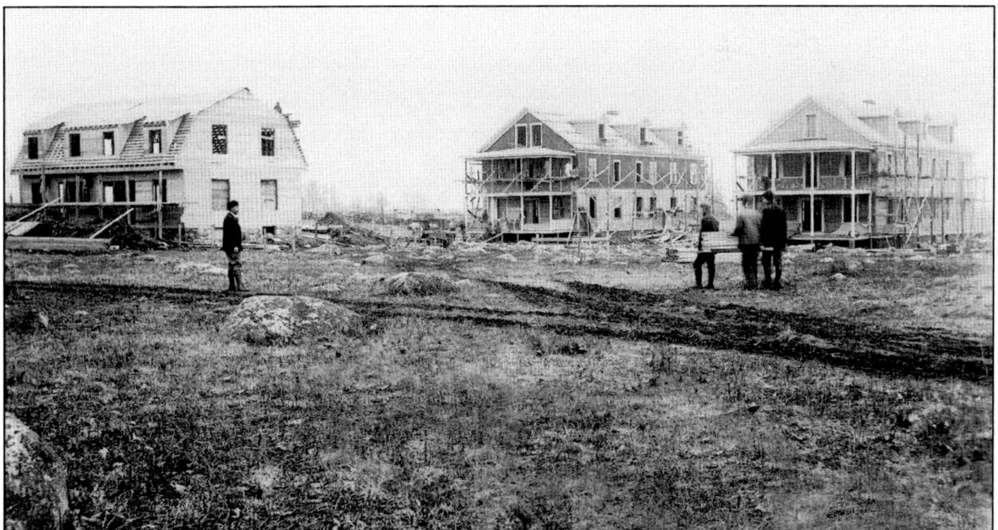

To accommodate the huge workforce of Groton Iron Works during World War I, the U.S. Shipping Board started a housing project in Groton that called for 92 new structures. These are some of them under construction. Some of those duplex houses still stand on Hynes Avenue. (Carol W. Kimball.)

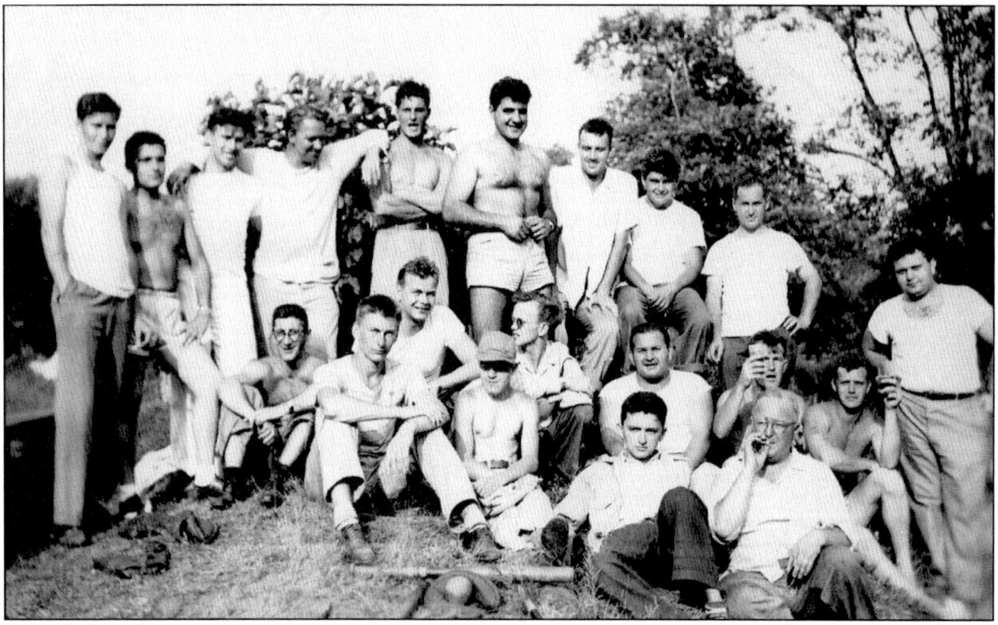

A group of Groton men, home from World War II, get together for some summer fun. Pictured are, from left to right, (first row) William Burgess (with the bat at his feet), George Brustolon (with hat), Everest Brustolon, and John Birchail (smoking); (second row) Mario Peruzzotti (wearing glasses), Richard Jaquith, Harry Jaquith, "Chub" Cataldi, Riggie Frattali, "Gizzy" Griswold, and Jerry Cataldi; (third row) "Bubsy" Giesing, Remo Fusconi, Tim Giesing, John Hoey, "Buck" Scarano, Marty Artale, Ed Kolnasky, "Toady" Sullivan, and Anthony Pisapia. (Marty Artale.)

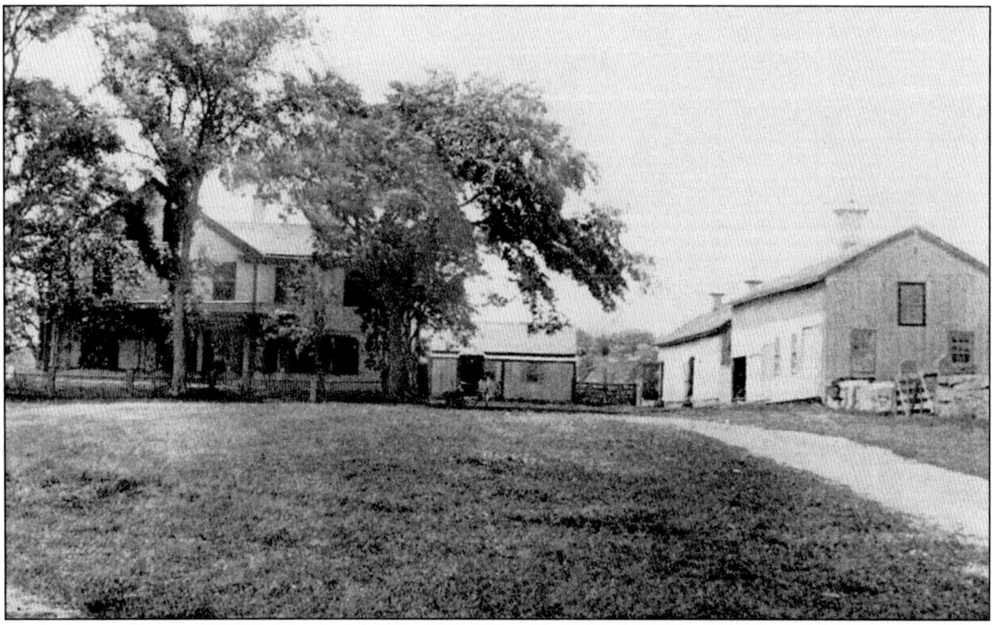

This 1960 photograph shows the Haley Farm near Noank. Caleb Haley, a Mystic native who made his fortune at the Fulton Fish Market in New York City, bought the property in 1868, making it into a model farm where he spent his vacations. His granddaughter Juliet inherited the property, which today is part of the town's green space. (James L. Streeter.)

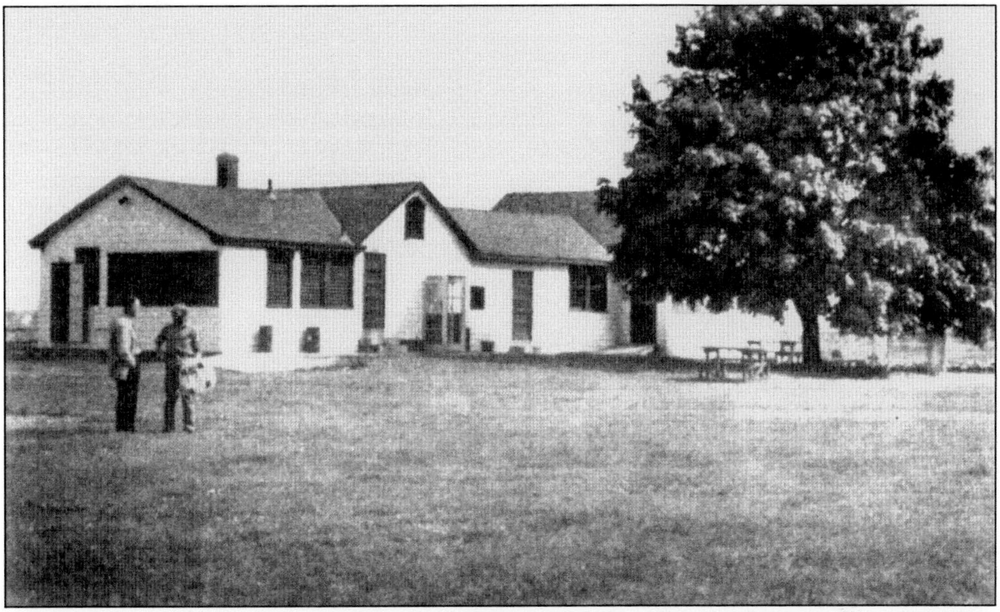

Although Groton has water on three sides, it did not have a town beach until 1956, when land adjacent to Groton-New London Airport was opened as a public beach. Tons of sand were spread along the shore to make a small beach, and the old Vasa Health Club building was used to serve refreshments. Although sometimes plagued by jellyfish and subject to silting, the beach was popular with townspeople until expansion of the airport forced it to close. (James L. Streeter.)

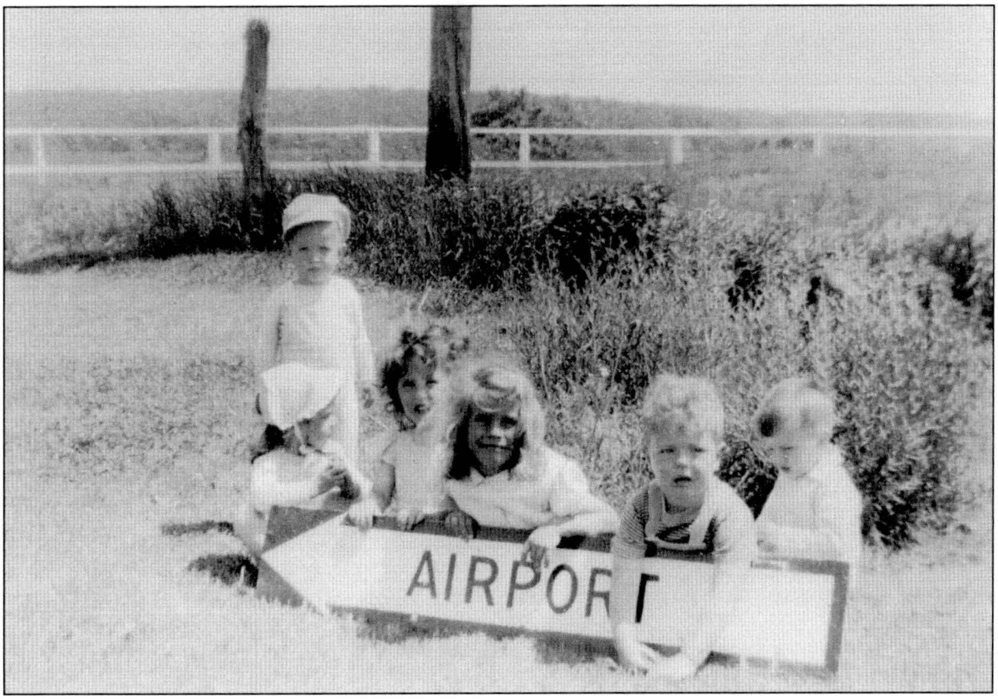

Children on South Road in Groton hold a sign for nearby Trumbull Airport. Pictured are, from left to right, Carol Sawyer, Linda Hansen, Gail McGrath, Jane Pollard, Mark Sullivan, and a toddler who is looking at the sign. (Lil Hansen)

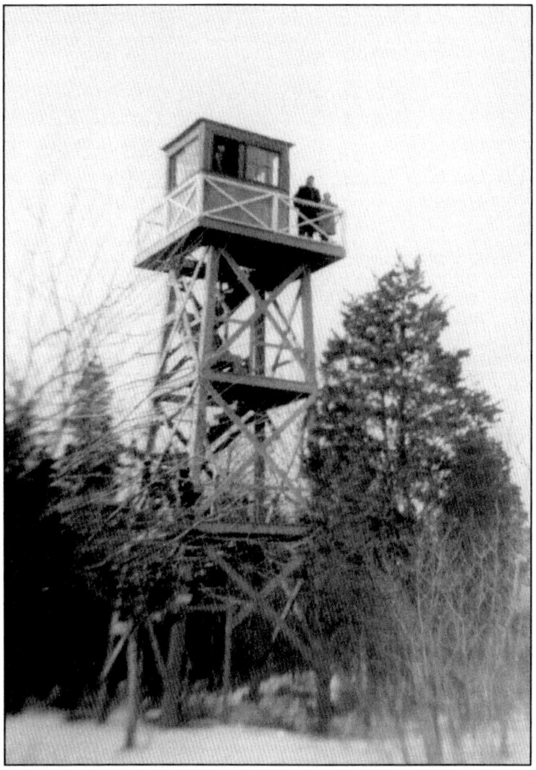

In the 1930s, a fire tower was erected at the top of Fort Hill and was used in the fall and spring to detect any evidence of forest fires. Crews were summoned to preserve the woodlands. (Grace McGrath.)

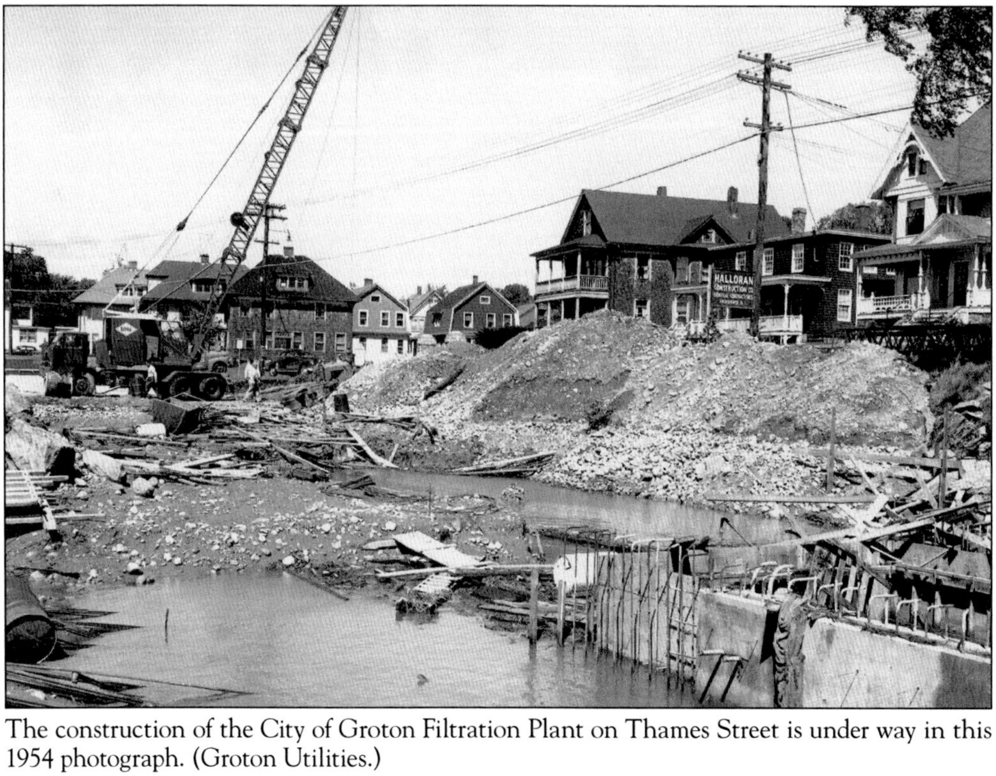

The construction of the City of Groton Filtration Plant on Thames Street is under way in this 1954 photograph. (Groton Utilities.)

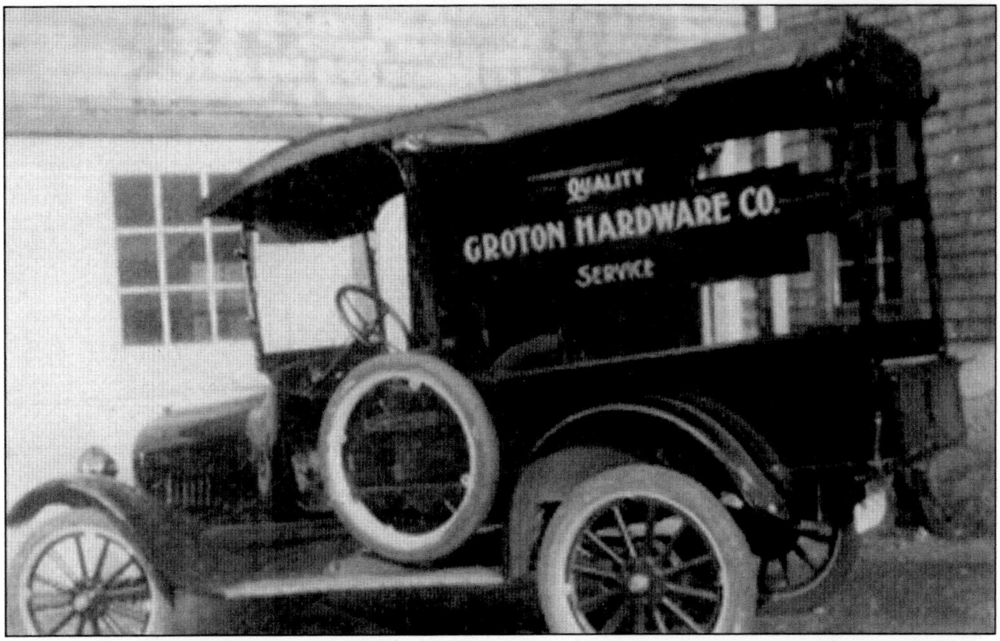

This truck made deliveries for Groton Hardware at 169 Thames Street. The store, whose proprietor was John L. Couch, sold housewares, toys, and marine hardware. It also was a fix-it shop. (Ann C. Brown and Barbara Parfitt)

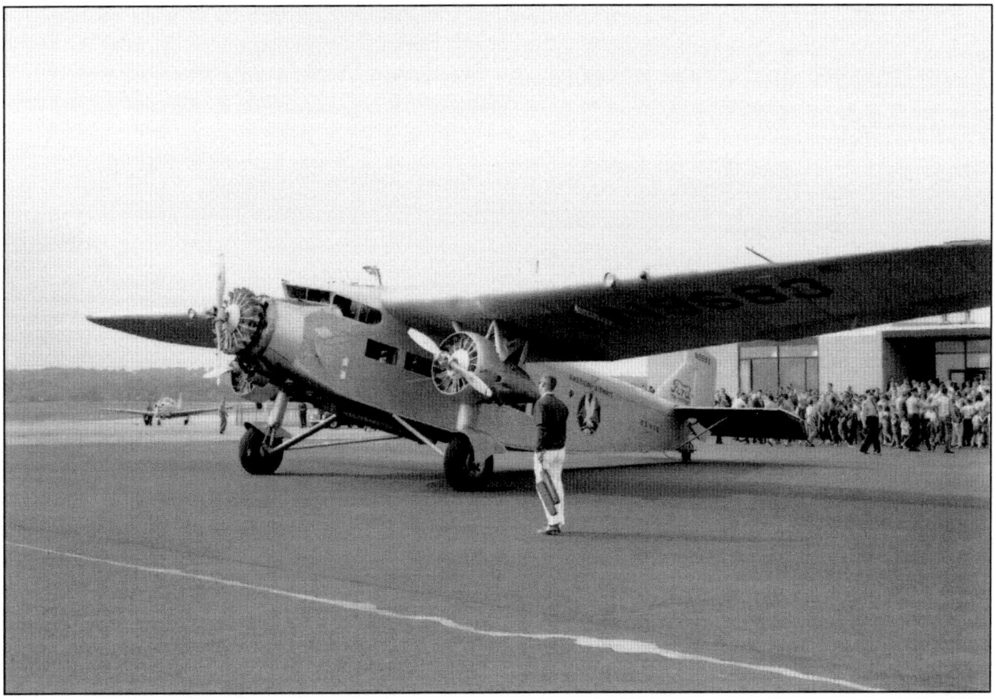

A Ford Tri-Motor airplane sits on the runway at Trumbull Airport in Groton in 1962. The airplane, one of 198 built by Henry Ford between 1926 and 1933, was on a nationwide tour, showing what travel was like in the 1930s. The Ford Tri-Motor was made of aluminum and was nicknamed the "Tin Goose." (Marty Artale.)

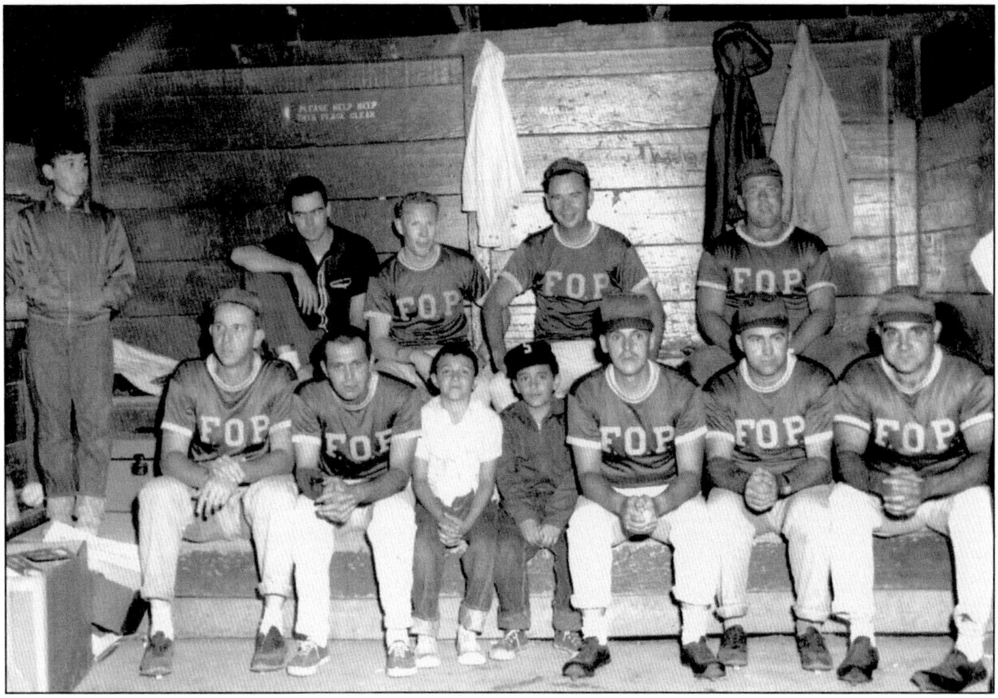

The Borough of Groton Fraternal Order of Police baseball team sits in the dugout in 1962. The boy standing at the left is Marty Artale Jr. The rest are, from left to right, (first row) Joe Sandora, Nick DeNoia, Eddie Artale, Ross Gencarella, Frank Bailey, Tim Giesing, and Marty Artale Sr.; (second row) Bob Sharp, Wally Trolan, Forest Carberg, and Mack Lyon. (James L. Streeter.)

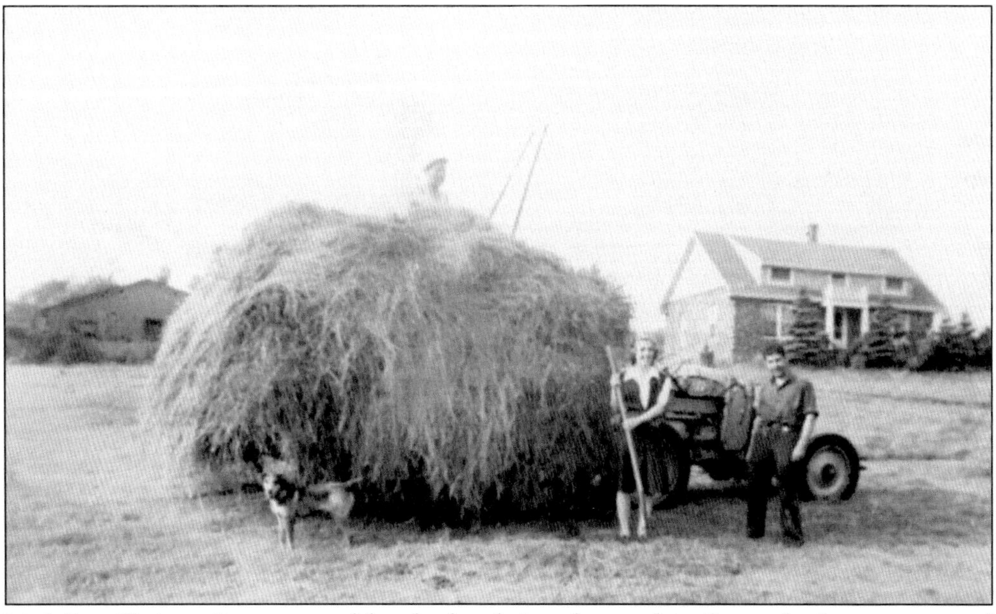

Madeline Chrissos Bongarro and her husband, Joseph, stand in front of a hay wagon, and Christopher Chrissos is on top of the hay in this 1945 photograph. Before the expansion of the naval submarine base, the Pleasant Valley section of town was devoted to farming. The hay field on the Chrissos farm sloped down to Grove Avenue. (Dorothy Chrissos.)

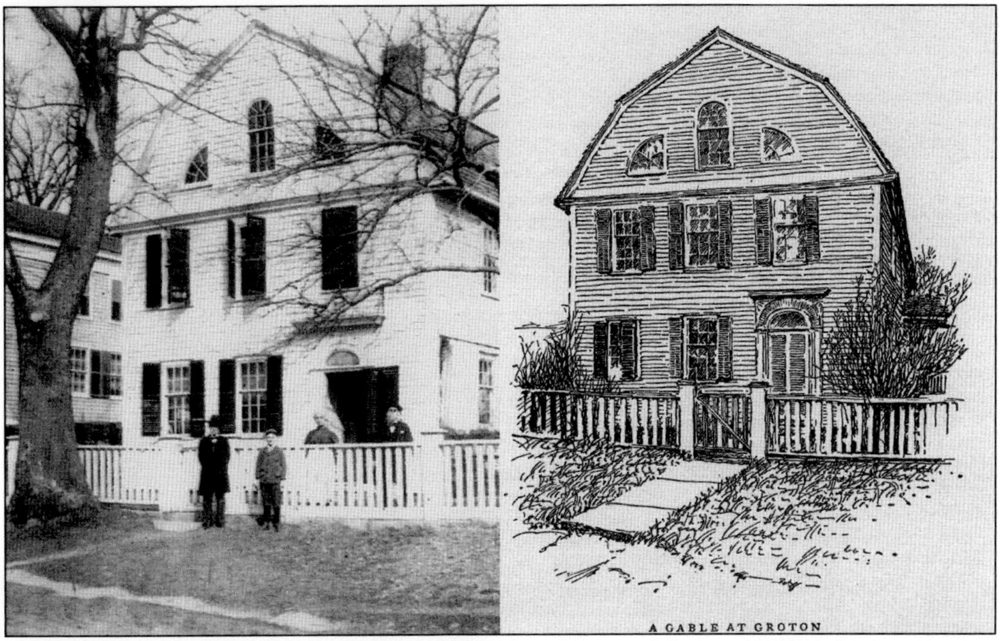

In his book *Connecticut Beautiful*, painter, photographer, and author Wallace Nutting depicts what he calls "A Gable at Groton," which was a drawing of the house at 118 Thames Street. In the foreword to the book, Nutting writes, "It is the country homes of Connecticut that constitute her greatest charm." (James L. Streeter.)

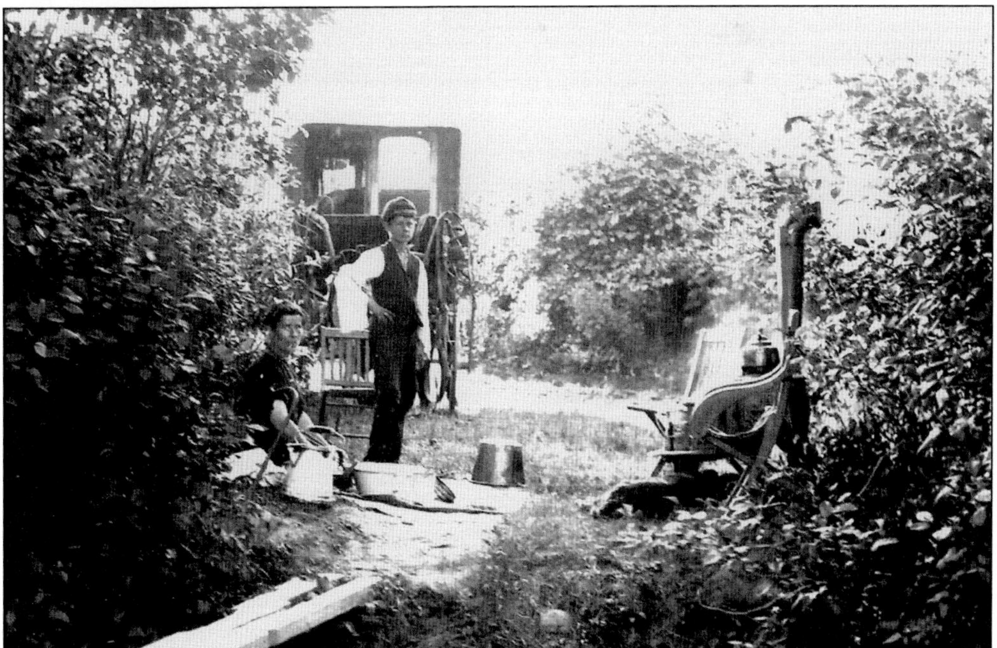

Gypsies are camped by the brook at the foot of Fort Hill in this 1904 photograph. The presence of gypsies caused distress to the village of Poquonnock Bridge. The gypsies drove their teams down from Boston, where they spent the winter. They often told fortunes in Poquonnock Bridge. (Carol W. Kimball.)

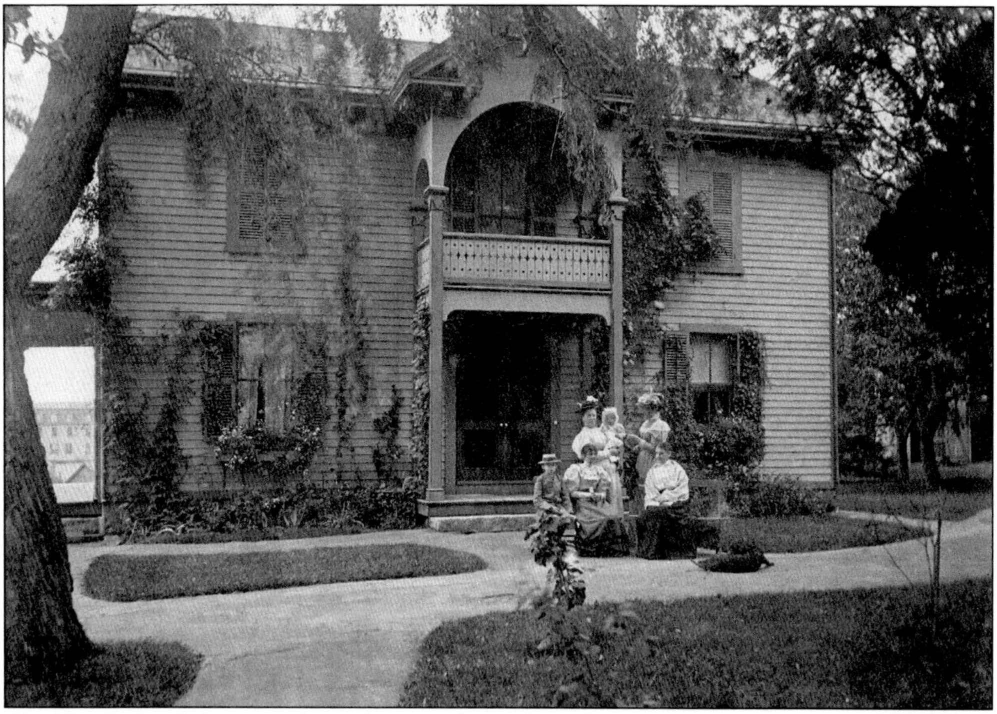

The Meech family home is shown here in the early 20th century. It is on Eastern Point Road, across from the Shennecossett Golf Club and borders the property where the Griswold Hotel once stood. The house and land were purchased by Robert Watrous and converted to a bed-and-breakfast inn. (Spicer family.)

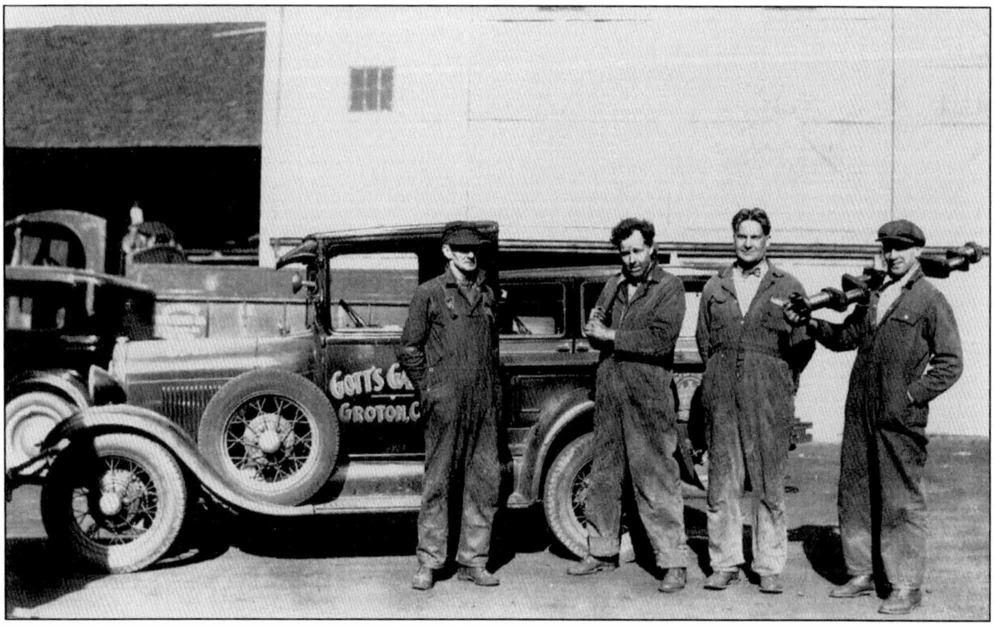

Workers from Gott's Garage on Thames Street were always busy repairing automobiles and providing towing for motor vehicles in distress. Gott Guhering opened the business in 1936, and it ran until his death in the late 1960s. (Dale Treadway.)

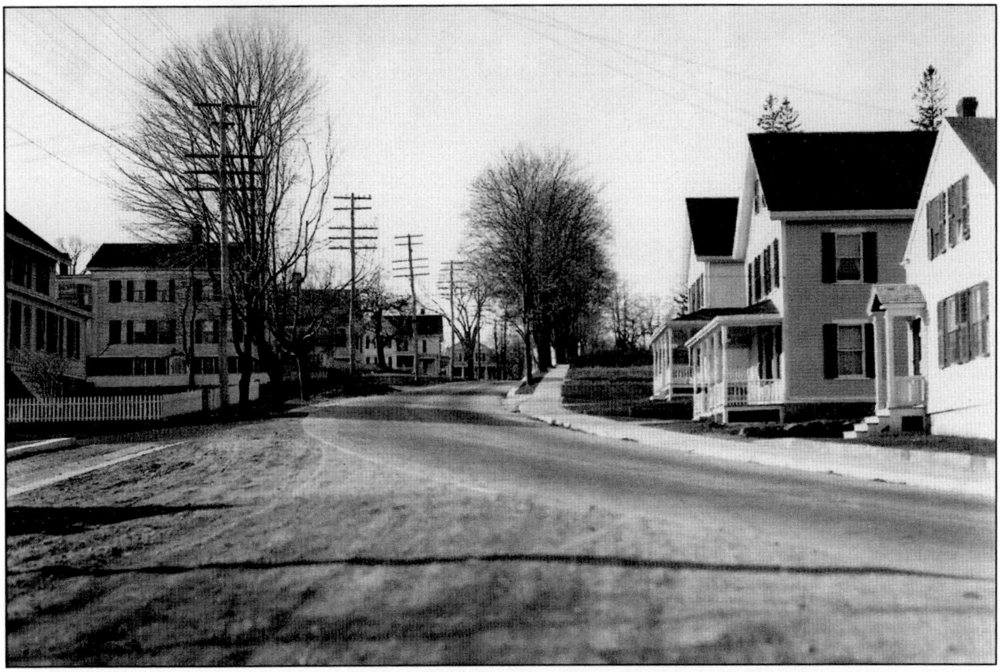

New London Road meets West Main Street in this 1924 photograph that shows the new road that takes automobile traffic down Baptist Hill and into downtown Mystic, making the lower end of New London Road the path less traveled by motorized vehicles. (Connecticut Department of Transportation.)

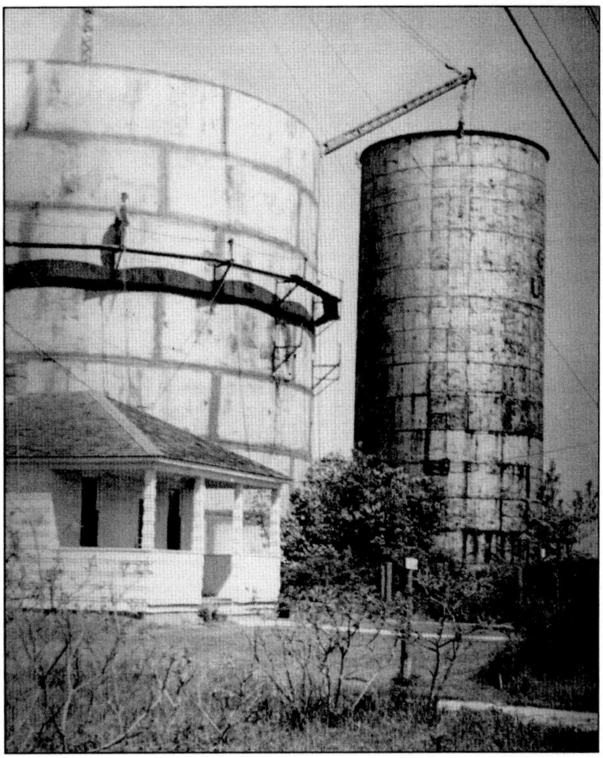

The original water storage tank on Brandegee Avenue is seen here in the 1940s being replaced with a new steel tank. The tank is owned and maintained by Groton Utilities. (Groton Utilities.)

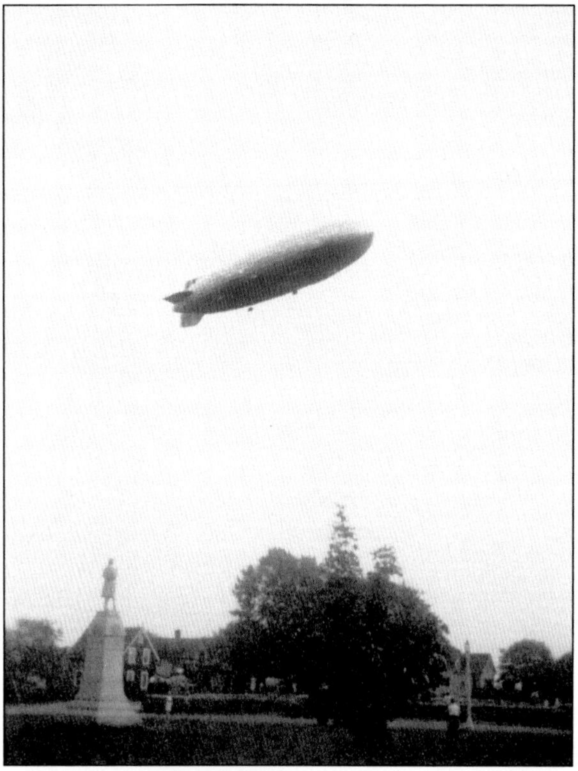

The dirigible *Hindenburg* passes over Fort Griswold on October 9, 1936. The famous airship was in service from March 1936 until it exploded and crashed at Lakehurst on May 6, 1937. On at least half of its transatlantic flights, including its final one, the ship traveled directly over southeastern Connecticut. Kindergarten teacher Eleanor Byles took this photograph when her class from Groton Heights School went out to see the airship pass overhead. (Eleanor Byles.)

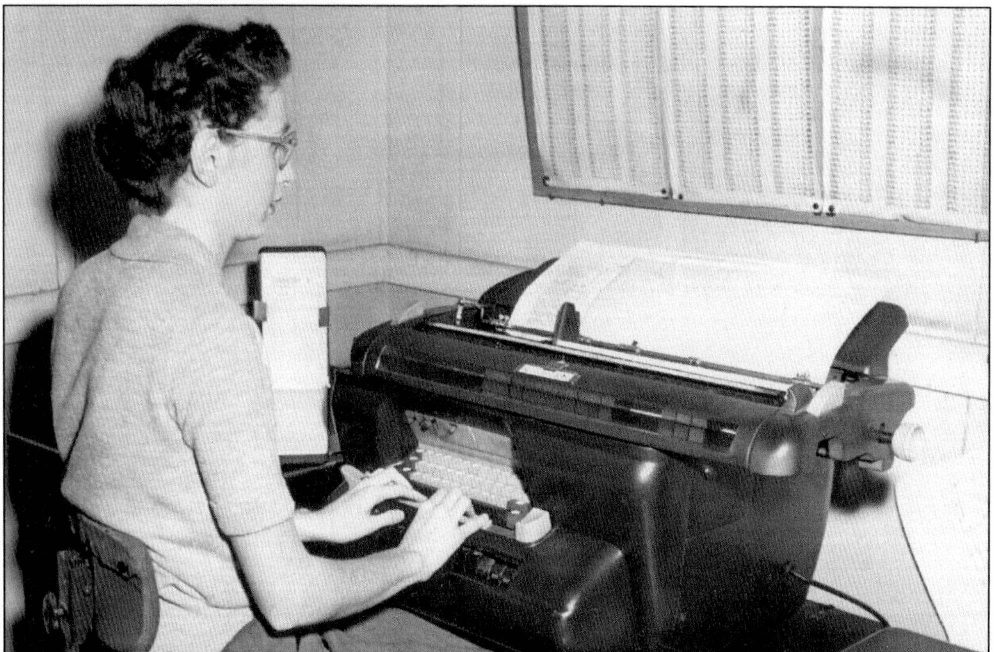

Carol Sanford works in the billing room at Groton Utilities in 1954. Groton owns its own utilities company, which provides electricity for most of the town, except the most eastern part. (Groton Utilities.)

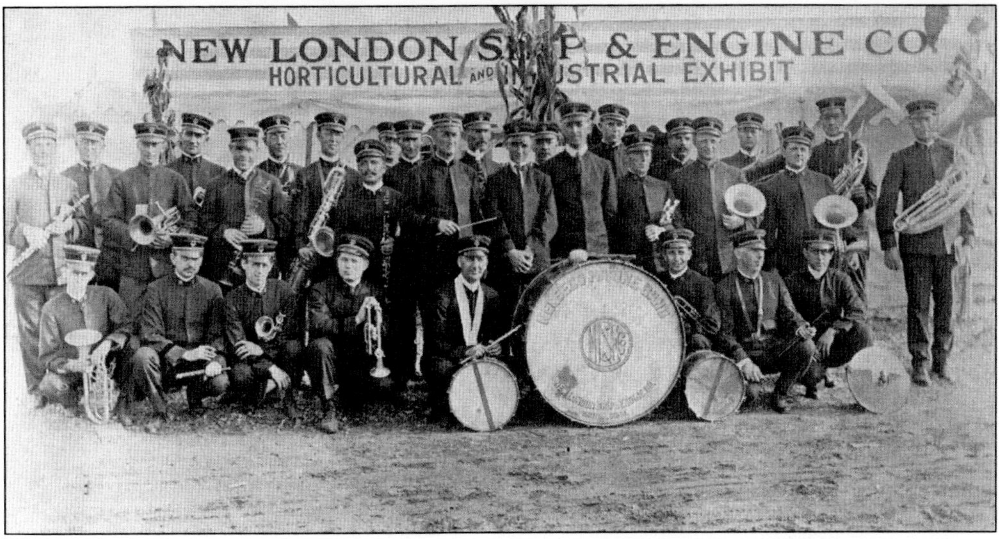

In October 1918, the New London Ship and Engine Company (NELSECO) Marine Band poses in front of a banner for NELSECO's Horticultural and Industrial Exhibit at the Norwich Fair. The band was organized in April 1917 by workers at NELSECO. It is believed that after NELSECO became a division of Electric Boat in 1928, the band's name was changed to Electric Boat Band. It played at ship launchings and other occasions. (James L. Streeter.)

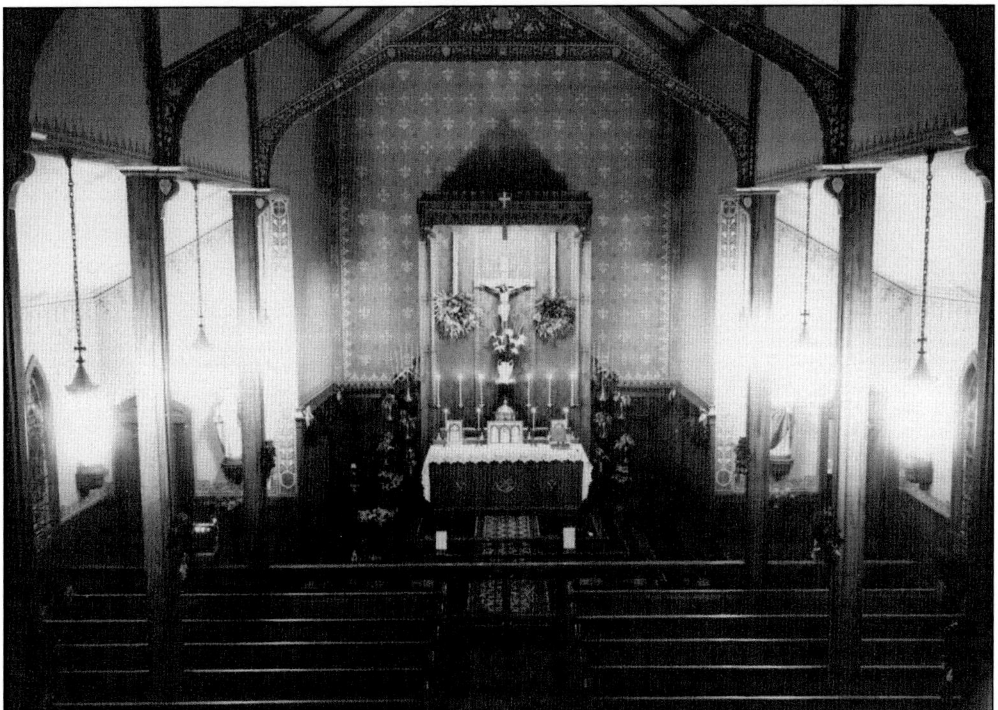

Sacred Heart Church stood on land across from the main gate of Electric Boat from 1913 to 1961. This 1940s photograph shows the interior of the church, which was built on land donated by Morton F. Plant. The building was torn down and replaced with a multistory parking garage. (James L. Streeter.)

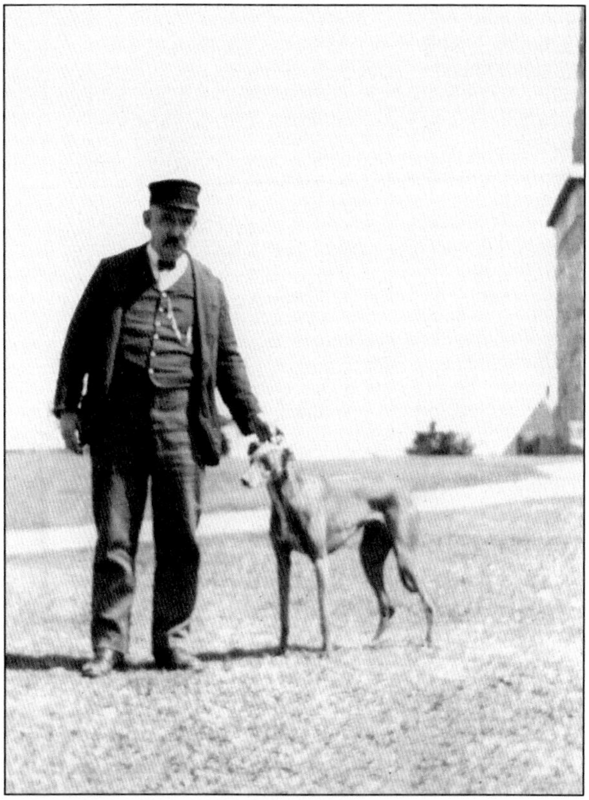

A Mr. Deon and his dog stand on the grounds of Fort Griswold, where he was the caretaker of the Fort Griswold Monument. The front section of the present Monument House Museum originally was the caretaker's house. (Winifred Newbury.)

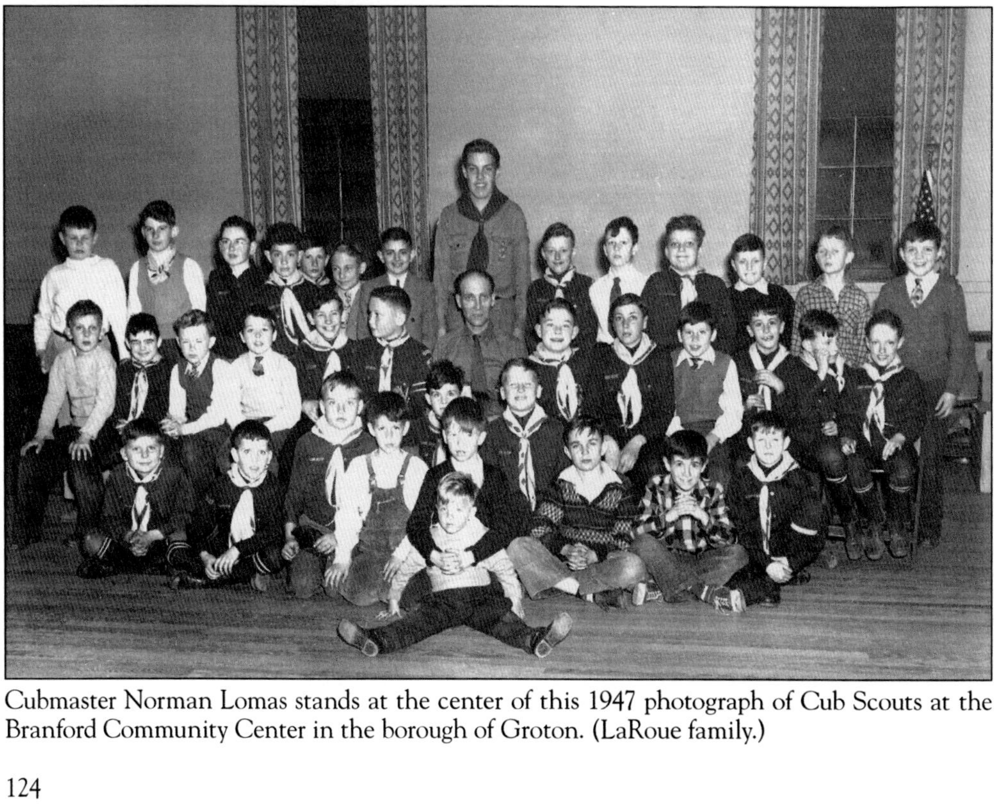

Cubmaster Norman Lomas stands at the center of this 1947 photograph of Cub Scouts at the Branford Community Center in the borough of Groton. (LaRoue family.)

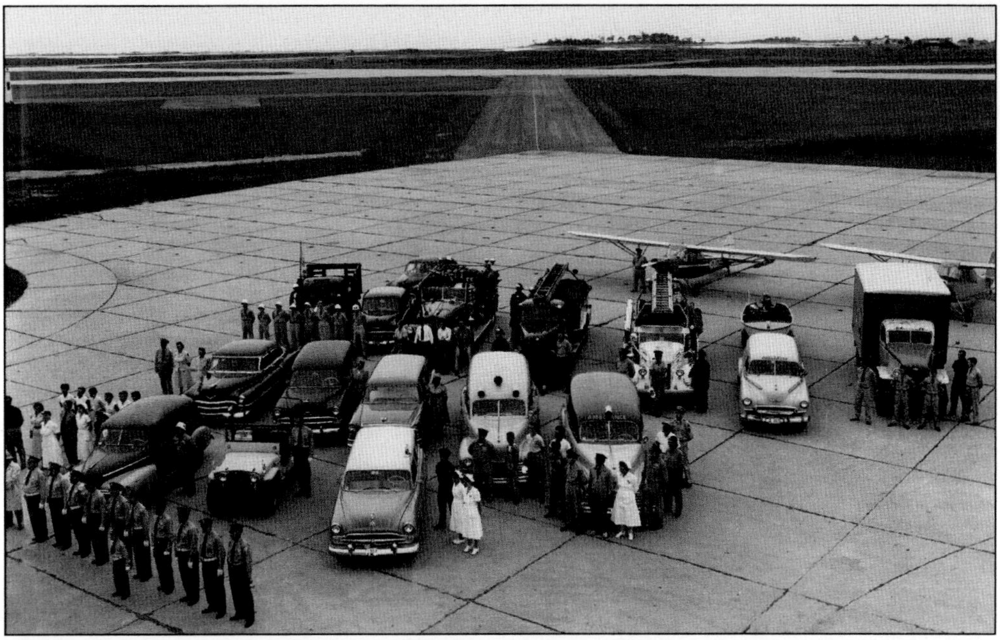

Emergency personnel from Groton's ambulances, police and fire departments, and Red Cross line up at Trumbull Airport (now Groton-New London Airport) in 1956. They were taking part in Operation Alert, a nationwide emergency drill that simulated an evacuation of Groton. (Groton Ambulance Association.)

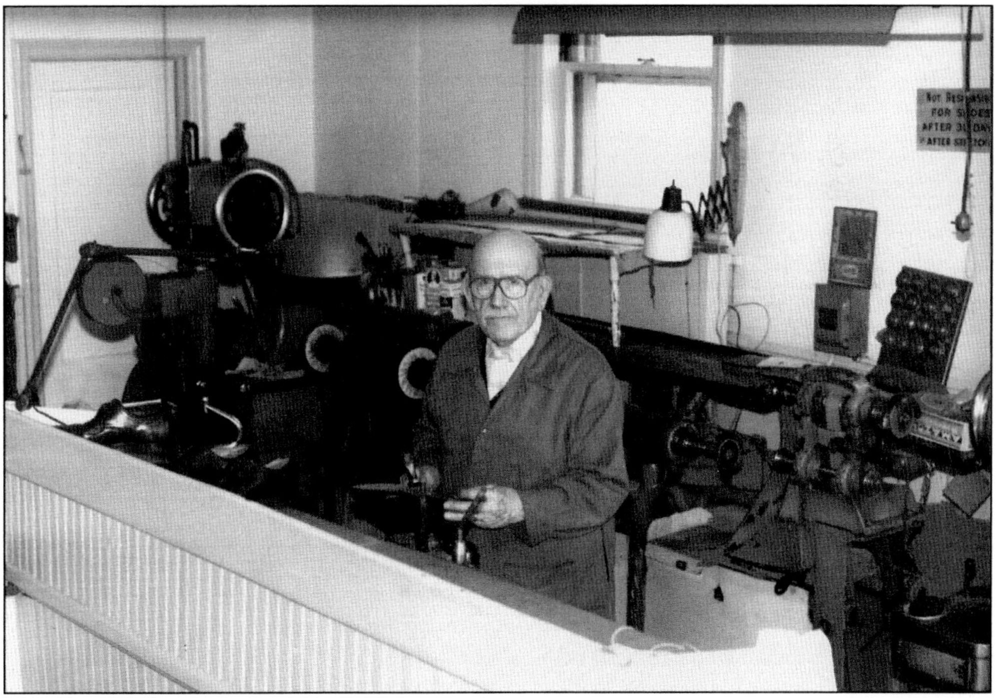

William DeCarolis ran a shoe repair shop at 470 Thames Street in the borough of Groton during the 1930s. His shop was very popular during the Great Depression, when resoled shoes, rather than a new pair, were the rule. (James L. Streeter.)

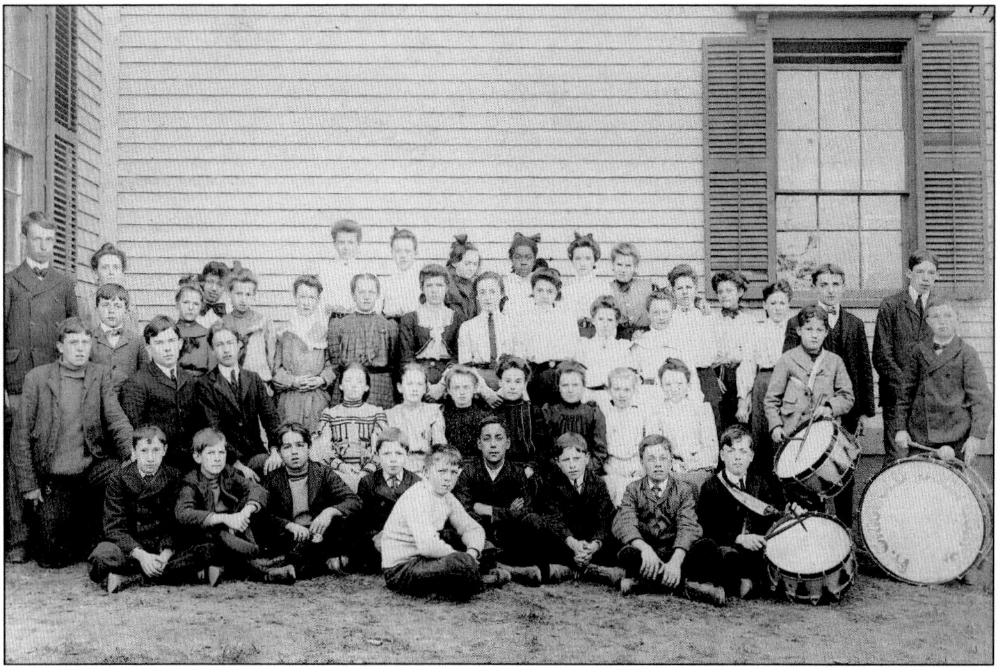

In the early 1900s, a group of youths organized the Fort Griswold Drum Corps, which at its peak had more than 40 members. The marching corps was considered among the best in southeastern Connecticut and often would lead parades. The group's manager and musical director was Ozzie O. Smith. (James L. Streeter.)

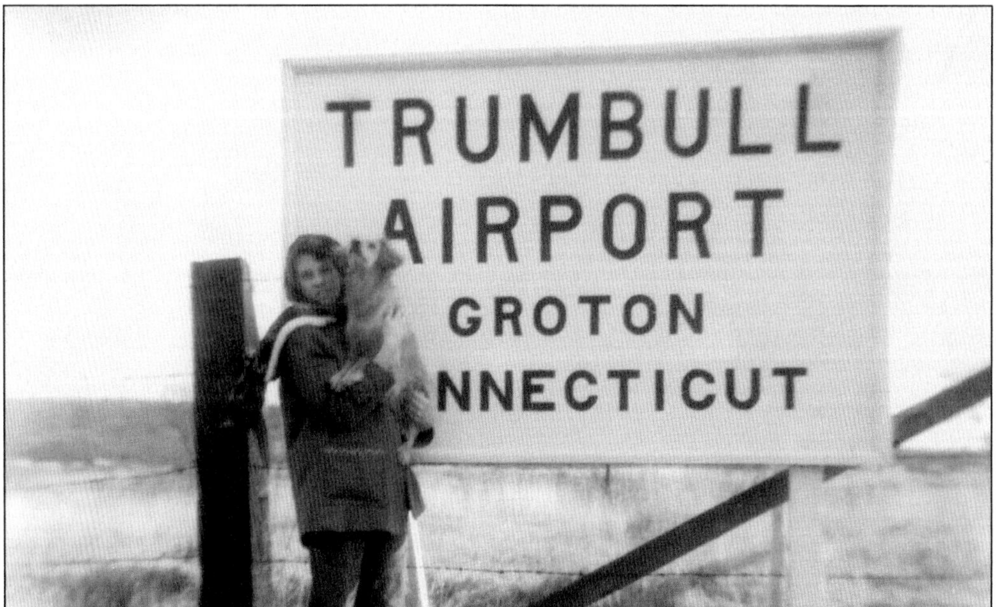

Linda Hansen Corteville stands in front of the sign for Trumbull Airport in this early 1960s photograph. The airport, named for Gov. John Trumbull, a licensed pilot, opened in 1928. In the 1970s, its name was changed to Groton-New London Airport to avoid confusion with the town of Trumbull, Connecticut. (Lil Hansen.)

INDEX

Ackley, John "Jack" Abbott, 29
Akeley, Mary Jobe, 23
Allyn, Carlos W., 98
Avery-Copp House, 100, 101
Avery, Ebenezer, house, 100
Bailey, Anna Warner, 34
Beebe, Capt. Silas, 35
Branford House, 32, 106, 111
Bucklyn, Capt. John Knight, 25
Burfoot, Amby, 22, 38
Chrissos farm, 94, 118
Coe and Bailey General Store, 30, 95
Colonel Ledyard School, 45
Croaker Memorial, 18
Cutler, Carl C., 25
C. W. Allyn Groceries and Provisions, 97, 98
Eastern Point School, 40, 41
Edgcomb and Poppe store, 26, 97
Edgcomb, Howard A., 26
Electric Boat, 12
Fitch, Robert E., schools, 46, 47
Fort Griswold, 19
Fort Hill School, 43
Goodale, Mary, 36
Goodman, Mary Virginia, 37
Gott's Garage, 120
Gray, Robert A., 24
Griswold Hotel, 79, 106
Groton Grain Company, 97
Groton Hardware, 96, 117
Groton Heights Elementary School, 47, 48
Groton Iron Works, 10, 11, 113
Groton Long Point, 22, 67–69, 71
Groton Monument, 105
Haley, John Ross, 90
Haley, Juliet, 30
Jones Garage, 101
Kelley, Johnny, 38
Macht, Stephen, 34, 48
Marie Gilbert, 12
Midway Yard, 86
Morrisson, Mary, 36
Mystic Academy, 39, 43, 48, 63
naval submarine base, 20, 76, 77
New London Ship and Engine Company (NELSECO) Marine Band, 123
Noank, 21, 85
Pioneer Hose Company, 108
Pleasant Valley School, 44
Poppe, Irving, 26
Plant, Morton F., 32
Sacred Heart Church, 123
Santacroce, Rudy, 103
Seely, William, 27
Sharp, Clarence B., 33
Shennecossett Yacht Club, 81, 104
Slocomb, Abby Day, 35
Strickland, Capt. Martin, 91
Tingley, George E., 37
Trumbull Airport, 115, 117, 125, 126
Union Baptist Church, 73, 87
Welles, Edward Randall, 31
Willow Spring Farm, 4, 92
Winthrop, John, Jr., 28